Also by Peter Young
The Blue Team

STOP THE TALL MAN, SAVE THE TIGER

STOP THE TALL MAN, SAVE THE TIGER

A Memoir

PETER YOUNG

ISBN: 979-8-88759-523-8 - paperback
ISBN: 979-8-88759-524-5 - ebook
ISBN: 979-8-88759-660-0 - hardcover

For my children

CONTENTS

III THE AWAKENING 2017 and on

AUTHOR'S NOTE

This book is a memoir. It reflects the author's recollections of experiences over time. While all persons within are actual individuals, some names have been changed.

PROLOGUE

WHEN I WAS a little boy, I had a recurring dream, more like a nightmare, actually. It went like this: I was next to a rock, boulder, or ball of some kind. There was very little color to the dream, and the surroundings were nebulous to the point that it didn't matter where I was. All there was, was me and this thing. And this thing kept getting bigger and bigger. It simply kept growing, and the bigger it got, the more terrified I became. And that was it. The thing would eventually get so big and terrifying that I would wake up, every time. And I had no idea what it was about or why it was so frightening.

I remember once my mother coming to console me at the top of the stairs just outside my bedroom. I had been asleep when the dream visited me again. In the dark of night with this large thing crowding out all comfort and security, it drove me to tears, and I burst out of my room and into my mother's arms. This probably wasn't the first time I'd done this, but was the only one I remember. As I stood there in my colorful one-piece pajamas, tears still fresh on my checks, my mother knelt down beside me and asked me to describe the dream. What was it that was terrorizing me? I had such a hard time telling her. I couldn't find the right words to accurately capture the sheer panic that this simple and obscure dream created. Even now, it's hard to describe. It's so simple, so lacking in nuance or story, just me and this object that starts out small and then gets bigger until I wake up crying. By the time I was ten the dream was seldom an intruder into my nights. I can still remember the fear, but I never figured out what it really meant.

That's the closest I've ever come to having a dream of any significance. I dreamt it so many times there must have been a good reason for it. Prior to meeting my ex-wife Paige and hearing about her important dream, I had never given much thought to the idea that the Lord still speaks to us in dreams. But why wouldn't He? He's God. He can do what He wants.

The Bible makes over twenty references to God speaking to people through dreams. Dreams occurred in both the Old and New Testament. Some are highly symbolic, other contain explicit instructions. Several, like the one below, are warnings.

> *When they had gone, an angel of the Lord appeared to Joseph in a dream. "Get up," he said, "take the child and his mother and escape to Egypt. Stay there until I tell you, for Herod is going to search for the child to kill him."*
> *Matthew 2:13*

I find it quite rational and reasonable that God can and does speak to people through dreams. But God isn't the God of confusion or contradiction. He doesn't change. He is the same yesterday and today and forever. He will not give anyone a dream that contradicts His word. A friend of mine said if a dream doesn't agree with the Bible one hundred percent, then it is not from God. It may leave you with a burning in your bosom, but that feeling is more likely from the pepperoni pizza you ate rather than from the Lord.

Paige's dream was so important to her, the timing so fascinating, the implications so astounding, that it's the perfect place to start our story. So much revolves around the characters in her dream, the interpretation of it, and how that interpretation affected our lives. And even if Paige's dream wasn't from the Lord, its impact is profound because it's such a prescient synopsis of the relationships that connected the three of us: Paige, her beloved Uncle Robert, and me, her husband for over twenty years.

Paige told me about her tiger dream shortly after we met in 1996. I found it odd, not just the dream but the importance she gave to it. The whole thing became even more odd when Paige showed me a long letter from the mysterious Uncle Robert with his bizarre interpretation of the dream. At the time I had no idea that the dream and the letter would be the cause of so much confusion, pain, and heartache. The dream was simultaneously the introduction and warning, compass and complex riddle, treasure map and Trojan horse. Its blunt warning and obfuscated meaning has impacted generations and continues to wreak havoc to this day. And it wasn't until Paige left me that I realized she had spent the better part of our marriage trying to stop me, a tall man, from exposing and expunging the tiger, Uncle Robert, from our lives.

It was a very long and complicated road from our wedding day, when Paige promised to love, honor, and respect me her entire life, to twenty years later when she called me a devil and labeled me abusive, insane, manipulative, serpentine, and treacherous. But this book isn't meant to be just another sad story of marriage and divorce. Rather it is a fascinating tale of discovery and redemption that magnify three key principles of the Christian life. First, a healthy marriage has Christ in the center. No one person—pastor, priest, parent, child, mentor, counselor, or friend—should get in between the husband and wife. Those people can and should help strengthen and maintain the health of a marriage, but from the outside. Second, Christian fellowship is crucial to maintaining a strong relationship with the Lord.

Forgoing fellowship with other believers, the body of Christ, and allowing yourself to be isolated makes you vulnerable to unhealthy false teachers, just like severing a toe from the body would kill the toe. And third, salvation is a free gift from God. Once we receive salvation, we are then sanctified by the work of the Holy Spirit. *You can't switch the order.* Anyone who tells you that you need to do certain things or grow in certain areas *before* you can be saved is trying to act as a gatekeeper to God.

In my life, that gatekeeper was Uncle Robert. He became the cult leader for me, Paige, her parents, and our family, but I didn't know it. After all, we didn't look like a cult; we didn't recite weird chants, shave our heads, or commit mass suicide. But we did drink the Kool-Aid. Steven Hassan, cult expert and author of *Combating Cult Mind Control* said in his introduction to the 2016 Edition, *"One of the biggest changes I have seen over the past decades is the rise of 'mini-cults,' which consist of anywhere from two to twelve people."* I lived in one of these mini-cults for twenty years, escaped, and then recovered.

Someone suggested that instead of writing a memoir about my experience in the cult, I fictionalize this story and turn it into a novel. My response? No one would believe it.

I
THE DREAM 1996-2014

CHAPTER 1
POCATELLO

———◦◉◦———

IN JUNE OF 1995, I packed my belongings into my little red Toyota Tercel, left Boulder, Colorado, and set out for fame and fortune. I was headed to the remote outpost of Pocatello, Idaho to start my first full-time job in sports broadcasting. As a teenager, I wanted to be the next Larry Bird, but never came close. Then I started coaching basketball with the goal of being the next John Wooden. That too didn't happen. Finally, in my mid-twenties, I decided I wanted to be a sports broadcaster. But not just any broadcaster, the next Bob Costas. With that dream still alive, I applied for and got the job as a sports reporter and anchor for the local NBC affiliate in Pocatello.

After driving over ten hours and covering hundreds of desolate, windswept, sagebrush-covered miles through Wyoming and south-east Idaho, I arrived in Pocatello. Looking to the north, beyond the town, at the seemingly empty Snake River plain, I thought, *This place may not be on the edge of the earth, but you can certainly see it from here.* Then, while sitting in the lobby of a local hotel waiting to meet with the TV station's news director, a business man in a suit and tie walked past. I thought, *What in the world would you need a suit and tie for in this Podunk town? Men wear suits in New York City, not Pocatello.* Having been raised in New Jersey and attended college in

1

Washington, DC, my East Coast arrogance was still strong.

I also wondered if I would ever meet somebody in Idaho whom I could marry. I was twenty-seven when I moved to Pocatello and figured I'd be married by that age. But I wasn't and Eastern Idaho is predominantly inhabited by Mormons or Latter-day Saints (LDS). And even though I have the same last name as one of the most famous Mormon leaders, I wasn't Mormon. I didn't even know what LDS meant until I moved to Pocatello. So, before I left Boulder, I prayed very specifically: I asked the Lord to return me to Boulder in two years (my contract at the NBC affiliate was for two years), and have me working on TV covering outdoor sports like climbing, skiing, and mountain biking, and, most importantly, be married to a tall, athletic, beautiful Christian woman.

I ended up falling in love with Idaho first as the small towns and wide-open spaces of the Gem State won my affection. I spent days driving deserted highways, passing through lonely towns that were nothing more than a handful of buildings, captivated by the scenery as ribbons of pavement led me down wide river valleys and over rugged mountain passes. With new discoveries waiting around every curve in the road, I didn't want to stop. I blistered my feet hiking miles of wilderness trails in the Sawtooth Mountains of Central Idaho or in the less majestic peaks cradling Pocatello. I have spent more time exploring the backcountry roads and forest trails of Idaho than any other state. Gritty little Pocatello is where I truly fell in love with the West and the outdoors, and I left behind any and all affinity for the crowded places I used to know.

The town of Pocatello isn't especially attractive. The railroad and attendant hump yard, fueling station, and repair shops cuts an enormous gash right through the center of it, and the one natural feature that could provide beauty, the Portneuf River, is imprisoned in an ugly concrete channel to prevent flooding. Sprinkled with junipers and sage, the mountains overlooking town aren't exactly beautiful either, but they're an outdoorsman's paradise. People come from all over the world to visit nearby Yellowstone National Park, Teton National Park, and the ski resorts of Grand Targhee and Jackson Hole. Few come to visit the area around Pocatello, even though the trails are beautiful and uncrowded, great for hiking and mountain biking. There is hunting and fishing and plenty of places to pitch a tent. I was hiking one such trail, the West Fork of Mink Creek, in the fall of 1996 when I kicked something loose in the dirt. Bending over, I saw it was a horseshoe and picked it up. Even though I'm not a believer in luck, I couldn't help but keep the horseshoe as a hopeful indicator of good things to come.

I had been in Pocatello for over a year, and, as much as I liked the place, I planned on moving to another town for a better TV job once my two-year contract was up. I had dated a gal for a while but was single again and still hadn't met the beautiful Christian woman I hoped would one day be my wife.

PAIGE KLASSEN WAS the second of five children born to Jack and Cathy Klassen. When the children were very young, they packed up the family station wagon and fled the big city of Vancouver and moved east to the lush green mountains and narrow river valleys of interior British Columbia, away from the rest of the extended Klassen clan of siblings, cousins, aunts, uncles, and grandparents. Having to figure out life on their own in this remote setting they bounced around from place to place, unable to sink roots. At one point, the entire family lived in a tent for several months. Their existence was backwoods in every sense: they homeschooled, sewed many of their own clothes, raised animals, drank raw milk, grew a garden, and canned their homegrown fruit and vegetables. Some years, they ran a little fruit stand next to the road by their home. Eventually, that humble stand grew into a small country store.

Between milking cows, canning food, and running the till at the store, Paige learned how to work hard and grew up fast. When her older brother, Jeff, headed south of the border to go to school at North Idaho College (NIC) in Coeur d'Alene, Idaho, Paige followed. Soon the rest of the family decided to follow as well. They sold the store and eventually settled in Hayden, Idaho. After two years at NIC, Paige finished her undergraduate degree at Albertson College (now College of Idaho) just outside of Boise. She came to Pocatello a year before me to get her master's degree at Idaho State University (ISU). She ended up getting two, and after graduating in the spring of 1996, started working for ISU. She lived in an apartment just off campus with her younger sister, Rebecca, who was still working on her undergraduate degree. The two were the best of friends.

Before I met Paige, I knew her as the blonde girl. I had seen her a few times on the ISU campus, and she was impossible to miss. Standing a statuesque six feet tall with an attractive athletic figure, she was crowned with the most beautiful blonde hair I'd ever seen. Long and curly, her shimmering golden mane cascaded well past her shoulders. One Sunday during the fall of 1996 I saw her at the University Bible Church (UBC) on the ISU campus. I had recently started attending there and couldn't take my eyes off her. We sat far apart, and, not knowing anything about her (did she have a boyfriend, was she already married?), my shyness got the best of me, and I didn't introduce myself that day. About a week later I saw her again during an ISU football game in Holt Arena, the school's domed multi-purpose stadium. I stood on the sidelines, videotaping the game for my station (a year earlier, we switched affiliations and were now the local ABC station). Standing next to me were the guys who had the same job at the NBC and CBS affiliates. In between plays, we would chit-chat or look up into the crowd and people watch. In a crowd of thousands, I spotted Paige instantly as she gracefully skipped down the stairs and turned into a row of seats. For the rest of the game, I nearly got whiplash, turning my head and camera to record the action while the game was going on, then turning back to gaze into the stands at the blonde girl.

I knew very little about this mysterious blonde girl until I talked with a mutual friend, Gary Ramos. Gary was a friendly, outgoing and confident guy. I knew him from UBC and the gym where we both worked out. We were at the gym lifting weights and the topic of Paige came up. I still didn't know her name, but as soon as I started describing the blonde girl, he knew exactly who I was talking about. He told me her name and that of her younger sister. He also told me about Uncle Robert. Moments after learning Paige's name, Gary told me about the Klassens' "family guru." He didn't mention Uncle Robert by name, nor did he elaborate much, but it was clear he found the guy weird, and the Klassens' relationship with him even weirder. Gary could tell I was interested in Paige and his mention of a "family guru" wasn't just another bit of background information—it was a word of caution.

PAIGE AND I finally met on Sunday, October 27, 1996. UBC had just created a singles' Bible study that met in the ISU student union building near the church. This Sunday was the third meeting of the group. The first two had been complete duds. I was a single guy in my late 20s; I wasn't going to a singles' Bible study to soak in the pastor's teaching. I was there to meet a beautiful, single, Christian woman and the first two meetings offered nothing of the sort. Walking down the hall toward the meeting room, I rounded a corner and saw Paige heading towards the same room. I'll never forget the warm and inviting smile she gave me, as if she couldn't have been happier to see me. The blonde girl was going to the same singles' Bible study as me. I was ecstatic.

I sat near the back of the room, and Paige sat up front next to her friend, Nan Nordby, who introduced us after the meeting was over. Like Gary, I knew Nan from UBC and the local gym but had never seen her with Paige before this moment. She was a short powerhouse of a woman who loved to lift heavy weights and study the Bible. Nan informed Paige what I did for a living and asked her if she'd ever seen me on TV. Paige hadn't and I was pleasantly surprised. Those of us on local TV were sort of big fish in a very little pond, and I hoped my future wife would get to know me before she knew *of* me as a broadcaster. Now that she'd met me, I was determined to give a knock-out performance during my live broadcast later that day in the hopes Paige would be watching. I wore my best jacket and tie and smiled back at her through the camera with the same warmth she'd shown me earlier in the day.

One week later, I saw Paige again at the same singles' Bible study. I'd been counting the days leading up to Sunday in the hopes she would be there. But when she arrived with a guy, my heart sank. Was he her boyfriend? My mind started to jump to negative conclusions, insisting she was too good to be true, and, of course, they were dating. But they didn't hold hands or act like boyfriend and girlfriend, so I held out hope. She looked stunningly gorgeous that day and he was much shorter than her, so they seemed an odd pair. During the Bible study, I sat across the table from Paige and her friend, a guy named Chad, who in my eyes, was nothing more than a wretched interloper. At one point, she gracefully brushed aside a strand of hair from her face. It was a simple gesture, but replete with such delicate charm and beauty that I was completely and utterly smitten. An earthquake could have shaken the building to its core and I would have sat there and continued to gaze at her. Later, after the study, she came up to me and we talked. She conversed as gracefully as she looked. As she left, she confidently reached out and shook my hand, leaving me with little else to think of but this remarkable woman.

A few days later, on November 7th, I was in Reed Gymnasium on the ISU campus, ostensibly to get an interview with their men's basketball head coach, Herb Williams. Herb and I got along great, and he always gave me interesting sound bites, like the time he mistakenly called his best player the "*clog* in our wheel." Practice ran late, so I put my camera gear down and wandered the halls outside the gym while I waited. Having wandered the main level, I went downstairs. I stopped at a glass frame on the wall that contained black and white portrait photos of people who worked in various offices in the building. There was Paige's picture with her name and office room number beneath. Looking at the nearest room number I realized her room must be just down the hall. So down the hall I went. The door was open, I knocked then peeked in. There she was, greeting me with that same inviting smile. I sat and we chatted. She was so easy to talk to and despite wanting to make a good impression, I was incredibly comfortable around her. After about an hour (with no mention of Chad I might add) she said she was going to go lift weights and asked if I'd like to join her. I said sure, but I had to change clothes first.

I casually walked out of her office then broke into a sprint as I ran upstairs, grabbed my camera gear, and raced to the TV station across town. There I grabbed my gym clothes and called my boss, sports director Mark Browning. He was in our main studio in Idaho Falls, waiting on that interview from Coach Williams to use in the

6pm sportscast.

"Sorry, Mark," I breathlessly exclaimed, "but I didn't get the interview with Coach Williams. I met the blonde girl and we're going to go work out together."

He wasn't the least bit upset. "Don't worry about it. Good luck!"

I sped back to Reed Gym and met up with Paige in the weight room. I loved that she was willing to lift weights with me. She was feminine and beautiful, but also very strong and proud of it. She wasn't afraid to grunt when pushing out one final rep. I even found myself being challenged on a few exercises to make sure I was lifting sufficiently more than her to maintain my manhood. As we cooled down I offered to take her to dinner and she agreed.

The maitre d' at Buddy's Italian restaurant seated us at a small wooden table for two in a quiet corner. It was a small family-owned establishment close to downtown that was best known for giving patrons who ate their garlic infused salad "Buddy's Breath." The food was good, but nowhere near the high standards I was used to growing up in New Jersey. The atmosphere, however, was perfect. No interruptions, no loud music or misbehaving kids, just Paige and me getting to know each other. It was during this dinner that I first heard the name Uncle Robert. When Paige mentioned him, I was certain he had to be the weird "family guru" that Gary had warned me about. He came up rather innocuously and the conversation moved on. Maybe this Uncle Robert guy wasn't so weird after all. At dessert, the waiter brought spumoni and wondered if we'd like one spoon or two. With one spoon, he instructed, we could playfully lick the ice cream off each other's noses. Paige smiled and said, "We're not there yet." I think Paige surprised herself by saying that because she blushed like a rose. We got two spoons.

Later, I drove her home and dropped her off outside her

apartment. I told her I had a lot of fun and would love to do it again sometime, then left. It wasn't until I was a few blocks down the street that I realized I forgot to get her phone number. Trying not to panic, I spun the car around and drove right back. She was still outside and pleasantly surprised to see me.

When I left the second time, I had a phone number.

CHAPTER 2
THE LETTER

AFTER OUR FIRST date of lifting and dinner at Buddy's, Paige and I started spending most of our free time together. One night while hanging out in her apartment with her sister and some other friends, I made eye contact with Paige. Usually when I caught the gaze of a woman, I looked away because of my self-consciousness. But this was different. In fact, everything about Paige was different. I looked right at her and she held my gaze, her deep blue eyes inviting me to safely linger. The self-consciousness, the fear of rejection or whatever else causes a man to look away from the eyes of a beautiful woman, vanished. In its place was a feeling of comfort and connection as if we had known each other all our lives.

A few days later Paige and I went on a hike up Red Hill, which is perched like crown molding over the ISU campus. Halfway through the hike we took a break and found a large rock that was perfectly shaped for two people to sit on. It was a sunny yet brisk fall afternoon, so we sat and cuddled next to each other, sharing our warmth, gazing out over Pocatello. As we spoke of our thoughts and visions for the future, I smiled inwardly at how similar they were, knowing I was falling in love.

After dating Paige for two weeks, I was ninety percent certain I wanted to marry her. This was something I had never experienced before. I knew we needed to spend more time getting to know each other, but my only reservations about her, the other ten percent if you will, were doubts about Uncle Robert and her father, Jack Klassen. Before we went further, I needed to meet them. Paige talked about them constantly. It was clear they were a huge influence in her life, so much so that, were we to marry, it was inescapable that they would become huge influences in my life too. I was head over heels in love with Paige, but had no idea what to think about these two men, especially Uncle Robert. No doubt, Gary's comments about the Klassen's "family guru" was lurking in the back of my mind, but Paige talked about him so frequently, with such undiluted praise and borderline glorification, so much so it was uncomfortable listening to, I would have had concerns even without Gary's cryptic warning.

THERE ARE NO professional sports teams in Eastern Idaho, and Idaho State University is the only Division I college program. So covering local high school sports was one of my primary assignments at our TV station. I spent many nights driving around the area gathering highlights from local football, volleyball, and basketball games. Paige started to come with me, and we'd have wonderful conversations in the car on the way to and from these games. By now, we had both fallen in love and wanted to be around each other all the time. Around Thanksgiving, we were off to another game when Paige said she had something she wanted me to read. It was a recent letter from Uncle Robert concerning a dream she had about a tiger. I could tell the letter was extremely important to her, and she was anxious for me read it.

The letter was my first interaction, so to speak, with Uncle Robert. It was several pages long, written in shaky cursive using several different colors of ink, and contained his bizarre in-depth interpretation of Paige's dream; a dream that seemed to hold incredible significance to her and Uncle Robert. As I read the letter, I failed to see the significance. He rambled on and on and wrote in an incoherent and grandiloquent style that had me completely baffled.

As far as I could ascertain, Paige dreamt she was in a house with an old boyfriend, Chad. The two of them were looking for a tiger. Paige wanted to find the tiger and keep it isolated in the house. For its part, the tiger wanted to find and kill her. And even though she knew this, Paige didn't want the tiger killed. The tiger possessed many qualities she admired: independence, strength, power, and courage. It was precisely because of these traits that she wanted to keep the tiger in her life, even though she knew the tiger had gotten her into trouble in the past. Then the front door to the house opened and a tall man entered. Paige hid from the tall man and was afraid for the tiger. She knew the tall man was there to kill the tiger, which, whether he did or not, I couldn't tell from the letter.

What I gathered from the letter, and what Paige had shared with me, was that Uncle Robert said the tiger in the dream was Paige's ego, her mind. And since the tiger was still alive, and Paige really didn't want to kill it, it meant she probably hadn't surrendered her mind or her life to the Lord. This meant that unless the tall man killed the tiger, she wasn't truly a Christian.

Not for a second did I think Paige wasn't a Christian, and not just because I met her at a church. Everything she said and did exhibited a heart filled with the love of Christ. To suggest she wasn't a Christian seemed absurd.

There was one specific point in Uncle Robert's letter that bothered me. In the dream, Paige said the man who entered the house to get rid of the tiger was tall. It was a specific detail and description in a dream that was otherwise short on both. No physical descriptors were given for the house or the tiger, just the *tall* man. It wasn't a casual remark, but an important point of the dream. If it hadn't been, Paige wouldn't have remembered it or bothered to mention it to Uncle Robert. In his letter to Paige, Uncle Robert tried to make the comparison between himself and the tall man in her dream. But from what I'd been told by Paige, Uncle Robert was a very short man. So why would this short man try to insert himself into Paige's dream and assume the role of the tall man? Why would he try to change her dream to make it about him? That, above all the other oddities in the letter, stood out the most. I didn't want to assume too much or be arrogant and think I was Paige's knight in shining armor, but at 6'5" I was tall. And I had just come into her life. But I kept my mouth shut.

I thanked her for letting me read the letter but didn't offer much else. It was so odd that I didn't know what to say. Paige was so different from anyone I'd ever met, from the way she communicated to how she made me feel. And I was captivated by all of it. So, I tried to keep an open mind about the letter. Without knowing much about Uncle Robert and the Klassen family background, most of the significance of the letter was lost on me at the time, and simply added another layer to Paige's fascinating mystique.

I GOT TO know the Klassens better that Thanksgiving. Paige invited me to her parents' home in Hayden, Idaho. Her parents were very welcoming and kind. Their home was spacious yet modest and set in a quaint subdivision seemingly hidden from the outside world by a towering rampart of pines and spruces. I hadn't been in the home for more than twenty minutes when I caught Jack staring at me. He was sitting on the couch in the living room while I was looking at a photo hanging on the wall in the dining room. You know that feeling you get when you know someone is looking at you? Well, I had it. So, I glanced over toward the living room and Jack, with his head turned, was staring right at me. It was awkward, borderline creepy, for a moment. But then I remembered, this was his home and I was his daughter's boyfriend. It was obvious things were getting serious between Paige and me, so I figured Jack, being a concerned father, had every right to check me out.

The only other event that stood out from that first trip to the Klassens' home was when I went to use the bathroom. As usual, I stood while urinating. When I opened the door to leave the bathroom, I was startled to see Jack standing in the hallway waiting for me. He didn't have great hearing, the result of years of using loud hand tools while in construction. To compensate, he stood very close when conversing; for me, it was always a bit too close, akin to an aggressive basketball defender trying to deny me the ball.

There he was invading my personal space when he told me that in his house, the men needed to sit down to pee. I guess his hearing was good enough to hear me standing up to pee. He explained that sitting down to pee prevented splashing and kept the toilet cleaner. Prior to that moment, I don't think I'd ever heard of a man sitting down to pee. He then said something I'd get used to hearing: "Uncle Robert taught us that." That phrase was always uttered in such a way that it put the thing we were discussing, whatever it was, above questioning or even discussion. If Uncle Robert had spoken on a topic, the issue was settled.

Despite these few odd moments, I found Jack to be a thoughtful and gentle man. A few days after I arrived, I left Hayden no longer concerned about the man I thought might soon be my father-in-law.

CHAPTER 3
CHRISTIAN OR NOT

---◦◉◦---

NOW THAT I had met Paige's father, all that I needed to be certain we should marry was to meet Uncle Robert. But that was going to take a while, since he lived in Southern California and I had no plans to drive down there and meet him. Over Christmas, Paige and I spent time with my family, and all the Youngs seemed to be smitten with her as well. We were together as much as possible and our love for each other grew by the day. Then, in mid-February of 1997, Paige went on a work trip that took her to Northern Idaho, where she stayed with her parents. It just so happened that Uncle Robert was there visiting the Klassens.

When it was time for Paige to fly home, Uncle Robert drove her to the airport in Spokane, Washington. During the car ride, they discussed Paige's dream about the tiger and the letter Uncle Robert had sent her. Paige told him she read his letter several times, as well as the many Bible verses he cited, and had come to the conclusion that she wasn't a Christian. She told him she wanted to be a Christian.

"Why not make today the day?" Uncle Robert asked.

So, there in the car, under the guidance and direction of Uncle Robert, Paige surrendered her life to the Lord. "That was the best day of my life!" she would later write in her testimony.

17

Of course, I wasn't there for that meeting, but Paige wrote about it many years later, and spoke to me about it the day she came back home to Pocatello. Her face glowed with excitement, and she couldn't wait to tell me her news. Sitting together on the edge of the bed in my apartment, she described the discussion with Uncle Robert with unbridled joy. Hearing her say she just became a Christian surprised me, but she was so happy and so convinced, so I didn't dare question her. She smiled at me, and her eyes were imbued with a deep and powerful love, yet there was also a question in them. I didn't need her to ask the question, I knew it.

"You don't think I'm a Christian, do you?" I asked.

Her reply was a loving no, but it was still a no. I pulled back and dropped my head. I was confused and hurt, but not angry. It seemed I was incapable of being angry with her. Nor did I blame this revelation on Uncle Robert. The belief that I wasn't a Christian, no doubt a consequence of her seeing herself as unsaved, seemed to be hers and hers alone, not something foisted on her by Uncle Robert. In that moment, I resolved not to try to convince her I was a Christian, but rather continue living my life and demonstrate my faith. And I was certain the Lord would show her.

PAIGE'S QUESTIONING OF my faith did nothing to dampen my love for her. I was absolutely convinced we were going to marry, and for her part, she acted no different toward me. But I still needed to meet Uncle Robert, and after witnessing the role he played in Paige's life during her recent conversion experience, it was now more critical than ever that I meet him. I finally got that chance in early April of 1997. Paige's older brother, Jeff, was getting married in Olympia, Washington, and I flew out to be there.

Uncle Robert, whose real name was Robert Booty, was there with his wife, Staci, and their younger son, Devin. When I first met Uncle Robert, I liked him. He was friendly, charismatic, and perhaps a bit eccentric, but seemingly harmless. Hovering halfway between 5 and 6 feet tall, he had a head that was completely bald on top with jet black hair on the sides, a bulbous nose, olive complexion, glasses, and an ample belly. He looked like a Middle Eastern Santa Claus without the white hair and beard. He didn't look anything like any of Paige's other relatives (because he wasn't actually related), and I learned the only reason he was referred to as *Uncle* Robert was because Paige's parents required their children when they were young to address adults as Uncle or Aunt as a sign of respect. For some reason, with Robert Booty, the Uncle moniker stuck. I didn't spend any one-on-one time with him, but nothing about him that I saw or heard at the wedding gave me pause. Nor was there anything remarkable about him that, in my mind, warranted the praise and adulation Paige showered on him.

Paige's immediate family was there as well as her aunts, uncles, and cousins who still lived in Canada. She seemed to get along great with everyone, but I did hear a few curious comments about how it was rare for the Klassens to get together like this. At the wedding reception, Paige caught the bouquet and I caught the garter. Everyone sensed we might be gathering for another wedding soon.

Paige hadn't said anything about my faith since she doubted it that day in February, and I assumed she became convinced I really was saved. Who knows? Perhaps Uncle Robert had given his blessing of me to Paige after meeting me at Jeff's wedding. Of this, I had no idea, but I did know we were in love. She had said, "I love you" first. It happened a few weeks after we had started dating when we were in the car, and she let it slip. She hadn't intended to say it; it just came out. Of course, I felt the same way about her and had for some time. I found myself irresistibly drawn to her. She had a bearing that cut against the grain from all women I had previously known: girlfriends, friends, and relatives. One night, we were once again driving to cover a sporting event, but I was subdued thanks to a headache. She told me to park the car away from the arena lights and turn off the engine, which I did. She then reached over and massaged my temples for several minutes until my headache went away. It wasn't so remarkable that she did that, but that she knew it would help, knew how to do it, knew I wouldn't ask her to do something like that, and cared enough for me to do it anyway.

After her brother's wedding, Paige and I talked about marriage and went ring shopping together. Later in April, I called her parents and asked for their blessing before I proposed to her. They gave it, and I was all set to ask Paige to marry me. There were two places I thought would make a great spot to ask my future wife to marry me: atop a mountain or on the steps of the Lincoln Memorial. The Lincoln Memorial was one of my favorite places to go in college when I needed time alone or a moment to reflect. At night the view of the city is spectacular, and I thought it would provide a wonderfully romantic and inspiring backdrop. But the Lincoln Memorial was in Washington, DC and, thus, out of the question. A mountaintop would have to do, only I hadn't hiked to the top of any local peaks to scout the location. Then I thought about Red Hill. It had a nice view of town and was a place Paige and I had been to before, so it had special memories.

On Sunday, April 27th, 1997, I asked Paige to go on a run with me. It was a beautiful sunny day, warm but not hot. We jogged around campus then headed up to Red Hill and eventually worked our way over to the large rock that we had sat on back in November. Taking a break, she sat down on the rock first while I quickly fumbled for the ring that was hidden in a small pouch in my running shorts. Instead of sitting down, I stood in front of her and produced the ring. It probably wasn't the most dramatic or romantic proposal in history, but I did surprise her. And she said yes.

On our way back down to her apartment, I felt like I could fly. When we walked into the apartment Rebecca was lounging in a chair reading. Somehow, the moment she saw Paige's face she knew. She burst out of her chair, and they embraced, squealing and laughing with delight.

CHAPTER 4
LOVE AND MARRIAGE

PAIGE AND I were married in Hayden, Idaho on July 19th, 1997, almost nine months after our initial meeting at the singles' Bible study. Our wedding was held outdoors in a gorgeous venue under brilliant cerulean blue skies with one hundred of our family and friends in attendance. Paige was simply beautiful in an understated white dress. Then again, she had the ability to take anything understated and turn it into something worthy of poetry. Paige's *real* uncle, Tim Klassen, older brother of Jack, was the pastor who married us. Uncle Robert spoke during the service, delivering a short homily, of which I can't remember a single word. However, I remember very clearly the words of Pastor Tim. He said we weren't perfect, but we were perfect for each other. I wondered if he said those words during all marriage ceremonies, or had he chosen those words specifically for that day and that audience? Were his words meant not just for Paige and me, but also for Jack, his self-righteous younger brother? I didn't know it at the time but later found out Jack had spent years isolating himself from the greater Klassen family thanks to his blind allegiance to Uncle Robert.

Nevertheless, marrying Paige was a dream come true, and our wedding day was one of the happiest of my life. As the years passed,

I learned more about the events of that day. Perhaps I was blinded by love, but there were undercurrents of depression and disgust that I was completely unaware of. Some of my family nearly walked out of the ceremony during Uncle Robert's brief talk. It wasn't because they were baking under the intense summer sun in wedding clothing, but rather because they were so bothered by what Uncle Robert shared. And, while Jack was walking his daughter down the aisle, it wasn't pride or joy he was experiencing, but rather thoughts of suicide. It was years later when he shared this, when he felt strong enough to look back and honestly speak of his struggles. Instead of enjoying that memorable day, Jack was tortured by the presence of Uncle Robert, for Uncle Robert represented the standard by which he judged himself, the archetype of the perfect Christian. When Uncle Robert was present, all Jack saw was a mirror reflecting his ugliness. Unfortunately, this wouldn't be the last time Jack obsessed over Uncle Robert on a day that he was supposed to focus on his daughter.

On that seminal day in July, I married my best friend and the love of my life. I married a tall, athletic, beautiful, Christian woman. Upon returning from our honeymoon in Bermuda, Paige and I moved into a condo in Boulder, Colorado, and I started working for my new company, the Outdoor Life Network (OLN). If the Lord could have answered my prayer from two years prior with more precision, I am unaware how. It was truly remarkable. In June of that year, during my last on-air broadcast at the local news station in Idaho, I told the audience I was moving on to my dream job and marrying my dream woman.

WHATEVER MARRYING Paige signified—the answer to a dream, a prayer, the Lord speaking to me, or me learning the Lord is capable of anything—it happened. About a month into our marriage something else happened. Paige told me she was late with her period. Having grown up in a household with four older brothers and no sisters, I barely even knew what that meant, let alone what that *could* mean. She picked up a pregnancy test at the store, took it at home, and just like that, we found out she was pregnant. As if taking a solid right from Mike Tyson, we were floored. Our plan was to wait a year or two before starting a family. *Our* plan. That must sound so silly to the Lord.

Once the initial shock subsided, Paige and I were ecstatic. We both came from big families and wanted a big family of our own. Very quickly, the nesting began: trips to doctors, baby clothes shopping, multivitamins for expecting mothers, birthing classes, etc.

In 1997, OLN was a fledgling cable network in need of signature events. They got one with the U.S. Winter Olympic Trials. My boss, a brilliant TV producer named Ric LaCivita, wanted me to host the coverage for a number of events. That would mean lots of travel and lots of time away for a newlywed whose wife was pregnant. Ric wasn't married and didn't have kids, but he was the consummate uncle. There was no way Ric was going to let me fly all over the country while Paige remained home alone and pregnant in Colorado. First, I took a brief solo trip to Duluth, Minnesota to cover the trials for curling. Interviewing the winning skip (or captain) to discuss his chances at the Olympics, while he held a cigarette in one hand and a Budweiser in the other, was one of the more bizarre moments of my broadcasting career. After curling, I again flew by myself, this time to Milwaukee, Wisconsin for the long track speed skating trials. But Ric decided that was enough time apart. For my next assignment, short track speed skating at Lake Placid, New York, he flew both Paige and me to the event.

The short track trials stretched out over two weekends, so Paige and I had plenty of time during the week to hang out and explore. While Paige's burgeoning belly made it obvious we were having a baby, it wasn't until she came back from a short shopping trip that it really sunk in what was coming. She'd gone to a used clothing store and picked up the most adorable baby outfit—a green and brown onesie with a cartoonish moose face covering the chest. When she laid it on the bed, it struck me that our baby would be wearing that outfit in a matter of months. I know it sounds silly, but in that moment, the cute moose outfit made the fact that we were having a child more real to me than anything else up to that point.

Five months later, in May of 1998, Thomas was born in a hospital just outside of Boulder. Ric sent a pair of baby Nike Air Jordans. In the course of our marriage, Paige and I had five children, and each of them wore those little shoes. We also have photos of each child in that silly moose outfit.

SHORTLY AFTER THOMAS' birth, Paige and I decided to move back to Idaho. For me, the bloom had long since fallen off the rose when it came to living in Boulder. I used to love that town; but after living in small town Idaho for two years, it felt like a big city. I was done living in cities. Paige liked Boulder, but she wanted to be closer to her parents. We got out a yellow legal pad of paper and wrote down the pros and cons of various places we considered moving to. Since all I needed for my career was a good airport nearby, we had lots of options. On the short list of possible places to move to were Pocatello, Coeur d'Alene, and Sun Valley, Idaho; Bozeman, Montana; Jackson, Wyoming, and a few others. Pocatello made the most sense because we knew the area, had friends there, and the cost of living was much lower than the other options. Uncle Robert didn't have much contact with us that one year we lived in Colorado, so this decision was made without any input from him.

But Uncle Robert was never out of our lives for long. We saw him again in the fall of 1998 while visiting Southern California for my brother Brad's wedding. Paige and I stopped by Uncle Robert's home on the way to the wedding. We spent a few hours visiting Uncle Robert and his oldest son, Thad Booty. It was the one and only time I ever met Thad. He wasn't married at the time, and I gathered it had been years since Paige had seen him. The two of them grew up knowing each other as the Bootys would occasionally visit the Klassens in Canada. Thad seemed very mature for an early twenty-something single guy. He even held Thomas for a few moments while Paige snapped photos. It's funny the things your mind chooses to remember, but what I remember most was what Paige said to her sister on the phone just after leaving the Booty's: "He's hot!"

Okay, a little context: Growing up, the Klassen girls idolized Uncle Robert, so a marriage between one of the Booty boys and one of the Klassen girls would have been a match made in heaven. Paige saw that Thad had developed into a mature, smart, good-looking guy, and, of course, he was the son of Uncle Robert. So, she couldn't wait to tell Rebecca, who was also single at the time. We had barely driven out the driveway when Paige got Rebecca on her cell phone and breathlessly exclaimed, "He's hot!" after Rebecca asked what Thad looked like. The two giggled like little girls and the call soon ended. As if she could read my mind, Paige assured me the only reason she called him "hot" was for Rebecca's benefit in the hopes of sparking a romantic relationship between the two.

I believed her then and I believe it now, but I have to admit it bothered me that she never once referred to me as hot. Was it a big deal to me at the time that she called another guy hot? Not really, but, obviously, it mattered; otherwise, I wouldn't have remembered it. Perhaps her comment remains such a strong memory because it was the only time I ever heard her call a man hot. And it wasn't me. To her credit (and perhaps mine), Paige did call me handsome on several occasions. For that, I was very grateful. I loved hearing positive comments from her, and as the years went by, I craved those comments more and more. Perhaps I craved them too much.

The relationship between Thad and Rebecca never materialized. The irony is that within two years, the thought of Rebecca having any connection with Uncle Robert, let alone being married to his son, would be considered blasphemous and unthinkable by both the Bootys and Klassens.

CHAPTER 5

INKOM

———◦◉◦———

IN NOVEMBER OF 1998, Paige and I bought our first house together in Inkom, Idaho. Inkom is a tiny one-horse town ten miles south of Pocatello that a few hundred people called home. The downtown had a bank, post office, gas station, small grocery store, bar, restaurant, and cement plant that covered everything within a quarter-mile radius with a fine, gray powder. Our house, located over a mile to the east and out of range of the cement dust, wasn't much—three small bedrooms, couple baths, and some shag carpeting in the basement that was ugly even by 1970s standards—but the land was amazing. Energetic little Rapid Creek ran through the backyard, and further beyond the cottonwood banked creek stood a ten-to-fifteen-foot-high basalt rock wall. Over the five years we owned that home, Paige's father came down and helped us make several substantial improvements. Jack had spent most of his adult life as a contractor, so he had the skills and tools. Together, he and I (mostly him; I was just a strong back helping out) installed a dishwasher and new flooring in the kitchen, bookshelves in the living room, a detached garage, and many more upgrades.

With all we did to the inside of the home, we altered the landscape on the outside just as much, if not more. We moved rocks and dirt, disgorged ugly shrubs, planted numerous quaking aspens, expanded the garden area, and installed underground sprinklers. I was particularly obsessed with creating a rock climbing paradise in the backyard beyond the creek. Over millennia the rock cliff had crumbled down and created a rocky hillside in spots, whereas in other places, a clean fifteen-foot vertical edge remained. I set out to improve upon nature and remove all the weeds, underbrush, dirt, and loose rocks to create a clean, ready-to-climb rock wall. I spent countless hours reclaiming the wall, but, ironically, I hardly ever climbed there.

Our Inkom home was truly an idyllic setting. During the frigid winter months, we snowboarded at the small ski hill just up the road, and deer would occasionally bed down outside our living room window. In spring, we would picnic in the backyard, with Paige and me smiling as little Thomas romped about in the green grass. I caught small brook trout in the creek in summer and picked berries from the chokecherry and elderberry bushes, which Paige used to make jams and syrup. In the fall, we enjoyed a bountiful harvest from our garden of sweet carrots, hefty potatoes, and plump zucchini.

The years we spent in Inkom were some of my happiest. My broadcasting career was on the rise at OLN, our family was growing, and we owned our own little private Idaho. But what made me most happy was Paige. She and I were in love and our marriage brought me immeasurable joy. We camped, hiked, rock climbed, and rode bikes together; we held hands when we walked, and every day, I told her I loved her; she was tender and affectionate and would laugh with delight as I chased her through the house and then tossed her on our bed. I adored her, and, it seemed to me, she adored me too. My position at OLN afforded me a great deal of free time and most of the events I traveled to lasted less than a week. In between events, I was free to do whatever I liked, and it was common to have several weeks off in a row. During these breaks, I was with Paige nearly the entire time. We made a good life together, and I treasured each day with her.

One event in particular stood out. On a cold winter day, when Thomas hadn't yet turned two, Paige, Thomas, and I hiked into a backcountry yurt. We drove a few miles up the road from our home to the Inman Creek trailhead. From there, we snowshoed a mile into the forest with Thomas hitching a ride on Paige's back in a cozy kid carrier. The yurt was a round canvas and wood structure that was completely surrounded by several feet of snow. At night the temperatures dropped well below freezing, but after making a roaring fire in the old wood-burning stove, it became so hot we could hardly sleep. After the fire died out during the middle of the night, it became bitterly cold again. Paige tucked Thomas into her sleeping bag to keep him warm. I barely slept a wink on the hard wooden bunk bed that supported me and my sleeping bag. Despite the lack of sleep, we had a great time. It was such a fun adventure. And that's what life with Paige felt like, an adventure.

EVEN NOW I find it hard not to be sentimental when I think of the trail at Inman Creek, the miles we spent riding our bikes on the nearby roads, climbing and camping, and all the other fun things we did during those five years we lived in Inkom. Compared to the years that followed, they seem so carefree and joyful. It was also a time when we saw little of Uncle Robert. I find the correlation obvious and inescapable.

That doesn't mean there weren't some difficult moments and signs of trouble. There were plenty. One such moment was on another trip to California and a brief visit to Uncle Robert's home. By this time Thomas was around two years old and able to communicate well.

We gathered in the living room with Paige and me sitting on a couch and Uncle Robert in a chair opposite us. Thomas, who was playing with a small toy airplane, climbed up and sat on Uncle Robert's lap. While we were casually chatting, Thomas interrupted and said something to Uncle Robert about the little plane in his hands. Uncle Robert corrected him. Thomas's brow furrowed and he dug his heels in. Thinking he knew better, he told Uncle Robert he was wrong. Uncle Robert glared down at him and said, "No," in a very loud and firm voice.

Seeing this man I still didn't know much about flash his anger at my two-year-old son, I practically jumped off the couch, walked over, and plucked Thomas from Uncle Robert's lap. Being polite and defusing the situation was only part of my thinking; I was also incredibly uncomfortable with Uncle Robert addressing my son that way. When I picked up Thomas, Uncle Robert smiled graciously and moved on with the conversation. Clearly flustered, Paige sat there, not knowing what to say. Only later did she unload both barrels and tell me she was livid with the way I handled that situation. To her, I had stepped in and completely ruined a golden opportunity for Uncle Robert to discipline and train Thomas, as only Uncle Robert could. On top of that, I had diminished Uncle Robert in Thomas's eyes and, thus, done Thomas irreparable harm.

At this time, I still didn't know Uncle Robert that well. We'd probably only met in person three or four times, and I doubt I had ever spoken to him on the phone. I was also completely unaware of how much Paige relied on him for wisdom and emotional support. As the years passed, that moment gained significance in Paige's mind and seemed destined to be yet another of the iconic, almost reverential stories the Klassens loved to tell about Uncle Robert.

One such story involved Jeff, Paige's older brother. Jeff had just learned to walk when the Klassens visited Uncle Robert in the early 1970s. Standing next to the bed and clinging to his parents, someone asked Jeff to walk to Uncle Robert. Jeff, being a very young child and not sure who this Uncle Robert guy was, refused. None of the adults forced Jeff to go to Uncle Robert, they all just waited. And waited. Roughly thirty minutes later, with his parents sitting there with bated breath, Jeff finally relented and walked to Uncle Robert on his own accord. That moment for Jeff, one I doubt he remembers, was recounted as if it was the most important moment in his life. I had heard this story, and, like many other stories the Klassens told of Uncle Robert (or ones he told of himself), it seemed a bit odd or, at least, odd the way they attached such significance to it. It seemed every little trivial moment with Uncle Robert turned into a seminal event for the person lucky enough to cross paths with him. It irritated me that this episode with Thomas on Uncle Robert's lap seemed destined to become another famous Uncle Robert moment, albeit one that I had ruined.

ANOTHER ODD MOMENT with Thomas occurred around the same time, but not with Uncle Robert present. Our little family was visiting Paige's parents in Hayden right before I left for Italy to cover the Giro d'Italia bike race in the spring of 2000. To enjoy some privacy and reduce our exposure to the increasing weirdness that went on at Paige's parents' house, we stayed at a hotel in nearby Coeur d'Alene. An example of that weirdness happened one night before we headed back to our hotel. Thomas was on the floor playing with a bunch of matchbox cars and Grandpa Jack got down on the floor to play with him, sort of. I sat on a nearby couch, close enough to hear what was said. Jack asked Thomas for the car Thomas was playing with. Thomas clearly liked this car and offered Jack another car. Jack refused it and repeated his request for the car Thomas was playing with. I could see Thomas was confused and he again offered his grandpa another car. Again, Jack asked for the car in Thomas's hand. This went on and on. Thomas, barely two years old at the time, was getting upset, but Jack kept pressing. I watched this with both amazement and horror and wondered at what point I should intervene. Eventually, Jack gave up, but I knew exactly what he was doing. He was trying to channel his inner Uncle Robert and create another formative moment for Thomas. He was trying to get Thomas to give up the thing he wanted most so that his grandpa could have it, and thus teach Thomas the valuable lesson of putting loved ones ahead of loved things. He was also dealing with a two-year-old, and, by trying to force the moment with all the subtly of a punch in the face, Jack antagonized, confused, and irritated Thomas. I wondered, and worried, how much further Jack would have taken things if I hadn't been in the room.

I told Paige about the incident, and she too was concerned by it. Later that night, when the Klassens offered to babysit Thomas the next day so Paige and I could go on a date, Paige agreed, but only if Cathy, Paige's mom, was around as well. This didn't sit well with Jack. We could tell his wheels were spinning, but he was utterly speechless as he stared at Paige, trying to make sense of her words. She smiled and hugged her parents and off we went to our hotel for the night.

Sure enough, as soon as we got to our hotel, Jack called and said he wanted to talk in person. When he showed up, Thomas was already asleep, so the three of us sat down on the hallway floor right outside our hotel room. He asked Paige why she said what she did, and she explained our concern about the incident with the toy car and Thomas. He vigorously defended himself, declaring that through his actions, he was teaching Thomas the very foundations of Christianity. He was trying to create another memorable moment, just like the ones with Uncle Robert. Only he wasn't Uncle Robert, and neither Paige nor I saw his actions as beneficial. We argued for a while and held our ground. He eventually got up and left in disgust. Because of moments like this, I often breathed a sigh of relief when I saw Hayden in my rearview mirror.

BY FAR, THE most bizarre and disturbing incident during this time happened one morning at our home in Inkom while Paige's parents were visiting. Jack asked to meet with Paige, Cathy, and I. Paige put Thomas down for his nap and we all met in the basement. Cathy, Paige, and I sat on our dingy old red couch and Jack pulled a metal folding chair across the ugly shag carpet and sat down in front of us. When Jack, in a very calm, matter-of-fact voice, said he was leaving Cathy, I was stunned. Reflexively, I glanced over at Cathy, who was scowling and shaking her head in disgust. After a split-second pause, perhaps to make sure her father wasn't playing some sick joke, Paige started sobbing uncontrollably. She dropped to her knees in front of her father and, once her sobbing had subsided enough for her to speak, begged him not to do it. Paige stayed there at her father's feet, crying and talking to Jack for a good twenty minutes. It was clear to me that Cathy didn't want Jack to leave her, but she seemed so disgusted with him, she hardly said a word the entire time.

At one point, Jack told Paige, "Uncle Robert has been your true father all these years, not me."

Again, I was shocked at such nonsense. Paige, too, seemed to brush this comment aside as absurd. Eventually Jack listened to Paige and didn't leave his wife that day. Later that afternoon, when Rebecca showed up at our house, Jack had settled down and whatever storms had been raging in his mind seemed to have dissipated. Incredibly, no one said a word to her. Rebecca had no idea what had happened earlier in the day with her parents, and it baffled me why she was kept in the dark. Unfortunately, Jack's remark about Uncle Robert being Paige's true father would be repeated years later.

Looking back on that moment, I was in awe of Paige. She was so fiercely committed to the concept of marriage, even more committed to her parents' marriage than her father. Once, during the first year of our marriage, when the breakup of another couple we knew was discussed, she said she would never agree to a divorce. No matter what the lawyers or courts said, she would simply refuse to sign a divorce decree because it went against the Word of God. I thanked the Lord for blessing me with a wife who was so devoted to me and the Biblical institution of marriage that divorce was something I would never have to worry about.

CHAPTER 6
THE BIRTH OF DAVID

---◦◉◦---

DESPITE THE CRAZINESS that permeated my in-laws' lives, life was good for Paige and me in the summer of 2000. I was married to my best friend and love of my life. Our son Thomas was a bright, inquisitive boy who brought us incalculable joy. Our joy was about to be doubled as Paige was pregnant with our second child. We had an adorable home with creeks and forests and mountains right out our back door. And I was well on my way to becoming the Bob Costas of adventure sports, or so I thought. I flew around the country covering mountain biking and road cycling races, bull riding and rodeo events, lumberjack competitions, and just about every other obscure athletic event you could imagine. Sometimes, I traveled the highways and, other times I took the road less traveled. I saw airport terminals not much bigger than a drive through espresso shack and drove through tiny rural towns that hadn't seen a fresh coat of paint since the Kennedy administration.

Like all sports broadcasters, I spent a lot of time in airports. Flights out of Pocatello, Idaho, went to one of two places—Boise or Salt Lake City. From there, I made my connecting flight. It seemed like I was always in the Salt Lake City airport waiting to catch a plane. Traveling home was always the most difficult part of the journey because my work was done, and I was anxious to see my family. I usually had to wait for hours, devouring junk food and lattes, then catch the last flight out of Salt Lake City in a sardine-can-sized turbo-prop airplane. The small plane would bump along the clouds for half an hour, like a small child bouncing on his father's knee, and land in Pocatello just before midnight.

In July of that year, after yet another work trip back East, I arrived to a dark and silent home. I dropped my luggage on the floor, brushed my teeth, then, thinking Paige was asleep, I quietly crawled into bed with her. But she immediately rolled over, round belly and all, and said, "I'm leaking." I had no idea what she meant. She explained she was leaking amniotic fluid and that wasn't a good thing. At the time she was only twenty-six weeks pregnant. Despite the late hour, she was concerned enough to call our midwife, who happened to live down the street. When the time came, we were hoping for a home birth, but our midwife was very conservative and didn't mince her words. "You need to get to the hospital right away." Within minutes, she appeared at our side door in her pajamas and robe to look after Thomas while Paige and I got in our car and sped off.

When we arrived at the hospital in Pocatello, we couldn't find anyone to help us. My calls of "Hello" echoed through the empty hallways with no response. After wandering a bit, Paige was leaking so much, she found a chair and sat while I continued to search for a nurse or doctor to help. Eventually, I found a nurse who attended to Paige immediately. Shortly after she gathered information about Paige's pregnancy and discovered how much she was leaking, the nurse grimly told us to name this child, as in this child might not live or might be delivered at any minute. We already had the name David picked out, so we were prepared for that, but little else.

That day was a blur, and the start of twelve straight weeks of stress, anxiety, fear, struggle, and hope that tested our faith and endurance. The doctors placed Paige on bed rest indefinitely while the nurses monitored her amniotic fluid levels. At the end of that long first day, I was exhausted, and it was late when Thomas (who had been brought to the hospital at some point during the day) and I left the hospital and went home to sleep. As we drove south on the interstate, I noticed in the distance bright jagged lines of flickering orange piercing the dark country night. Fires. Approaching the exit for Inkom, I slowed down, driving within one hundred feet of the fires that were devouring the parched sagebrush-covered hills. State patrol cars, with their lights flashing, had blocked the on-ramp to the highway, but the off-ramp was still open. As we crawled past, the glow of burning grass and sage reflected off our faces. When we got home, I put Thomas to bed, then walked outside. The fires were close, illuminating the sky just over the horizon. With an unfavorable shift in the wind, the fire could easily consume the mile or two between us and be at our doorstep very quickly. While Thomas slept, I packed our car with keepsakes and other valuable possessions in case we needed to make a fast getaway.

The wind, however, didn't shift, the fires died out, and Paige lay in her hospital bed drinking water like a fish in order to keep her fluids as high as possible. And she did this for weeks, all while lying in a hospital bedroom that had a commanding view of Pocatello. The fires near Inkom were gone, but larger ones were burning in the Arbon Valley to the south and west. The smoke drifted, hanging thick over that valley and the one Pocatello occupied. Thomas and I visited Paige nearly every day, but during the times when we weren't there, Uncle Robert was always just a phone call away.

THE DOCTORS NEVER figured out why Paige's amniotic sac

started leaking, but she knew. And, of course, it all had to do with Uncle Robert. Going back a few months, Paige's sister, Rebecca, had been having serious misgivings about Uncle Robert. Unbeknownst to me, she had shared with Paige and her parents some very disturbing accusations against him. Because of these accusations, and what she saw as a history of manipulation and abuse, she called him out as an evil fraud that the Klassens should immediately reject for their safety and sanity. It all came to a head that summer, while Paige was pregnant, in a dramatic showdown at the home of George Bookman.

George lived near the Klassens in Northern Idaho and was a close friend of both Jack and Uncle Robert. A kind and trusting man, George had met Jack roughly a decade earlier. Before long, he was sucked into the close circle of friendship that revolved around Uncle Robert. Whenever Uncle Robert traveled to Idaho to visit the Klassens, chances were that George would come by as well. On this fateful night, Jack and Uncle Robert had gathered at George's home. Rebecca showed up at George's ready to confront her father in the hopes of convincing him to sever his ties with Uncle Robert. But when she walked in the door, she discovered Uncle Robert was there at the house. Thrown off guard, she never stood a chance. Rebecca was an emotionally fragile young woman, and pitted against the smooth-talking, manipulative Uncle Robert, she was eaten alive. Jack, who had briefly believed Rebecca's allegations (as had Cathy) did a one hundred eighty degree turn that night and, from then on, fully supported Uncle Robert.

Prior to that confrontation at George's house, Rebecca had also shared her accusations against Uncle Robert with Paige. For a time, Paige believed her sister, just like her parents did. But then she too became convinced Rebecca was dead wrong. Paige was so distraught over believing the accusations Rebecca levied against Uncle Robert, she became absolutely certain the breach in her amniotic sac and the resultant leaking of fluid which endangered David's life was the Lord's judgment on her. Many years later, when Paige wrote her testimony, this is what she had to say about this moment.

"In July 2000, I was chastened by the Lord when I failed to stand up for the truth when the one who led me to Christ was being attacked. I am ashamed to say that I stood by and waited, therefore condoning the words and actions of the one viciously attacking him. The Lord allowed me a chance, however, by letting my pregnancy of the time become endangered through an amniotic fluid leak. I knew at once why I was there in the hospital with my unborn baby's life in danger. I called Uncle Robert the next morning and confessed and apologized through tears of anguish at what my lack of action had caused. I asked the Lord for forgiveness and for the life of my unborn child."

At the time Paige went into the hospital with David, I had no idea any of this was going on. Over that summer, I heard bits and pieces of Rebecca's accusations, and it sounded like she was accusing Uncle Robert of molesting her. While I thought Uncle Robert was weird, I didn't think him capable of that. When Paige finally told me that she believed her pregnancy was endangered because she believed Rebecca's lies about Uncle Robert, I was baffled and annoyed. Why would the Lord nearly kill our unborn son simply because someone slighted Uncle Robert? And who cared what Rebecca, or anyone else for that matter, thought of Uncle Robert? Knowing Paige was going through an extremely difficult situation, I tried to be sympathetic and focused on supporting her, rather than questioning her judgment. As for the showdown at George's house, I didn't find out about that for another eighteen years.

Perhaps Paige didn't tell me her true feelings regarding the amniotic leak right away because she was ashamed of herself or because she thought I would find her reasoning nonsensical. She knew I wasn't the biggest fan of Uncle Robert, so confessing that our unborn child nearly died because she hadn't been loyal enough to him wasn't going to go over very well with me. And it didn't. The idea that the Lord orchestrated this because Paige believed Rebecca's accusation was absurd. But I didn't share these opinions with Paige. I can't remember at what point Paige shared her feelings with me, but it was clearly after she confessed everything to Uncle Robert, begging for his forgiveness. I found out years later that this too was a disturbing pattern that continued throughout our marriage. When it came to Paige's inmost thoughts and feelings, Uncle Robert, not me, usually heard them first.

After the dust settled from the confrontation at George's, the Klassen family split apart over the issue of Uncle Robert. Brothers Lance and Phil believed Rebecca, while Jeff, Paige, and their parents sided with Uncle Robert. Once the battle lines had been drawn, Rebecca, Lance, and Phil were completely shunned and vilified by the rest of the family. Shortly thereafter, the rest of the extended Klassen family—all the aunts, uncles, and cousins in Canada—were shunned as well. What was a rift in the family evolved into Paige, Jeff, and their parents isolating themselves behind a moat of fear and self-righteousness, carried out for the sole purpose of protecting Uncle Robert. I went along with the shunning because my relationship with Paige was paramount, not because I agreed with it. I thought the shunning was bizarre and cruel, but whenever I brought it up with Paige, she made it clear she didn't want to talk about it. So, once again, in order to get along with my wife, I simply stopped bringing it up.

Not only did we cut off all contact with Rebecca, Paige wouldn't even allow her name to be uttered in our house. From then on, Rebecca, with her beautiful red hair being the first thing you'd notice about her, was dismissively referred to as the "Redhead." Rebecca went from being Paige's best friend to public enemy number one. Paige even went so far as to remove all framed pictures on walls or photos in albums that had Rebecca in them. Her chief concern seemed to be Thomas. Prior to the split over Uncle Robert, we would see Rebecca regularly since she still lived in Pocatello. Rebecca was incredibly fond of her cute little nephew, and the two got along great. But after the split, Paige was determined to purge Rebecca from not only her life but also from Thomas's. She didn't want Rebecca poisoning his young and impressionable mind. And anyone wicked enough to oppose Uncle Robert had to be just that: poisonous. Thus, the sooner Thomas forgot about his beloved Aunt Rebecca, the better.

As for my family (my parents, my four older brothers, and their spouses and children) no one really knew what was going on with the Klassens and my family. And that was fine with me. I didn't really understand it myself so how could I explain it to my parents and brothers? We lived in Idaho, far away from my relatives, so they rarely saw us, and never saw the Klassens. Over the years when my family would ask about Paige's family, our answers were always vague and evasive. Just as Paige made it clear to me she didn't want to discuss Rebecca or her other brothers, we made that same point clear to my family. At the time, it didn't seem to me like evidence of a dangerous metastasizing veil of secrecy. It just seemed weird. Later, it became crystal clear.

AFTER THIRTY-TWO weeks of pregnancy and dropping amniotic fluid levels, the doctors decided to deliver David via cesarean section. When he was born, David weighed just shy of five pounds, much heavier than we thought he'd be. As soon as the doctor plucked him from Paige's womb, a nurse whisked him to the Neonatal Intensive Care Unit (NICU), with me fast on her heels. It was hard to leave Paige who was lying on an operating table with a small curtain strung across her chest so she wouldn't see the bloody mess that was her abdomen. But she gamely smiled and asked me to stay with David. I'll never forget the sight of him, minutes after birth, lying on a warming pad in the NICU, fighting for air. Every breath seemed like a life-or-death struggle as his tiny chest cavity would expand on the inhale then sink to the width of my index finger on the exhale. He was so tiny, so fragile. As tears trickled down my face I prayed to the Lord and asked him to save my precious little son. Then I spoke directly to David. I told him I loved him. I told him he was strong, and with the Lord's help, he would survive.

I find it hard to accurately describe the terrifying feeling of vulnerability when my wife was on the operating table, her abdomen cut wide open, and my newborn son a breath away from having his life snuffed out. Repeatedly, Christ told his followers not to fear, and it is in these frightening moments that we should trust Him the most. Did I trust in the Lord at that moment? Absolutely. Was I still afraid? Yes.

Because he was born eight weeks premature, David's lungs were dangerously underdeveloped. During his six weeks in the NICU, he had a few near-death moments, but, thankfully, the Lord provided great doctors and a few miracles too. A week or so after the C-section, Paige came home, but for the next five weeks she took daily trips back to the hospital to help feed David. One morning, while Paige was at the hospital feeding David, I was at home in the shower with the bathroom door open so I could hear Thomas if he needed me.

Suddenly Paige appeared in the doorway with a look of utter astonishment and glee. She held onto a car seat, and sitting there snug and cozy was little David. I had no idea he was coming home that day and it remains for me one of the best surprises of my life.

JUXTAPOSED AGAINST THE inspiring birth and survival of David was a lot of weirdness going on with Uncle Robert and the Klassen family. Just prior to the birth of David, Jack became aware, with ample help from Uncle Robert, that he hadn't really been a Christian all these years. We were told that through many tears of anguish and countless hours of counseling, Uncle Robert led Jack to Christ. Just as with Paige a few years earlier, I had assumed Jack already was a Christian. He had grown up in a Christian home, attended seminary, read the Bible, and, most importantly, acknowledged he was a sinner, recognized Jesus as Lord, and—again, I assumed—had accepted the Lord's gift of salvation. Apparently, Uncle Robert convinced him all that history was fraudulent and he, Jack, was also a fraud. Then, not long after his conversion, it dawned on Jack that Cathy, his wife of over thirty years, must not be a Christian either. After all, if he had been faking it all these years, then she must have been doing it too. Of course, Uncle Robert was in full agreement with Jack's assessment of Cathy. So, Jack, under the guidance of Uncle Robert, set out to show Cathy tough love, the kind of love that would leave her with no option other than admitting she was a demonic fraud, had always faked her Christian faith, and had never truly believed in Christ Jesus.

To demonstrate this tough love for her, Jack treated Cathy like dirt. One of the ways he did that was preventing her from visiting David while he was still in the hospital. So, when Jack came down from northern Idaho to support Paige and visit David, he came alone. Aside from Jack's trip to visit David, I didn't see much of Jack or Cathy during this time, and I certainly had no idea this was going on. There was, however, one time during this episode between Jack and Cathy that Paige and I were around both her parents. We were on a short visit to Hayden, and we all went out to dinner. It was perhaps the most awkward dinner I've ever had to sit through. Jack was rude and dismissive and mostly ignored Cathy, but the few questions of hers he did answer dripped with judgment and condescension. Obviously, Jack was up to something, and I suspected that Uncle Robert was somehow involved, but nothing was explained to me at the moment. So, I swallowed my questions and simply observed, but at an angle because watching the ugly and bizarre scene that played out in front of me was too embarrassing to face head on.

Paige and I were led to believe that Jack and Uncle Robert's ploy to save Cathy by rejecting her false claim of being a Christian had actually worked. Apparently, the deliverance of Cathy was so dramatic and hard fought, that when Uncle Robert exorcised the demons within her, Cathy shouted like a horse (I'm not sure what a shouting horse sounds like but that is how Uncle Robert described it to me). After this amazing, life altering event, Jack and Cathy again visited our home in Inkom and once again we gathered in the now infamous basement with the ugly shag carpet. This time, though, Paige and I sat on the dingy old couch together while Jack and Cathy sat next to each other on metal chairs facing us. While Jack patiently watched, Cathy spilled her guts to Paige, confessing she never truly loved her or any of her siblings, that she had pitted Paige and her siblings against each other when they were young, and numerous other sins. It was an incredibly weird meeting. It was also very exhausting and difficult to listen to, and I barely knew my mother-in-law. I couldn't imagine what it was like for Paige to hear those words come from her own mother. I would have been devastated had my mother confessed to never loving me. Unlike the time when her father threatened to leave Cathy and Paige sobbed unabashedly, Paige remained stoic as she listened to her mother confess the sins of her past and the ugliness of her soul. It seemed she wasn't the least bit surprised and knew the truth all along. Remarkably, Paige hardly ever talked about it with me.

With the benefit of time and distance to reflect and ponder carefully, I am struck by how odd it now seems that immediately after these events took place—Cathy's confession that she never loved Paige, Jack's declaration he was leaving Cathy, the absolute and complete discarding of Rebecca—it was back to life as usual for Paige. Time to wash the laundry, plant the garden, make lunch, feed Thomas, keep moving and don't look back. I don't recall much discussion between us about what we'd just heard and experienced. It was as if it wasn't that big a deal to Paige. Had it been my parents and siblings who had said or done these things there would have been days, weeks, perhaps even years of discussion, healing, and processing for me. And I would have involved Paige in all of it, for I trusted her opinion above all others. However, if Paige had needed help processing everything her family was throwing at her, she didn't seek my help.

Cathy was now the third member of the Klassen family that was supposedly led to the Lord by Uncle Robert after falsely believing they had already been saved. I couldn't help but wonder if this had happened to other members of the Klassen family, but I just didn't know. Had Paige's older brother Jeff also gone through this recipe of salvation with Uncle Robert? One of the other brothers? Were there other families who followed Uncle Robert and experienced these same things? And who would be next?

CHAPTER 7
ROOTS OF HATE

—◉◉◉—

IT SEEMED CLEAR in the fall of 2000, that none of Paige's younger siblings—Rebecca, Lance, or Phil—would be the next family member to receive a spiritual epiphany at the hands of Uncle Robert. They wanted nothing to do with him. Thus, after Jack and Cathy had been saved, and David's life had been spared, Paige's family became deeply divided between those who trusted and believed in Uncle Robert and those who didn't. You had to pick a side; there was no Switzerland option. And no one related to Paige was spared from having to declare their allegiance for or against Uncle Robert, including her maternal grandmother.

Cathy Klassen was an only child and had very few relatives of her own: just her father, mother, and an aunt and uncle. In fact, Cathy's mother, Ellen Hansen, was only married to her father, John Hansen, for about a year. He was in the merchant marine and left Ellen shortly after Cathy's birth. Cathy never saw her father growing up and only reunited with him when she was in her 50s. By then, he lived in upstate New York with relatives who had immigrated with him from Norway. When Paige and I got to meet him a few times before he passed away, he seemed like a wonderful old man with lots of spunk and a twinkle in his eye. Because he had removed himself

49

from Cathy's life for so long and was living his final years thousands of miles away, he knew precious little about Uncle Robert and everything that went along with knowing him.

That left Cathy's mother, Ellen, and Ellen's brother, Paul, and sister, June. Paul and June never married, and once Ellen was divorced, she moved back in with her siblings. The three of them lived together for decades and, together, raised Cathy. I'm not sure how much Paul and June knew about Uncle Robert, but Ellen knew enough to be skeptical of him. So, when Jack and Cathy drove down to Southern California where Ellen lived and tried to convince her that Cathy had only now become a Christian, thanks, of course, to Uncle Robert, Ellen didn't believe it. Perhaps recalling a lifetime of memories that convinced her Cathy had already believed in the Lord, Ellen didn't accept what she was now being told. And that was all it took for Jack and Cathy to throw Ellen out of their lives.

Ellen was in poor health, and on that last visit from her daughter and son-in-law, she was enduring the humiliation of needing a colostomy bag. She died a few years later. Jack and Cathy didn't find out Ellen had died for months, if not years, after the fact. They simply didn't care. Not one letter or card or bouquet of flowers for the funeral ever came from Jack and Cathy. The last time I ever heard Cathy talk about her mom, she described that final meeting in California where her mom was tethered to the colostomy bag. She kept referring to her mother's "bag of shit," insinuating that her mother was a "bag of shit." I was stunned by the incredible animosity and vitriol Cathy directed toward her mother. Perhaps equally disturbing was the fact that neither Jack nor Paige spoke up to defend Ellen.

The Klassens on Jack's side of the family were treated just as poorly. Jack had two brothers, Tim the oldest, and Donnie the youngest. They both were married with several children, and the entire extended Klassen clan lived in and around Vancouver, B.C. Jack had been feuding with his brothers and parents off and on for years. Now the split seemed permanent. Jack and Cathy, as well as Paige and Jeff, lived in a world where you were either for Uncle Robert or against him. It was that simple. The last time we saw any of Paige's aunts, uncles, and cousins was at Phil's wedding in Seattle just prior to Paige going into the hospital pregnant with David. Tim, who officiated at both Paige and Phil's weddings, was a favorite target of criticism for Uncle Robert. Tim was an ordained minister and thus a threat to Uncle Robert. Often, when Uncle Robert shared one of his unique insights from God's Word, he would turn to Jack and say something like, "I'll bet your so-called brother never told you that."

The shunning of Rebecca was the most severe and vicious because she was the one who came forward with the allegations against Uncle Robert. But with her name no longer mentioned and pictures of her removed from sight, as if she'd been erased from existence, life moved on, and I stopped asking questions about her. Then around seven years later, Rebecca reached out to Paige and tried to mend the fences. I don't know how I knew, but within seconds of Paige answering her cell phone, I knew it was Rebecca. Paige's face became stern and rigid, and she walked into another room so the children wouldn't hear, but I could. The conversation was brief. Rebecca gave a blanket apology and Paige asked her what had caused her to change her mind. Rebecca then said something that set Paige off. She screamed at Rebecca through the phone, calling her a snake, and just before hanging up, warned her to stay away from our family and never call again. Just like that, it was over. Paige hadn't spoken with her in years, and when Rebecca reached out in the hope of reuniting with her older sister, Paige shut it down in less than a minute.

It was all so strange and bizarre to me. Within a very short time every single relative of Paige, other than her parents and older brother, had been shunned and vilified. While it's much clearer to me now what happened, back then I wasn't really sure what was going on. The shunning may have been complete, exhaustive, and assiduous, but the explanations were anything but. It seemed to me nobody wanted to discuss why we now had to completely ignore Rebecca, Phil, Lance, and the rest of the Klassen relatives. I tried not to ask too many questions and, in essence, went along to get along. Still, I wondered. Why didn't someone reach out to these relatives and start a dialogue seeking some kind of resolution? Why didn't Jack and Cathy embrace the role of parent and reach out to their children? It seemed like no one in the family wanted to start talking, except Uncle Robert. And he did a lot of it.

MOST OF US can remember where we were when we first heard what was happening on September 11, 2001. Paige and I were about as far away from the tragic events of that day as any American in the country could be. We had stayed the previous night in a small cabin at the Redfish Lake Resort in the Sawtooth Mountains of Central Idaho. There was no cell reception, no TV, no radio, no internet, nothing. The outside world seemed light-years away. That was the point and I loved it there. Even though the devastation had already unfolded on the East Coast, there was nothing out of the ordinary as Paige and I, along with Thomas and David, ate a late breakfast at the resort restaurant. But I remember vaguely hearing the wait staff mumble something under their breath about fires and planes and burning buildings. I had no idea what they were talking about and paid it no mind.

After breakfast, we left for home, but along the way, Paige and I took turns riding our bikes. Paige went first: I dropped her off on the side of the highway and drove ahead in the car with the boys to our meet up location. About an hour later she showed up and we switched. I hopped on my bike and took off for the top of Galena Summit where Paige would pick me up. At the top of the pass, around mid-afternoon, I stopped to wait for Paige and met a friendly Canadian couple who had pulled off to a small parking area along the side of the road. They were enjoying a snack while taking in the breathtaking view of the surrounding mountain ranges. We exchanged pleasantries and chitchat for a few minutes, then they asked me if I'd seen what was happening back in New York City and Washington, DC. It strikes me now as very odd that we would chat for a few minutes before they brought up the carnage. And what they told me had me doubting their sanity or sobriety. Planes knocking down skyscrapers in New York? Planes flying into buildings in DC? I thought they were crazy. But when Paige, who'd been listening to the news on the radio, drove up in our car and got out, I knew it was all true the moment I looked at her face.

Most Americans old enough to remember 9/11 have their own stories from that day or stories related to those events. A number of people from my hometown of Ridgewood, New Jersey died in the Twin Towers. One of my high school classmates was widowed that day. I remember flying out of the ridiculously small airport in Pierre, South Dakota about a week before 9/11 and never even going through a metal detector. And I remember flying in the first-class section of a large jet about a week after 9/11. While the plane sat on the tarmac, many of the passengers still shaken up over 9/11, the pilot came out and talked to the first-class cabin and calmly assured us we were all safe. It was one of the most memorable displays of leadership and professionalism I've ever seen.

9/11 changed all our lives. I flew frequently for work and the new government restrictions made airline travel odious. But the most dramatic change in my life that was a result of the events on 9/11 didn't occur until about a year later. We were visiting Paige's parents in Hayden and—you guessed it—Uncle Robert was there. With all of the shunning of family members that happened because of Uncle Robert, I was more leery of him than ever. Then he started talking about 9/11 and it opened up a whole new world for me. I would imagine, for many, the horrific events of 9/11 made the world seem a more dark and dangerous place. For me, that happened while sitting in the living room of Paige's parents' house listening to Uncle Robert.

I don't know how we got on the subject, but Uncle Robert adamantly claimed that over 80,000 people died on 9/11. I had always heard or read a death toll of around 3,000. When I questioned him on his figure, he bristled at my suggestion that the number was inflated. Then he proceeded to lay the blame for the entire event, and pretty much every other controversial event of the last one hundred years, on the Jews. He said that both President Franklin D. Roosevelt and President Harry S. Truman were Jews. That wasn't all he said, but those are the details I vividly remember from that particular discussion.

Growing up in New Jersey, I had a melting pot for a neighborhood. My childhood friends were Jewish, Catholic, Christian, Black, White, Polish, Italian, Greek, Irish—you name it. And because we grew up around each other, we often cracked jokes and teased each other about our religions or ethnicities. No one was immune, so no one really got too bothered by it. But when Uncle Robert called FDR and Truman Jews, it was more than just a political or religious jab, or some kind of locker room talk. There was an angry, sinister tone to his comments that unnerved me. I had majored in history at college and loved to read about history, but I had never heard anything like this. A sinister Jewish conspiracy was behind every catastrophic event in recorded history? I was shocked and, frankly, scared.

Later that night, in the downstairs spare bedroom that often felt like a dungeon with its dim lighting and low ceiling, I told Paige what Uncle Robert said about the Jews. And I told her something along the lines that I thought he was dangerous and that we shouldn't have anything to do with him. She listened, her face pinched with concern, but remained silent. I should have continued the conversation, pressed the issue, demanded we take action. I should have asked her if she believed him and all his theories about the Jews. But I didn't. Instead, she got up, left the room to get ready for bed and that was it.

In some ways, this was a repeat of Paige not believing I was a Christian back in 1997 prior to our marriage. She brought it up once and we never discussed it again. Likewise, after that night, I never again told Paige that I thought we should have nothing to do with Uncle Robert. We never discussed Uncle Robert from the perspective of questioning our involvement with him. I wonder what Paige would have done if I had been more assertive. Of course, she wouldn't have allowed me to get rid of Uncle Robert, but what would the fight or confrontation have looked like? Would she have left me right away? Called a meeting with Uncle Robert and her parents so they could gang up on me and shame me into an apology? Start shunning me like she did Rebecca?

What if ...

I will never know because I didn't follow up, didn't follow through. I let it go, and for the most part, silently grew more and more suspicious of Uncle Robert. Unfortunately, our reliance on Uncle Robert for wisdom and advice on just about everything grew exponentially. And because of that dependency, I was exposed to one radical and bizarre belief after another.

I don't want to turn this story into a laborious theological dissertation, but knowing a bit of Uncle Robert's theology is crucial to understanding him and how his theology affected all of us. Robert Booty was born and raised in Syria in the 1940s by Christian parents. The influences of Muslim and Arabic culture and religion were strong on him, despite coming from a Christian home. He grew up in a culture where hatred of Jews was pervasive. When he emigrated to this country as a young adult, he wholeheartedly embraced the American dream, but brought with him his Middle Eastern passions and prejudices. While at a small seminary in Fresno, California, which is where he first met and befriended Jack Klassen, he wrote his dissertation on the controversial early 20th century document, the *Protocols of the Learned Elders of Zion,* that supposedly details Jewish plans for world domination. Uncle Robert pompously said that it didn't matter if the document was an antisemitic forgery if all the things it planned for the world were coming to fruition.

He believed the answer to the Jewish question was found in the Bible with the Old Testament story of Isaac's family and the identity of his two sons, Jacob and Esau. According to him, Esau eventually became Edom, or the Edomites, who eventually became modern Jewry. Conversely, Jacob was the father of the twelve tribes of Israel and eventually greater Christendom in Europe and America. He also taught that when the Bible speaks of Jew and Gentile, Jew is really referring to the tribe of Judah, and Gentile to the Nations, or the other tribes of Israel. Which, through a byzantine reconstruction of world history, led to our modern-day problem where the vast majority of Christians think the Jews are the chosen people spoken of in the Bible. However, according to Uncle Robert, the Jews are mostly the descendants of Esau, people that God hated. And Gentiles, while a pejorative to the Jews, really means the Nations, or the tribes of Israel, the true chosen people of God. What really mystified me was his implication that, somehow, nearly every Jew knew this, while nearly every Gentile or Christian didn't. Moreover, ever since Jacob stole the birthright from Esau (see Genesis Chapter 27), the descendants of Esau, the Edomites and Jews, have been trying to get it back. And the way they've been doing that is to rule over the Gentiles, the Christians, through bloody warfare, central banking, usury, anti-Christian education, Communism, and being the culprit behind every conspiracy or calamity the world has known for the past several centuries.

Thus, it didn't matter to Uncle Robert if the infamous *Protocols of the Learned Elders of Zion* was a forgery or not. In his mind, what the supposed elders called for (Jewish world domination) was happening in our world, and that's all that mattered. Hopefully, you can see the obvious danger in thinking this way: every conspiracy, every bad world event (war, depression, recession, Communism, etc.) had Jewish roots. And it wasn't really necessary to come up with any evidence to back it. This was supposedly biblically ordained and prophesied, something that only Uncle Robert was wise enough to glean from the Word of God. So, if there was evidence of Jewish complicity in 9/11 or any other catastrophe, great, but evidence wasn't necessary. All that was necessary was to simply believe in what Uncle Robert said and not ask too many questions. And that proved difficult for me.

CHAPTER 8
CONFERENCES

AFTER OUR SON David was born, and Paige's family splintered into two camps, we circled the wagons around Uncle Robert, and his beliefs took on a much larger role in our lives. At least they did for me. To my surprise, I started finding some of his teachings beneficial. I learned more about the Declaration of Independence and U.S. Constitution through him than I did while obtaining my history degree from George Washington University. Paige encouraged me to talk with him more so I could accelerate my learning, and, realizing he wasn't going away, I reluctantly started calling and emailing him. I was still wary of him and *never* comfortable around him. He was so unpredictable and immune to questioning that I found him hard to approach and could never let my guard down. If I erred in asking Uncle Robert the wrong question or asking it the wrong way, I was not only bluntly scolded by Uncle Robert, but also felt the sting of disapproval from Paige. With her, it was subtle (a look, a gesture, the cold shoulder) but it was unmistakable. And in the back of my mind, I wondered if I really messed up, would I get the same treatment as Rebecca?

Meanwhile, Paige seemed to adore and respect everything about Uncle Robert, hanging on his every word, no matter how off-the-wall it was. And when it came to off-the-wall comments, nobody could hold a candle to Uncle Robert. Most of those comments were shared during what became our annual conferences in Hayden. Usually when friends or relatives get together it's called a gathering or meeting or reunion; or if people at church gather to study the Word of God, it's a Bible study. But when we gathered with Uncle Robert, it was always elevated in importance to a conference. Which was a glorified way of describing all of us, my family and Paige's parents and brother, sitting around listening to Uncle Robert talk.

We usually congregated in the Klassen's living room. Uncle Robert's hairless dome, which was covered by his black cowboy hat when outside, glistened as light filtered in through the large picture windows. The Klassens supplied a small card table for Uncle Robert to place his Arabic Bible, English Bible, and other notes and papers. From behind this humble dais, he sat, pontificating for hours on end with his sonorous voice and Middle Eastern accent. The rest of us, occupying chairs, couches, or a spot on the carpet, sat in a semicircle around him. The adults, myself included, took extensive notes, and Jeff, being the most technically savvy, recorded all the sessions with a video camera. Only our very young children received a special dispensation and were allowed to remain downstairs and play quietly. Once old enough to sit relatively still, we required the kids to join us in the living room, stifle their wiggles and at least pretend to listen to Uncle Robert's long-winded sermons.

The agenda for the Conferences was always set by Uncle Robert. What was covered and for how long was entirely his domain. Despite my doubts about him, it became apparent to me how Paige and her parents could view Uncle Robert, with his command of the Bible and knowledge of history, as the most brilliant man to walk the face of the earth. He could talk extemporaneously for extended lengths of time, cleverly weaving back and forth between memorized passages of scripture and dubious sounding tales from his colorful past.

There was very little back and forth, discussion, or debate at any of the Conferences. One voice dominated. Uncle Robert wasn't interested in what anyone else thought. He was only interested in hearing himself talk and became irritated if anyone wasn't listening to him at all times. He was the master of the dramatic pause and would employ it to extinguish all other conversations. If we were at the dinner table, and idle chatter was taking place but he wanted to make an important point, he would loudly start a thought then pause. He'd peek around the room, hoping to make eye contact, enticing us like we were little children and he was hiding candy in his hand. Like a loyal dog, Jack was *always* listening, ready to gobble up whatever morsel of wisdom Uncle Robert had to share. But the other conversations would slowly end as it became apparent Uncle Robert wouldn't continue until all eyes and ears were on him. Only after everyone was paying attention to him, would he continue his thought.

Much of what he shared sounded, at least the first time, so crazy I had a million questions, and not just for Uncle Robert. I had questions like, *Paige, do you really believe this nonsense?* Or *Jack, why are you acting like a child around him?* But questions weren't encouraged. It was the Word of Uncle Robert. If you didn't understand, it was always your fault, never his. So, just trust him anyway; eventually, you'd catch on.

That certainly seemed to be the modus operandi of Uncle Robert's sidekick, Michael Erving. Michael wasn't around when I first met Uncle Robert but started showing up to the Conferences a few years later. He was somewhere in his late 50s or early 60s with thinning unkempt hair and an unruly beard or mustache. His clothing was perpetually wrinkled and dated as if he pulled his wardrobe out of the bargain bin at a thrift store. Like Uncle Robert, he didn't seem to have much money and never talked about a job or career, so I saw him somewhere near the intersection of vaguely unemployed but not yet retired. And he either suffered from narcolepsy or simply found Uncle Robert's monologues too boring to keep himself awake. He constantly nodded off during the Conferences. Thomas and David would quietly giggle as Michael's head would bob, swivel, then jerk. To compensate for his inability to focus and stay awake, Michael would often change sitting positions, wandering all over his chair, shifting about on the couch, and dropping to the floor to kneel down, lay down, or sit down. At one Conference, Michael, whose devotion to Uncle Robert was dangerously infantile, spoke up and said he enjoyed being a follower and had no problems being submissive to authority. He was kneeling on the floor as he said this, just a few feet away from where Uncle Robert sat. He jokingly raised his hands above his head then elaborately bowed down to Uncle Robert. Uncle Robert didn't find it funny and imperiously barked at him to sit up and stay awake. I was shocked that Uncle Robert didn't reprimand Michael for bowing down to him, even though it was mostly in jest. As Christians, the only person we should ever bow down to is Jesus, and any true Christian leader would have made that clear. Uncle Robert's only objection to Michael's antics was that he had been interrupted.

It's easy to see, then, why the story of Uncle Robert and the imaginary deer is my favorite story about him. It was at one of our Conferences in Hayden where my family, Jeff, Jack and Cathy, and Uncle Robert and his wife, Staci, were all there. (Aunt Staci, as she was called, hardly ever came with Uncle Robert to Idaho, ostensibly because she had to stay behind in California and work. She had a good job at a hospital and was the family's breadwinner.) It was a gorgeous summer day and we were gathered on the large, covered back deck. Food was spread out on a table and we were snacking on watermelon while some of the adults sipped wine. It was a festive atmosphere and, of course, Uncle Robert did most of the talking. It was rare for him to not talk. He was pontificating about something while holding onto his glass of wine. Jack hovered over his shoulder as always. Uncle Robert's thoughts turned to the dense woods behind the house and the deer that frequented the area.

Suddenly, Uncle Robert sat up straight and pointed, claiming he saw a deer in the woods. We all looked to where he pointed. The afternoon sunlight sifted through the trees with leaves, branches, and needles creating a tangled mosaic of colors and shadows. In that brief moment, when we all looked, I am confident Jack, Jeff, and, perhaps, Cathy were all ready to describe the deer that Uncle Robert claimed to see but wasn't really there.

But then Staci spoke up, *"Yeah right, maybe I should have some of that wine!"*

After a split-second pause, Uncle Robert laughed heartily at her comment. In essence he laughed at himself; so then, and only then, did everyone else feel free to laugh as well.

Staci was the only one who could have gotten away with that. Had I said what she did, I would have been immediately vilified as disrespectfully sarcastic, arrogant, and who knows what else. None of the other adults there would have dreamed of doing such a thing. And had Staci not said what she did, I am convinced those other adults, especially Jack, would have believed there was a deer there. They might have even started to describe what it looked like, so deep was their trust for all words spoken by Uncle Robert. But for me, at that moment, Staci made Uncle Robert human and fallible. He was more relatable and likable in that moment than any other.

AUNT STACI'S DEVOTION to Uncle Robert was strong, but different than the Klassens. She was fully committed to her husband, but her devotion was seasoned with maturity, and she wasn't awed by him. Paige's devotion was fierce and bulletproof. Jack's devotion was childlike, unquestioning; he was constantly humbled to be in the presence of such savior-like brilliance. And Uncle Robert's most brilliant manifesto, the *piece de resistance* of his political and financial philosophies, was his American Sovereign National Credit proposal. I knew Jack and everyone else who followed Uncle Robert didn't understand this harebrained idea, because if they did, they would have realized its implementation would guarantee economic destruction. Uncle Robert loved talking about America's Sovereign National Credit. He even claimed to have met and spoken with former Chairman of the Federal Reserve, Alan Greenspan, about the concept. It was so big and grandiose, that, of course, only Uncle Robert could really understand it. The point wasn't for us to understand it, but simply go along with it and trust him.

Giving a clear explanation of Uncle Robert's vision of America's Sovereign National Credit is difficult because the concept is so stupid and opaque. But I'll try anyway. He claimed the citizens of the United States of America owned the nation's credit, not the Federal Reserve (the FED). And of course, Uncle Robert assured us, the FED was under the complete and total control of the international Jew, the descendants of Esau. Thus, the FED and America's Sovereign National Credit dovetailed nicely with Uncle Robert's theology. Admittedly, I was a big fan of Congressman and former Presidential candidate Ron Paul, and fully agreed with him and his critique of the FED. But while Congressman Paul brilliantly and patiently advocated a return to free markets and real money, Uncle Robert's solution to the problem was akin to a witch doctor giving his sick patient rat poison.

Uncle Robert claimed that by collectively owning our nation's credit, each and every American has their own Sovereign Credit and we should be able to do with it as we please. If you, an American citizen, need money to buy a car or house, you can simply tap into your Sovereign Credit and float a loan to yourself. Not only that, but you can float loans like this as often as you want, for any amount of money, pay it off when you want, and not have to pay any interest. In essence, all the money we need already exists, we Americans just need to tap into it and start claiming our credit. On an individual level you wouldn't need to work for a living or go to a bank for a loan. As a nation, we wouldn't need the FED, and there would never be another recession or depression.

In addition to spawning many other problems, Uncle Robert's Sovereign National Credit idea would lead to hyperinflation and the collapse of the currency (whatever currency it would be called by then) almost overnight. Picture this: you want to buy a house for sale down the street. It's gorgeous, and the price tag is one million dollars. Problem is, you don't have one million dollars. However, thanks to Uncle Robert, you can float yourself a loan and "borrow" the money to pay for the home. So, you offer the seller one million dollars, drawn on the bank of you. But wait, another neighbor wants to buy the same home. He too doesn't have any money, but he floats himself a loan of one million dollars and offers the seller that amount. You get wind of the other one million dollar offer and immediately increase your offer to two million dollars by floating yourself more money. After all, you really want the house and you can pay the money back whenever you want at no interest. If it takes thirty or forty or even fifty years, who cares? The second buyer responds in kind by increasing his offer to three million. Genius, right? See where this is headed?

If everyone had immediate access to unlimited amounts of money that they didn't have to work for, could choose to pay off the loans for this borrowed money whenever they wanted, and never had to worry about paying interest, prices on everything would skyrocket. The flood of money in the form of these new loans would make the money practically worthless. Prices would rise so fast and so high that nothing could be accurately priced. Without accurate prices and stable money, business would collapse shortly thereafter. Not to mention the damage being able to conjure up endless amounts of money from thin air would do to the vital principles of thrift, saving, hard work, and delayed gratification.

If you're waiting for a "Surprise!" or "Gotcha!" to all this, it's not coming. Uncle Robert really believed that America's Sovereign National Credit would not only work fabulously well but was also enshrined in the U.S. Constitution. I tried hard to find anything written that would explain and support Uncle Robert's position. I couldn't. The idea is so nutty that it's not supported by anyone. When I persisted in questioning him on the subject, I received responses like this:

> If your mind cannot comprehend the question as to how credit was withdrawn from the American People and redirected to this colossal destruction before, during and after the wars, then you should not be in the business of understanding the causes and the effects, but should go into politics where you can paint any color you want with any brush you desire, in the party line coloring book, and they will call it abstract art.

Many years later, when it became clear that I didn't think Uncle Robert's idea had any merit, it became a source of tension not only between him and me but also between Paige and me. She believed it wholeheartedly and thought she understood it, but I knew she didn't because to understand it was to immediately reject it. I tried to gently point out to her the inherent flaws, but by that time, she wasn't going to believe me over Uncle Robert on any subject.

IT MAY SEEM like all this is just a bunch of harmless economic, political, and religious theory. Who cares if Uncle Robert had some weird ideas? It's a free country, we're allowed to think what we want. Sure, he was odd, but his ideas had no real-life negative consequences. If you're thinking that, just wait. I'm only getting started. The real danger that Uncle Robert represented, wasn't just his ideas, but how he created a cult of secrecy and paranoia to insulate himself from criticism while simultaneously brainwashing those closest to him to do whatever he asked and believe whatever he said.

An example of the paranoia and secrecy playing out in everyday activities had to do with cell phones. One day, while Paige's parents were visiting us, Jack and I went to play golf. On the drive to the course, I got a call on my cell phone from a friend of mine, Tim Martin, who lived in Montana. He was a window washer in rural Montana, and I was a sports broadcaster from rural Idaho. I mentioned to Tim a book about Zionism that Uncle Robert suggested I read, and I thought he'd like it too. Jack spoke up, alarmed that I would mention a dangerous trigger word like Zionism on a cell phone call. After I hung up with Tim, Jack made it clear that I should never use words like Zionism or Jew or Gentile on a cell phone because all cell phone calls are listened to. And using words like that would make me a target because those listening in on all our phone calls were, of course, Jewish and there to protect Jewish interests, presumably the same ones mentioned in the *Protocols of the Learned Elders of Zion*.

It is true that years later, thanks to Edward Snowden, the National Security Agency got caught red-handed listening in on cell phone calls between Americans. However, to think that a call between a lowly window washer in Montana and an equally lowly sports broadcaster in Idaho was important enough to be monitored or presented a threat to anyone is absurd. If people in the employ of the Jewish New World Order really were wasting their time monitoring phone calls from people like me, then people like Uncle Robert had nothing to worry about. That very same New World Order would be so bogged down with worthless and inane cell phone monitoring they'd never have time to do any real harm.

The absurdity of it all is precisely the point. Because Uncle Robert gave it credence and made it important, it made *us* important. Because Uncle Robert was so wise and knew of the Jewish threat, his life was in constant danger. And if his life was in danger, so was ours. Thus, we needed to be vigilant in keeping him and ourselves safe. We had to be careful on cell phone calls, shred all important documents rather than just throwing them in the trash, post little to no photos on social media, and, most importantly, be careful whom we shared all this knowledge with. Several times, I heard from either Paige or Uncle Robert the refrain about throwing our pearls before swine.

What I couldn't understand was, if Uncle Robert's ideas were so brilliant and his teachings so sublime, why were we so focused on keeping him and his ideas to ourselves? Why weren't we sharing his light like the city on the hill Jesus talked about in Matthew 5:14? Why weren't we inviting all the Young family members to our Conferences in Idaho? If we benefited from Uncle Robert's wisdom, wouldn't my parents? Wouldn't all my brothers and their families too? While questions like these would become much more nuanced and harder for me to answer years later, at this point in my marriage to Paige, I knew the answers the moment the questions came to mind. Uncle Robert's teachings weren't brilliant; they were asinine.

If the Emperor is prancing around without any clothes, he must make sure only those subjects blind to this fact are allowed to see him. God forbid a child show up and let everyone know the Emperor's naked. Paige and her parents were blind to Uncle Robert's manipulation and control and to the stupidity of many of his ideas. While not blind yet, my eyesight was starting to get blurry. And what would eventually be one of the more obvious signs of Uncle Robert's control over Paige can be seen in the miraculous birth of Naomi, and the distorted retelling of it many years later.

CHAPTER 9
THE BIRTH OF NAOMI

———◦◉◦———

AFTER DAVID WAS born in September of 2000, Paige needed time to physically recover from the C-section and eight weeks of lying on her back. In addition, we needed to focus on the needs of David who was small and still very vulnerable, even after he came home from the hospital. Given our track record, there was a good chance Paige could become pregnant again, and if we had another child quickly, David might not get the attention he required, and Paige wouldn't get the rest she needed.

While I always wanted to have a big family, I was very concerned about what another pregnancy might do to Paige. When I first met Paige, she was in amazing physical shape, strong and lean thanks to near daily work outs. After giving birth to David, she looked like a completely different woman, aged, fragile, folding in on herself at the waistline scar. Could her body handle another pregnancy? Was it fair to put her through that again? While I sensed it was wrong of me to make a decision in fear of losing Paige or David or both, I felt the best thing to do was to have a vasectomy. Paige didn't want me to, but she didn't argue much and respected my decision.

As the years passed, David grew strong and his development caught up with other children his age, so much so you couldn't tell he was born eight weeks premature. Paige recovered also. Before long she returned to lifting, riding her bike, and playing volleyball, so her body once again became toned and muscular. Several times, Paige expressed her regret at agreeing to the vasectomy, and felt strongly led by the Lord to encourage me to get a reversal so we could have more children. Again, she left the final decision to me. She was a wonderful mother to the boys and clearly had the energy and passion to raise more children. I had been at peace with the decision to stop having children after David. I was convinced the decision was made for the right reason—protecting the loved ones already in my life. But now those loved ones were strong enough to welcome another child into the world. I prayed and asked the Lord for direction and felt a strong confirmation: get the surgery, have more kids.

So, I did. I had the reversal surgery, and about a month later, Paige was pregnant again. By this time, we had moved from our beloved home in Inkom and settled a few hours north in Fremont County, Idaho. We had purchased a gorgeous seven-acre piece of land to build on outside the town of Ashton, replete with aspens, pines, incredible views of the Teton mountain range, and close to great fly fishing. We didn't have the money then to build our dream log home, so we moved into a temporary rental in nearby St. Anthony. Despite having a C-section last time around, Paige was determined to have a natural birth with our next child. But the doctors we interviewed were squeamish, if not downright hostile, to allowing Paige a natural birth under their watch. It quickly became clear to both of us that if we went to the hospital to deliver the baby, there was a zero percent chance the doctors would refrain from intervening and perform a C-section. Paige felt like her only option was to have a home birth. The idea made me nervous, but I had such faith and trust in her abilities, I agreed. Paige was so driven and focused; if anyone could have a natural home birth after a C-section, it was her.

As pessimistic as the doctors were about Paige's chances of having a natural birth, Michelle Bartlett, a local midwife Paige discovered, was equally optimistic. Like Paige, Michelle was a strong, confident, take-charge kind of person. The two of them immediately hit it off and made a great team. With her on board and fully supportive of Paige, I felt better about the home birth. Paige wanted a water birth, so we rented a tub, filled it up in our living room, then waited.

More than a week after the due date, we were still waiting. Paige finally started pre-labor on a Friday and the two of us didn't get any sleep Friday night, and none again on Saturday night as labor continued. I was at home with Paige the entire time, as was Michelle and her assistant. Meanwhile, Thomas and David, who were six and four at the time, were being attended to by Paige's close friend at the time, Sheila Patriquin. Like Paige, Sheila was an alpha-female, tall, beautiful, her long red hair flowing as she confidently entered a room. She took the boys to her house and had them play with her children. Finally, after a long and arduous weekend, our daughter, Naomi, was born shortly after midnight, on Monday morning. I was standing in the tub with Paige and caught Naomi when she came out. I quickly pulled Naomi up out of the water and handed her to Paige, who put her next to her bare chest. It was immediately apparent Naomi's life was in danger as she struggled to breathe. Her skin turned a ghostly grey pallor, and her heartbeat dropped dramatically. My heartbeat skyrocketed as Michelle sprang into action, vigorously massaging Naomi's chest to get her heart beating faster. Within seconds, Naomi's skin bloomed into a healthier color, like a chameleon changing from the colors of death to life, and the immediate danger passed. But there was something else; Naomi's head was abnormally large, and at the time, we didn't know why.

An hour or so later, with Naomi resting, Michelle and her assistant left, and Paige and I managed to get a few hours of sleep. Later that morning, Michelle called and urged us to take Naomi to the local hospital to check on her head. Once again, Sheila stepped in to help, taking care of Thomas and David while I drove Paige and Naomi to the hospital in Rexburg. Right away they diagnosed Naomi with hydrocephalus, which is excess fluid on the brain caused by a blockage somewhere in one of the brain's four ventricles. I'd never heard of such a thing. The doctor didn't seem overly alarmed by the diagnosis, and while it wasn't immediately life-threatening, he made it clear the only fix was brain surgery. Naomi didn't seem to be in a lot of pain, but she would whimper every time we touched her head. We thanked the doctor but left and went for a second opinion in Idaho Falls. Again, I drove, and again, the diagnosis was hydrocephalus. This time though the doctor was much more concerned about Naomi's condition and urged immediate intervention. The best place to have the needed surgery, he said, was at Children's Primary Hospital in Salt Lake City, UT. He was so concerned with Naomi's health (or so concerned with a lawsuit should something happen to her) he urged us to have her life-flighted via helicopter to Salt Lake City. We declined and drove the three hours to Utah ourselves. Having the benefit of only a few hours of sleep over the last three days, we were both exhausted, surviving on adrenaline to keep going.

While Sheila continued to watch over Thomas and David, my parents flew out from California to be with us. Based on the due date, they had planned their flight to arrive about a week after Naomi was born. Instead, they arrived in the middle of the chaos. My mother took over the duties of watching the boys in Idaho while my father drove a rental car down to Utah in case we needed help there. Mrs.

Bartlett came back to the home in St. Anthony and drained the tub of water and cleaned up our disheveled living room. And, thanks to a phone call from the nervous doctor in Idaho Falls, bureaucrats from the Idaho Department of Health and Welfare paid an unannounced visit to our house to supposedly check up on us.

Paige and I slept that Monday night in the Utah hospital with Naomi. Early Tuesday morning the nurse came into our room to take Naomi into surgery. Handing over her suffering, newborn baby girl must have been one of the hardest things Paige ever had to do. When the nurse left with Naomi cradled in her arms, Paige buried her head into my chest and cried. And then we prayed, asking the Lord to protect and save our precious little girl. Thankfully, the surgery was a success; the skilled neurosurgeon inserted a tiny tube into one of the ventricles in Naomi's brain. That tube was connected to an equally tiny valve that controlled the amount of excess fluid that would be drained. The tubing snaked its way down Naomi's neck and chest and emptied into her abdominal cavity. Incredibly this is a fairly standard procedure that is performed on thousands of babies every year.

As if this moment wasn't chaotic and stressful enough, I was already late to arrive for an event I was supposed to be hosting in Mississippi for OLN. I had been on the phone with the producer every day for the past week as he nervously waited for my child to be born so I could come do my job. So, the next day, Wednesday, I flew out of the Salt Lake City airport while Naomi stayed with Paige and recovered in the hospital. As I left, my father arrived in Salt Lake City and a day later drove Paige and his new granddaughter back home to Idaho.

THE BIRTH OF Naomi was a very challenging moment in our

marriage and family, but also a wonderful moment of teamwork and togetherness. When I came back from my broadcasting trip a few days later, Paige and Naomi were home safe in Idaho along with my parents and the boys. When I walked in the door, a physically and emotionally drained Paige rose from the couch and gave me a long, genuine, tearful embrace. Out of all the years we spent together, that hug remains the most heartfelt and tender hug we ever shared. I felt truly appreciated and loved by her.

For the first few years Paige and I were together, I felt like we had the best marriage in the world; I was the best husband ever, she the best wife ever. But things were different between us now. While I was still head over heels in love with Paige, I could tell she didn't think I was the best husband in the world. We hardly ever argued, I never raised my voice at her, and there wasn't even a hint of infidelity, or even a desire. Yet, subtle clues clearly conveyed discontent on her part, like fewer compliments directed toward me and more time on the phone with Uncle Robert. It was clear that her feelings of unhappiness and dissatisfaction always increased whenever she spent time around Uncle Robert. It seemed she increasingly sought solace and guidance from him and not me. Despite all that, when I walked through the front door of our home and Paige wrapped her tired arms around me and hugged me tight, I felt like Lou Gehrig, the luckiest man on the face of the earth.

The reason I went into such detail with Naomi's birth is because, many years later the story was rewritten by Paige to denigrate me in the eyes of our children. The children were told that I neglected their mother right after Naomi was born and forced Paige to drive all the way to Salt Lake City from Idaho while I slept in the backseat of the car. Paige's efforts, along with the doctors and midwives, were truly heroic, but it's simply not accurate to say I neglected her and made

76

her do that drive on her own. And not only were my efforts later disregarded, nearly everyone else who helped out during this ordeal was vilified, shunned, alienated, and ostracized by Paige and Uncle Robert, just like Rebecca and the rest of the Klassens had been years prior.

Not long after Naomi's birth, Sheila, the helpful friend, had a heated argument with Paige over Christian doctrine. Paige spoke with Uncle Robert about it, and he advised her to confront Sheila and demand an apology. Paige then called and asked Sheila to come over to our house for a talk and said I would be there as a witness. Sensing an ambush, Sheila declined and the two were never friends after that.

Years later, Michelle, the courageous midwife who also helped deliver our fourth child, told Paige she planned to divorce her husband. By this time, Paige and Michelle had become friends; she'd delivered two of our children and Paige had supported Michelle in her efforts to help pass key legislation in Idaho meant to protect midwives. Once again, Paige spoke to Uncle Robert, he advised her, and Paige confronted Michelle about the divorce. That caused a breakup of some sort, and the two were never friends again. Knowing little else about the incident, I called Michelle while writing this book. Reluctantly she agreed to speak with me and told about a letter she received from Paige. It was condemning, judgmental, and hurtful. "All I remember," she said to me over the phone, "was sitting in my living room, crying as I read her letter."

After Paige left me many years later, my parents, along with the rest of the extended Young family, were tarred and feathered as people who display a "chronic indifference to others." But my parents flew out to Idaho, babysat the boys, drove back and forth between Utah and Idaho so Paige and Naomi could come home from the hospital safely, and stayed for a week to look after us, feed us, and shower us with love.

As I stood in the living room hugging Paige in March of 2005, all of the ugly aftermath—the shunning and vilifying of friends and relatives—was still years off in the future. But soon, the dark side of following Uncle Robert would become painfully obvious to me. And the victims of his judgment and wrath would start to pile up.

CHAPTER 10
UNCLE ROBERT KNOWS BEST

---◦◉◦---

WHEN PAIGE AND I sold our home in Inkom and moved north to Fremont County to build on our land with the Teton views, it wasn't just our address that changed. My career changed too. My dream job with the Outdoor Life Network as a sports broadcaster took a hit when Ric LaCivita, the man who hired me, retired in 2000. He was always my biggest supporter, and with him gone, I became far more susceptible to the opinions and capriciousness of upper management.

The story, as told to me around Christmastime of 2003, had most of the OLN executives in a meeting at their headquarters in Stamford, CT. In each of the offices a small TV sat perched high in a corner with OLN on 24/7. Most of the time the TVs were mute. During this meeting, somebody mentioned what a great job we were doing with our Alpine World Cup ski coverage. The President and CEO of OLN effectively stopped the meeting as he turned up the volume on the TV with the remote and listened. "Who's doing the play by play?" he asked.

Someone answered, "That's Peter Young."

"Who's Peter Young?" the CEO asked.

Several of the executives in the room knew me and shared

awkward glances. I'd been with the network for six years and was on air all the time. "He's one of our main play-by-play guys," came the response.

"Well, his voice is flat," the CEO responded.

Here's a little bit of advice for anyone considering a broadcasting career: if the president and CEO of the network you work at doesn't like the sound of your voice, start looking for another job. And that I did. When in February of 2005, I didn't get my contract renewed at OLN, I already had my feet wet as a real estate agent in Idaho. During my first few months selling real estate, I'd go to the office and hope that my broadcasting agent in New York City would call with another job in TV. But he never did. So, I reluctantly became a full-time real estate broker and former sports broadcaster who still called a few local games on the side.

Prior to losing my position at OLN, everything in my life seemed to be going according to plan. I had a great career, a beautiful wife, a happy marriage, a growing family, and my own little slice of paradise on which to build a home and make memories. Then life started throwing curveballs, one after another. The OLN debacle was just the first. Unfortunately, I wasn't very good at hitting curveballs. Perhaps this was the Lord's way of making me more reliant on Him, more humble and trusting. Perhaps *my* plan wouldn't accomplish the eternal goals *His* plan had in store for me.

OBVIOUSLY, THE DEMISE of my broadcasting career had nothing to do with Uncle Robert, but I hoped traveling less and spending more time at home would help Paige and me draw closer together. Unfortunately, that didn't happen. Real estate kept me plenty busy, but more importantly, Paige kept herself busy with more frequent and longer phone calls with Uncle Robert. It seemed they spoke on the phone several times a week. You may be thinking, *What was your wife doing spending so much time talking on the phone with another man?* That's a good question. The short answer is, what was inappropriate for everyone else was acceptable when it came to Uncle Robert. That's how he was always treated. He did and said things that, if they came from anyone else, Paige would have been offended, outraged, or simply would have ignored it as utter nonsense. But Uncle Robert's words were never ignored. Instead, they were held in the highest esteem and elevated in importance above all other voices, no matter the topic. The best example of this is what happened when Thomas nearly knocked out his two front teeth.

It started out as the kind of moment that you want to soak in and remember forever, but, in an instant, it turned into the kind of moment you want to forget immediately. Roughly eight and six years old respectively, Thomas and David were laughing and wrestling like two little bear cubs on our king-sized bed. I was right there enjoying the sights and sounds of their unbridled joy. Then with one wrong move, innocent enough and impossible to predict or prevent, Thomas's mouth met the back of David's head with a sickening thud. It was an unmistakable sound, and I knew it was bad. Both boys immediately started crying. David grabbed the back of his head and Thomas reached for his mouth.

Knowing it was Thomas's front teeth that hit David, I turned my attention to him first. His front teeth dangled from his maxilla like two towels hanging on a clothesline. Somehow, the teeth didn't fall out, and we were able to calm him down and alleviate his pain. The next morning, we took him to our dentist, Dr. Kunz, who had been working in town for decades and had already seen our boys for cleanings on other occasions. While I was off working, Paige took Thomas there by herself, and Dr. Kunz seemed to indicate no intervention was necessary. But then we all went back in the afternoon, and Dr. Kunz highly recommended installing a small brace to stabilize the teeth so they could be protected and properly reset. This simple procedure sounded like the best course of action to me, but Paige was unconvinced. We asked Dr. Kunz for a few moments to discuss what to do, and he respectfully left and went to work with another patient.

While Thomas sat in the dentist chair wondering what was going on, Paige made it clear she wouldn't agree to Dr. Kunz's recommendation until she had first spoken with Uncle Robert. Dr. Kunz's two different recommendations alarmed Paige, and she was adamant only Uncle Robert knew what was best for Thomas. Flabbergasted, I watched as she knelt by Thomas's dentist chair and dialed Uncle Robert. No answer. She tried again. And again. After a while Dr. Kunz came back into the room to see if we'd decided. I was embarrassed and frustrated that we were still waiting on some guy who had never been a dentist to tell us what to do. With more political deftness than agitation, Dr. Kunz said we were free to go elsewhere if we didn't agree with his professional opinion and left the room once again.

Finally, Paige was able to reach Uncle Robert. She explained the situation and he agreed with the dentist. Just like that, we were now ready to proceed with the brace for Thomas's teeth. It simply didn't matter to Paige that Uncle Robert had never been a dentist and wasn't even a doctor of any kind. He was Uncle Robert, and he knew more about everything than anyone else.

Another example of Uncle Robert's voice drowning out all others occurred when I became involved with the John Birch Society. Coinciding with our move to Fremont County, I became inspired to learn more about the principles of limited government and free market economics. I stumbled upon the John Birch Society (JBS) and quickly joined. At first, Uncle Robert was very supportive of the JBS and my involvement. I organized meetings, emceed events, and read as much as I could. Over the course of a few years, as my knowledge grew, I found support for some of Uncle Robert's ideas, but when it came to his most cherished beliefs—America's Sovereign National Credit, and the threat of a Jewish New World Order—it was hard to find any credible evidence. I emailed him questions he didn't like, and, suddenly, his support for my involvement in the JBS ended. The JBS was apparently not wary enough of Jewish plans for world domination and were, thus, part of the problem. And the simplest way for Uncle Robert to get me to turn my back on the JBS was to convince Paige that the JBS was the problem. While I was in Canada announcing the Calgary Stampede, which was one of my last big broadcasting jobs, Paige took our three children and spent the week with Uncle Robert at his home in California. Before the week was over, she had adopted his position on the JBS, and as far as she was concerned, I couldn't leave that group fast enough. That wasn't the only thing Uncle Robert convinced Paige she should leave.

Uncle Robert and Aunt Staci lived not far from Riverside, California, which had a horrible problem with violent crime. That area is also close to the San Andreas Fault line. On any given day, the odds of Uncle Robert and Aunt Staci being a victim of a violent crime or suffering the consequences of a major earthquake were relatively high, astronomically high if compared to where we lived in Idaho. But while Paige visited Uncle Robert in California, he scared the daylights out of her with tales of an imminent and catastrophic volcanic eruption in Yellowstone National Park that would kill everyone in nearby Fremont County, Idaho, in the blink of an eye. I'm not sure if he had studied this or just watched an overly dramatic episode of National Geographic on TV, but he was now convinced we were foolishly endangering ourselves by continuing to live in Fremont County. When Paige came home from that trip, not only was the JBS something I needed to give up, but so were my dreams of living in a beautiful log home on our land with Teton views. The danger of a deadly volcanic eruption was simply too great, and we needed to consider moving right away. Never mind that Yellowstone National Park hadn't experienced a serious eruption in several hundred thousand years, and scientists have no real idea when the next one will come. Uncle Robert said it was dangerous, and that's all that mattered.

THINGS THAT I had considered safe were now declared dangerous by Uncle Robert, and some things I usually associated with danger, Uncle Robert said were perfectly safe. I considered Southern California with its crime and earthquake problems a dangerous place to live, whereas Fremont County, Idaho with almost zero violent crime and zero natural disasters seemed rather safe. Not to Uncle Robert. Same thing with having an innocent cell phone call with a friend: safe to me, dangerous to Uncle Robert. Going to small JBS meetings in rural Idaho seemed okay to me, but not Uncle Robert. However, the most bizarre proclamation in this increasingly upside-down world Uncle Robert promoted was when Jack Klassen, fresh off a three-week stay with Uncle Robert, declared casinos the "true churches" in America.

Nope, still not trying to play a joke on you; he really said that. And Paige, Jack, Cathy, and Uncle Robert all believed that. I'll never forget the moment I first heard this theory because it was another one of those times when Jack stood really close to me. It was summer and Jack and Cathy were traveling home from California and stopped by to visit us. We were all standing in the kitchen, and Jack was singing the praises of casinos. Apparently, Jack, Cathy, and Uncle Robert had spent a lot of time in the casinos on their visit. Similar to Paige, Jack and Cathy exhibited an Uncle Robert halo effect after being with him; whatever Uncle Robert had been discussing with them was all they could talk about for the next few days. Thus, after this visit, Jack was saying casinos were the "true churches" in America, where true worship takes place, and that the church buildings that most people visit on Sunday mornings were useless.

The rationale for thinking casinos are the real places of worship in America lies in the fact that anyone, regardless of race, religion, sex, education, social status, or the size of your bank account, can go into a casino and be blessed by the Lord. While this is a true statement in a twisted way, whenever I went into a casino, I didn't see anyone worshiping the Lord. I saw people worshipping money. I saw desperation. I saw people who craved money pulling a lever, pushing a button, spinning a wheel, all in the hope that luck would bring them fortune. The Bible is full of verses that talk about the value of hard work and discipline and being good stewards of what we've been given. I don't recall reading anything in the Bible about casinos.

When Jack made the remark about casinos being churches, I didn't speak up. Not only was it so cockamamy that I didn't know what to say but I could tell he was totally convinced of its veracity and ready to passionately defend the comment with his life. Why? Because it came from Uncle Robert. Soon, our family's involvement with casinos and gambling blossomed to levels I could never have predicted. I don't want to sound like I was as pure as the driven snow or so self-righteous I couldn't accept people having fun playing cards or the slots. I'm not, and I have no problem going out with some buddies, playing cards or blowing a few bucks on the machines. But I've never had much extra money, so I've never gambled much. I simply couldn't afford to lose my money. And I'm no rocket scientist, but I figure the casinos are big, pretentious buildings where they give you free drinks for a reason: the house always wins.

Uncle Robert's preferred gambling sites were on Indian reservations and there just so happened to be one in Northern Idaho, not far from where the Klassens lived. The Coeur d'Alene Casino Resort and Hotel is located in the tiny town of Worley, Idaho, on the Coeur d'Alene Reservation, about a forty-five minute drive from the Klassen's home. Whenever Uncle Robert visited the Klassens, they would frequently pile into a car and drive down to the casino. Ironically, they didn't call it their church and they never said they were going to worship when they went to gamble. Instead, they said they were going to the *office*.

CHAPTER 11
THE OFFICE

ONE OF THE requirements for obtaining my history degree at George Washington University was completing a writing seminar. I chose to write on the 1919 Black Sox scandal in which eight players on the Chicago White Sox conspired, at varying levels of involvement and commitment, to throw the 1919 World Series. The scandal devastated the White Sox franchise and forever changed Major League Baseball. Ever since writing that report, I've generally regarded gambling and sports as bad bedfellows. The only gambling I do is filling out my NCAA Men's basketball tournament bracket each March, sometimes with a few dollars on the line, other times, with nothing but pride. And when it comes to actually walking into a casino, sitting down, and spending money on gambling, I could probably count on two hands the number of times I've done it. It has just never been my thing. With the sensory bombardment from all the blinking lights, incessant noises, and cigarette smoke, plus the overwhelming desperation of it all, I usually can't get out of a casino fast enough.

It's the desperation that really makes my stomach turn. You can see it on nearly every face, and the smell of it is worse than the cigarette smoke. Every person in the casino walked into the building that day thinking *they* would be the one to walk out a big winner. That same desperation, that obsession with money, was what drove some of those White Sox players a century ago to make a decision that destroyed their careers. It's one thing to go to a casino and have fun, then walk away afterwards with your sanity and bank account still intact. But frequenting casinos night after night in the vain hope that more time there will solve your financial troubles, like going to a job and real office, is simply absurd.

When I finally figured out that Uncle Robert, Paige, and her parents were referring to the casino when they said they were visiting the *office*, I was appalled. My guess is they used that word to hide from our children the fact that they were going to a casino. Whatever the reason, every time we gathered for our conferences in Hayden, at least one night, often more, was spent at the *office*. They could tell I didn't want to go, so I always stayed behind and watched the children. For Uncle Robert to call it the *office* made perfect sense. When I first met him in 1997, he would have been in his fifties, and in all the years I knew him, I never once saw him work. Never. As far as I could tell, he never had gainful employment but relied on his wife's salary as well as tithes from Paige and me and the Klassens to pay the bills. He loved to tell the story of asking Aunt Staci, before they got married, to commit to his ministry, so he could be her mission-field. By that, he meant she'd work and make the money to support him.

When I say I never saw Uncle Robert work, I mean I never saw him perform anything resembling physical labor for more than a few seconds. I recall him cooking onions once at his home in California while we were visiting, and at one of our conferences in Idaho, Uncle Robert rolled a few logs out of the way for Jeff to move around and operate the log splitter more efficiently. That's it. During all of our conferences, he never once helped out with the cooking, or clean up, or sweeping or … anything. This may be partly due to the Klassen's devotion and reverence for him—they didn't give him much of a chance to help out—but then again, I never heard him offer to help either.

The idea that wealth comes from hard work and discipline was simply lost on Uncle Robert. To him, all wealth was a gift from the Lord, which, again, is true. But Uncle Robert had a special and perverse ability to take the Word of God and twist it into something unrecognizable from the actual Scriptures. Hard work is a commandment from the Lord. Proverbs spells it out very clearly that we work hard because He has commanded us to, and when we are obedient to Him, he blesses us: *"All hard work brings a profit, but mere talk leads only to poverty." Proverbs 14:23*

Frequenting casinos to pull levers and push buttons in the hopes the Lord will bless you with a windfall of cash is the quintessential example of wanting the blessings without the obedience. And there is nothing productive about gambling. The farmer grows food that people eat, the doctor helps injured people heal, and the carpenter builds homes people live in. Gambling doesn't produce anything. I admit I was judgmental and self-righteous when I first realized Uncle Robert gambled. Over the years, I've softened my stance. If you want to go gamble and have fun, and you can do it without becoming addicted, then fine, go have fun. But to think you can outsmart the randomness of gambling at casinos and make a living at it is just silly to me. And while the Klassens loved to tout Uncle Robert's amazing ability to consistently win large sums of money at the casinos, nearly every time I sent Uncle Robert a tithe check, I would get an email from him thanking me for the money, for it couldn't have come at a better time. They were consistently strapped for cash. Go figure.

THE STORY THAT captures all the elements that made the *office* such a bizarre feature of Uncle Robert, was the time he helped a woman win at the slot machines. I don't recall how Uncle Robert figured he had helped her, but, nonetheless, this woman, while supposedly following his advice, won the jackpot and walked away with a few thousand dollars. She thanked Uncle Robert by giving him a chip worth roughly twenty dollars. Uncle Robert was so disgusted by her lack of proper gratitude that, in the telling of the story, he turned this unsuspecting woman into the most cheap, greedy, and ungrateful woman to ever set foot in a casino. His voice dripped with arrogance as he took all the credit for her win. Didn't she realize that it was Uncle Robert's magic touch that produced all that cash? And just like the plumber who, after fixing the clogged sink, deserved to be paid for his work, didn't she see that Uncle Robert needed to be properly paid? After all, this was his *office*. Jack soaked up the story and shook his head. If he had this woman's mailing address, he would have sent her a bill.

AS I DID with most things Uncle Robert promoted, I largely kept my mouth shut in regard to my true feelings about the casinos so as not to risk creating more distance between Paige and me. As far as I knew, Paige never gambled aside from the times she did with Uncle Robert and her parents. They gambled, not only because he did, but because if they didn't, it would be seen as a direct challenge to him. And that is something Paige and her parents weren't going to do. So, trips to the *office* became nighttime staples during our conferences in Hayden. And when my relationship with Paige was in serious jeopardy years later, I tried hard to embrace gambling in a failed attempt at earning her love and respect. But I hated gambling. I didn't want to embrace a slot machine; I wanted to embrace her. Even more, I wanted her to embrace me.

CHAPTER 12
Ashton, Adversity, and Alex

IN 2007, WE bought and moved into an older home on the edge of town in Ashton, Idaho. Surrounded by peaceful rolling fields of grain and seed potatoes, picturesque creeks and rivers, the actual town of Ashton looked like it had been forgotten by the farmers and the fly fishermen. Dilapidated store fronts dominated Main Street and aging homes with sagging roofs dotted most other streets. While in dire need of updating, our newly purchased home was in relatively good shape. It was the second and last home Paige and I bought together. Even though we had sold the beautiful land with the Teton views, I had managed to delay the move from Fremont County, despite risking immediate obliteration from the Yellowstone volcano. A few months before we moved into our home, we got two dogs: a golden retriever named Larry and a chocolate lab named Magic. Yes, I'm a big basketball fan who grew up watching the NBA in the 1980s. And around the time I picked up Larry and Magic, we found out Paige was pregnant with our fourth child.

As with our first home in Inkom, Jack Klassen was very gracious with his time and talents and helped us make several improvements to the home. However, no sooner had we moved into the home when Naomi started showing odd signs of lethargy. This continued for weeks and grew worse until, on June 20th, 2007, Paige met with a friend who suggested testing Naomi's blood sugar. It was sky high. She immediately took her to the hospital, and it didn't take long for the endocrinologist to diagnose Naomi with Type 1 Diabetes. She was only three months past her second birthday. Sitting in a big cushioned chair in the hospital room with an exhausted and confused Naomi cuddling on my lap, we listened to the endocrinologist tell us she'd have this disease the rest of her life. Then, as now, I refused to believe it. I was absolutely certain the Lord would find a way for Naomi to recover from this, beat this, live long enough for a cure—anything but have this the rest of her life.

The pain of seeing my two-year-old daughter endure daily blood sugar checks and insulin injections when she had no idea why we were doing this was incredibly difficult. The two people she trusted the most, her father and mother, were now seemingly punishing her by constantly poking her fingers to draw blood and stabbing needles into her arms. She must have been so confused and scared. We started a nightly routine that would last for years by setting an alarm for an hour or so past midnight so one of us, usually Paige, could get up and test Naomi's blood sugar. As I'm sure every parent who goes through this feels, both Paige and I would have gladly taken Naomi's diabetes on ourselves to spare her the pain. Hearing that nightly alarm, a maddening intrusion of my sleep as I dreamt of healthy children, where there was no diabetes or crazy uncles, was a splash of cold water in the face. Everything wasn't okay and Naomi still had diabetes. With Naomi's struggle came one more life-altering event that Paige and I tackled together. Dealing with a sick child is always difficult, but dealing with a type 1 diabetic child is consuming and relentless. It required sacrifice and commitment and hard work, and we were both up to the task. Despite feeling like another man constantly intruded into our marriage and diminishing the oneness we once had, I still felt that Paige and I made a great team and were drawn closer to each other because of this trial.

WE ADAPTED TO the new normal of our lives and managed as best as we could to carry on and enjoy that summer. With Paige's due date fast approaching and another big change coming, we decided to simplify our lives just a bit by getting rid of Magic, our chocolate lab. Larry was a wonderful dog from day one, always looking for ways to please us, but Magic had a strong independent streak and repeatedly escaped from our yard. He had become a huge nuisance and needed more time and attention than I could give. So, we found someone who lived out in the country that was happy to take him. While we had all gotten a little fed up with Magic running away so often, it was still an emotional day when he left for his new home.

That emotion seemed to be the needle that popped the bubble on Paige's pregnancy, literally. Within hours of saying goodbye to Magic, her water broke around dinnertime. We put the kids to bed early and Paige went off to catch whatever sleep she could before labor. She had been gearing up for this delivery for months by practicing calming techniques and self-hypnosis through a program called Hypnobabies. The idea is to learn how to keep the mind and body relaxed and ignore the pain of labor. Easier said than done, but Paige had gotten really good at it. So good that she nearly delivered the baby before any of us were ready. We'd planned for another home birth with Michelle Bartlett again acting as midwife (the blowup between her and Paige hadn't occurred yet). I called Michelle a few times to update her on Paige's contractions. Perhaps remembering the long labor that brought Naomi into the world, Michelle waited till the last minute to leave her home and head to ours. She lived about forty-five minutes away, and with Paige telling me she thought the baby was coming at any moment, my next call to Michelle took on a much more urgent tone. I have a feeling that experienced midwives like Michelle, spurred on by nervous fathers, become very proficient making midnight runs at breakneck speeds on dark, lonely roads and that night, after flying up Highway 20 with a flashing red light mounted on her car, she arrived at our home with only ten minutes to spare. When the other children woke up that morning, they had a new baby brother named Alex.

TWO MONTHS LATER, we visited Paige's parents for Thanksgiving. While there, Naomi's blood sugar numbers were completely normal and stable without any insulin. She'd had a stomachache and thrown up twice just before we left, and since then she hadn't needed insulin. After a few days of this, I thought it was the miracle I'd been praying for; I thought my child was cured. This was the latest turn of events in what had been an emotional roller coaster for Paige and me. Between the dogs, remodeling, and moving into our new house, Naomi's diagnosis, the birth of Alex, getting up every night to test Naomi and feed Alex, homeschooling our two older boys, and running a real estate business, we were emotionally, mentally, and physically exhausted. It was almost too overwhelming to comprehend Naomi no longer having diabetes. For our entire visit with the Klassens, I felt like Naomi truly had experienced something miraculous. It wasn't until a few days after Thanksgiving, when we arrived back home, that Naomi's blood sugars started to rise, and we knew the diabetes was still with her.

One night, instead of the adults going to the *office*, we all decided to go to the grand opening for a local Cabela's store. It was a huge store, and the place was packed for the grand opening weekend. The crowd was so big that there were police officers stationed at the front door for extra security. Jeff, Paige's older brother, was also there with his wife and daughter. This was all that remained of the extended Klassen family, since everyone else had been shunned and ostracized years earlier. Jeff thought it would be a good opportunity to take a photo of his parents with all their grandchildren, or at least the grandchildren they knew and cared about. As we were setting up for the photo, Naomi got upset over a piece of gum. Perhaps I hadn't given her one, perhaps she wanted a different one, or wanted more than one—I don't remember. All I remember is I had a very emotional two-year-old daughter nearly hyperventilating from crying so hard. I gave her what she wanted, and she started to calm down. But when I tried to hand Naomi to Jack for the photo, she refused to go to him and started crying again. I'd seen enough crying and suffering from Naomi to last me a couple years so, I didn't require that she go to her grandfather.

Jack became livid and the expression on his face, captured in the photo Jeff took in that moment, also captured the essence of what Uncle Robert's teachings had done to Jack. It was a toxic mix of self-righteous anger, condemnation, judgment, and a determination to inflict suffering as a prerequisite to obedience and salvation, in this case for Naomi. Later, while milling about the store and watching over Naomi, Jack came up to me and said, with severe conviction, that I couldn't let Naomi behave the way she did. He said she needed to be stopped and my coddling was going to destroy her. Then he delivered a threat; if I didn't stop her, he would. And by stopping her, I knew exactly what he meant—the same harsh, over the top, soul-crushing punishment that Uncle Robert gave Jack, Jack gave Cathy, and now Jack and Cathy were so fervently trying to accomplish with our children every time we visited. That Naomi was only two years old and experiencing incredible highs and lows emotionally and physically meant nothing to Jack in that moment. In his mind, she needed to be stopped, severely, right then and there, regardless of the crowds and police officers nearby, or else she was doomed.

Jack's angry and judgmental attitude toward Naomi was a direct reflection of how Uncle Robert treated him. That condemning posture convinced Jack and then Cathy that they weren't saved—and now, Jack wanted to use the same technique to save his granddaughter. He wanted the gospel of Uncle Robert to save her. I wanted no part of it.

In disgust, I shook my head, walked over to Naomi, picked her up in my arms, and walked away. I knew at that moment I needed to protect her from Jack, and by extension, Uncle Robert. I still feel that way.

In times like these, when Jack and Cathy were so overbearing in their zeal for disciplining the grandchildren, pouncing on every little misstep the children made, I couldn't stand being around them. Paige would defend them, explaining they were still learning how to parent and grandparent as Christians. Since Uncle Robert had convinced them they'd never been Christians until recently, that meant everything they did while raising their five children was wrong and needed to be corrected. And, of course, the correcting was done by Uncle Robert. Jack, figuring he was a babe in Christ, even though he was in his sixties and had professed faith in Christ for decades, would talk to Uncle Robert almost daily. What Uncle Robert was drumming into Jack's head during all those phone conversations, I don't know for sure, but what I saw were two people, Jack and Cathy, embracing a twisted all-or-nothing attitude. The *nothing* was their life prior to being saved by Uncle Robert, and the *all* was every word of Uncle Robert. Rather than giving their two-year-old granddaughter the grace to be disciplined and learn as she matured and grew, she had to be confronted and all traces of sin and disobedience stamped out immediately—or else. I would later come to realize what "or else" looked like.

OTHER THAN UNCLE Robert, the disciplining of the children was the one area that created the most friction between Paige and me. And since the disciplining issue could be traced back to Uncle Robert, everything really began and ended with him. For me, the best example of this friction can be illustrated in the events that took place about a year after the Thanksgiving fiasco at Cabela's. I was at my real estate office in Ashton and Paige was home with the four children. Naomi was acting out and disobeying. While Naomi continued to be defiant, Paige made repeated phone calls to Uncle Robert to get his advice on how to deal with her. Several times, Paige called me and filled me in on Naomi's behavior, after which I'd leave the office, drive the two minutes across town to our home and administer the spanking for Naomi's disobedience. Each time I spoke with her before and afterward about what she had done, hugged her, and told her I loved her.

After about the third or fourth time Paige called me home to deal with Naomi, I expressed my frustration with her and our approach. Naomi was still a very young child, probably no more than three years old. We weren't going to spank the sin and disobedience out of her that day. No matter what we did, she was still going to wake up the next morning a three-year-old child, still given to acts of sin and disobedience, still learning, and still a child of God that would mature and grow over time with love and grace and discipline. Paige didn't want to hear it. She grew agitated and accused me of not being willing to go "all the way" with Naomi. Eventually, Naomi settled down that afternoon, and the calls from Paige stopped, but I never asked Paige what she meant by going "all the way." What did going "all the way" in the area of discipline look like with a three-year-old child? Handing that child over to Uncle Robert so he could coax out a demonic horse?

ANOTHER INCIDENT AROUND that time that involved Naomi took place in California at my parents' home where all the Youngs had gathered to celebrate Christmas. One of Naomi's aunts, my sister-in-law Annie, was also a Type 1 diabetic and also diagnosed at the tender age of two. Because of the shared disease, Annie felt a strong connection with Naomi but lived far away from us and hardly ever got to see her young niece. Anxious to strengthen their connection and show Naomi that she wasn't alone in having to suffer with this disease, Annie asked me if Naomi could be in the room as she gave herself an insulin injection. I thought it would be fine but when I double-checked with Paige, she immediately and unequivocally said no. When I told Annie we weren't going to allow Naomi to watch, she stormed off to her bedroom to deliver the shot. Moments later she emerged even more angry, incredulous as to why we would make such a decision. The rest of the family was either watching TV in the den or in the kitchen helping my mother put the finishing touches on another masterpiece of a meal. Meanwhile, I was looking for Paige, fretting over a potentially epic fight between sisters-in-law. When I found her, I informed Paige of Annie's less than enthusiastic response and she rolled her eyes. Moments later when Paige tried to approach Annie and explain her reasoning for not allowing Naomi in the room, Annie bluntly replied she was too angry to even talk about it. The bruised feelings remained for the rest of the trip but, thankfully, there were no outbursts, yelling, or fighting.

Having seen the destruction of the Klassen family—the alienating and shunning of Lance, Rebecca, Phil, Grandma Hansen, and the Canadian Klassens—I was determined to not let something similar happen with my sister-in-law, Annie. Once back home, I asked Paige how she thought we could diplomatically mend the fence and put this incident behind us. But Paige had no interest in offering an olive branch, and apologizing was out of the question. She had already called Uncle Robert and shared the entire episode with him. And, not surprisingly, he promptly and pompously advised Paige to simply be done with Annie—have nothing to do with her until she, Annie, made a full and complete apology. I was furious that Uncle Robert would be so quick to condemn Annie. He didn't share a whiff of patience, love, or desire for reconciliation and peace. Just like with the outcast Klassens, it was either submit to Uncle Robert's judgment or be kicked out of our lives.

It was my turn to roll my eyes. Ignoring Uncle Robert's suggestion, I called my brother, Annie's husband, and after a few tense conversations we were able to come to a shaky detente that enabled us to move on. Naomi was oblivious to all of it. Annie and Paige were never close after that, and I took the event as a warning sign to share even less of the mysterious Klassen family guru with my family.

ALL IT REALLY boiled down to on every issue was whether or not Uncle Robert approved. If not, then we had to go "all the way" to rectify the situation. There was no dialogue or effort to lovingly work through the differences with the Klassen relatives and Paige's three ostracized siblings. They disagreed with Uncle Robert, so either they had to admit their fault and grovel at his feet for forgiveness, or they were to remain shunned. There was no room to patiently work within the John Birch Society and see if I could still be of service.

They didn't believe in Uncle Robert's worldview that pitted all the descendants of Esau (the Jews) versus all the descendants of Jacob (greater Christendom) so they remained shunned and opposed.

And, most importantly, there was no room for becoming a Christian in a way that didn't meet Uncle Robert's approval, nor was there room for growing in your Christian faith that didn't meet Uncle Robert's criteria. If you struggled with sin, didn't have a dramatic conversion to Christianity, or didn't see eye to eye with Uncle Robert on every bit of Christian doctrine, then you were a non-believer, a non-Christian. And you needed to either immediately agree with everything Uncle Robert said or immediately be kicked out of our lives.

With that attitude, it should come as no surprise that Paige and I didn't stick with one church for very long. When we were first married and lived in Boulder, Colorado, we attended First Presbyterian Church. It was a large, conservative church in an ultra-liberal town that had a thriving group of young people who loosely fell into the category of post-college, pre-family. We lived in Boulder a year, and I was very happy that Paige was able to make friends with several of the women in that group. Even early on in our relationship I could see Paige's stature, intensity, and Uncle Robert-style bluntness sometimes made it hard for her to make and keep female friends.

After we moved back to Idaho, we attended First Presbyterian Church in Pocatello, which was also conservative but had a much smaller congregation. The pastor was a kind man who tried his best, but wasn't a strong leader or eloquent speaker. We belonged to a couples Bible study for a few years before leaving that church to attend one closer to home. For the last few years we lived in Inkom, we attended the Inkom Community Bible Church which was housed in the town's old elementary school building. That pastor was also a kind and gentle man but, in Paige's eyes, not in the same league as Uncle Robert when it came to teaching and understanding the Word of God. In fact, no other man ever came even remotely close to claiming Paige's attention and loyalty the way Uncle Robert did.

When we moved to Fremont County, we settled on the Berean Baptist Church in Ashton. I had never attended a Baptist church before, but it didn't seem too different from the other churches we'd attended in Idaho, other than it was incredibly small. When we first arrived, the pastor was in an interim position. The congregation was so minuscule that I imagined it was hard to find a pastor who would be willing to uproot his family and move to Ashton to take such a low-paying job. The interim pastor, Mr. Glatz, was a semi-retired man with a shock of thick gray hair who wore old suits that sometimes made him look like a small-town mayor or mortician from the 1970s. He also had a remarkable gift for empathy. I liked him and Paige seemed to as well; however, she, of course, would always relay all she could about Pastor Glatz (and every other pastor or church leader) to Uncle Robert to get his condemnation or approval. About a year or two later, Pastor Glatz was replaced by a young man, fresh out of seminary, with a wife and two very young children. His name was Chris Lawrence and he didn't stand a chance. Chris was the first pastor that Paige became openly hostile to, and when it came to the Word of God, she regarded Chris as a pea shooter compared to Uncle Robert and his arsenal of nuclear tipped warheads.

Admittedly, Chris was a bit green and perhaps not ready for the position, but with not much to offer, the little Berean Baptist Church couldn't afford to be picky about whom they hired. The death knell for Chris, and by extension, the Berean Baptist Church, came the day Chris spoke of the death of a young boy who had accidentally killed himself. He was a local kid who lived in nearby Island Park and was playing the choking game by himself. He used ropes around his neck to temporarily cut off oxygen to his brain with the goal of achieving a momentary high of some kind. But it went tragically wrong, as it had in many other cases, and he died. The Sunday after everyone found out, Chris was in the pulpit and Paige and I were sitting in a pew near the front along with our children. Thomas and David were only a few years younger than the boy who died, and like all boys, curious and impressionable. When Chris started to describe what the boy did, alarm bells went off in my head. What could he be thinking? No one needed to know the details of what killed this boy, especially not my two young boys. It was incredibly poor judgment on Chris's part. I looked over at Paige. Way beyond alarmed, she was furiously mouthing words to Chris like "Stop" and "What are you doing?" But Chris either didn't see her or paid her no mind and kept on going. Paige couldn't stand it any longer. She bolted out of her seat and practically dragged our two boys with her as she stepped past me into the aisle and out of the small sanctuary.

Stunned by what just happened, I waited a moment to gather myself then followed. Outside the sanctuary, in the crude narthex of the Church, Paige was beside herself with rage, her face bright red and streaked with tears. She was about to storm back into the sanctuary and give Chris, and the entire congregation, a piece of her mind, but I convinced her not to. We continued to attend church there for a little while longer, but it was never the same.

Knowing I needed to find yet another church to attend, I started looking online and found one I thought would be a great fit. It was in Montana and required a long drive on our part, but I was convinced this was the place for our family. I had no idea the firestorm it would eventually unleash on our family and in our marriage

CHAPTER 13
WHITEHALL

WHILE WE WERE still attending the Berean Baptist Church in Ashton, Pastor Chris Lawrence followed up his misstep regarding the choking game death with fervent sermons on end-time theology. I didn't think it was possible for Chris to be diminished even further in Paige's eyes, but he somehow managed. He also became diminished in my eyes, too.

Even though many of Uncle Robert's ideas sounded like utter nonsense, there were times when his words carried the weight of truth. As the years passed, and I got used to his manner of speech, I gradually found myself agreeing with many of the thoughts he shared on politics and faith. On some issues, it may have been a matter of erosion—his never-ending stream of words simply wore down my resistance to them. Add the fact that everything Uncle Robert espoused was backed up with passionate fidelity by my wife and in-laws, it was perhaps surprising it took so long for me to come around. But when it came to end-time theology, my shift in thinking happened quickly.

After Paige left me and our marriage in 2017 and the Lord opened my eyes to the dangers of Uncle Robert, someone anonymously sent me a book on cults. *Combating Cult Mind Control* was written by Steven Hassan who used to be in the Moonie cult. His book is excellent. At first, I was offended by people suggesting that Uncle Robert's relationship with the Klassens sounded like a cult. How could people think we were in a cult? We didn't live together in a compound, wear similar clothing, cut our hair the same way, or walk around town banging a drum. "Cult" has a very strong negative emotional connotation and I wasn't ready to hear it yet. So, the book sat on my shelf for over a year before I finally read it. Hassan referred to the manipulation and dangers of a cult as *undue mind control.* That sounded better to me and seemed an exact fit for Uncle Robert's relationship with the Klassens. Hassan also brought up a great point for those dealing with loved ones who have been or are currently in a cult or suffering from undue mind control: not everything the cult leader says is wrong. Cult leaders don't convince people to abandon the truth by immediately spouting lies. Rather, they slowly and subtly twist the truth, until later down the road, the lie now seems to be the truth. The Bible states it even clearer: the wolf doesn't get close to the sheep fold, but the wolf in sheep's clothing does.

Hassan's point held true for my relationship with Uncle Robert as well. After all, Uncle Robert often read to us from the Bible at our conferences. The analogy that works best for me is this: if you miss-hit a golf ball by a fraction of an inch on impact, then two hundred yards down the fairway, the ball will likely travel off course one hundred feet to the left or right of the pin. In other words, Uncle Robert hit the right golf ball, but he twisted the Word of God just enough so that years later, he took us far from the Gospel. That's what happened to me, and I believe that's what happened to Paige and our family as well.

So out of all the crazy ideas Uncle Robert shared with us, some were solid. One came in the form of a book he gave to me and Paige early on in our marriage, *Beyond the End Times* written by John Noe.

It claims that Jesus Christ already returned to earth exactly when He said He would in the Bible. When I first heard the premise for the book, I couldn't wait to read it and rip it to shreds. What utter nonsense, I thought. I'd never even heard anybody express this thought before, nor had I ever considered it. I didn't study the book of Revelation or end-time theology much; in fact, I mostly avoided the subject because it seemed so confusing and controversial. Nevertheless, I looked forward to reading this book, so I could pick it apart point by point and knock both the author and Uncle Robert off their pedestal.

A funny thing happened, though. As I read the book, it started to make sense. I was having a hard time refuting the author. By the end of the book, I became absolutely convinced he was right. Even now, I read the Bible in a completely different way than I did before I read *Beyond the End Times*. While I don't claim to have all the answers, I simply can't see how one can read the New Testament and still think Christ is waiting to return to earth. This view of eschatology is called Preterism, but I don't really like the label. I don't think a label is necessary. To me, it's simply what the Bible is saying about Christ's return. And while this aspect of Christianity wasn't something contrived by Uncle Robert, nor did he discuss it much in our conferences, he was the person who introduced me to it. Of course, Paige accepted Preterism immediately, since it came from Uncle Robert.

Agreeing with Uncle Robert on Preterism certainly created some cognitive dissonance in me. On the one hand, he was the Klassen family guru, the guy who called casinos his office and saw Jewish conspiracies everywhere he looked. He was weird and dangerous, and I didn't like or trust him. On the other hand, he was the guy who introduced me to Preterism, and, because of that, we now shared common ground on a key theological issue for Christians. The matter of Preterism cemented Uncle Robert's position as the ultimate authority on Christian doctrine for our family, although I'm sure it wasn't necessary for Paige, as she already saw him in that role. How then could I possibly challenge or disagree with Uncle Robert now?

For years, Paige and I sat in church pews and listened to sermons we disagreed with. I would imagine many other Christians do the same thing. But when Chris Lawrence started preaching on the Rapture, we'd both had enough. I went online and searched for Preterist churches in the Northwest and came up with two options. The closest was in Whitehall, Montana. I looked on a map, found Whitehall, and figured it was about a two-and-a-half-hour drive. When I suggested we go pay a visit one coming Sunday, Paige was game to try.

COVENANT COMMUNITY CHURCH met in an odd little building on Main Street, just north of the railroad tracks in the dusty, unpolished town of Whitehall. The services were very informal and lacked elaborate production. They sang, prayed, read the Word of God, had a sermon, and then, after every single church service, they ate together. This time of fellowshipping over food, discussing the sermon and getting to know each other on a more personal level, was my favorite part of the gathering. Most of the small congregation belonged to one of two families that had joined through marriage; two brothers from one family had married two sisters from another family. There were parents and grandparents, adult children and little children. All the families homeschooled their children, and many worked together for the family landscaping business.

The patriarch of one of the families, and, it seemed to me, the de-facto leader of the church, was Shane Wagner. Standing around six feet tall with a receding hairline and smile so big it nearly curled his eyes shut, Shane was the father of the two boys who married sisters and thus father and grandfather to many. Energetic and stocky, he had hands and forearms thickened by years of hard work. He was well read, yet didn't take himself too seriously, nor did he need to hear himself speak all the time. In some ways, Shane and the Whitehall Church seemed the antithesis of Uncle Robert. Shane and his sons embraced hard manual labor and weren't just talkers but doers—up before the sun, back home at dark. They were always busy getting things done. Conversely, I never saw Uncle Robert work but heard him talk about lots of ideas, none of which I ever saw him act on. And, unlike the extended Klassen family, the Whitehall Church families worked together, worshiped together, learned together, and seemed to actually enjoy each other's company. In other ways though, Shane and the church sounded very similar to Uncle Robert. They embraced Preterism, operated well outside mainstream Christian churches, and, when it came to politics, believed fervently in the founding principles of our country.

Paige seemed to enjoy her time at Whitehall, and, pretty soon, I thought we'd found our new church home. However, with the drive from our home in Ashton taking up well over two hours, we didn't go to church every Sunday. This was just one more factor in eventually looking toward Montana as our future home. The allure of Ashton had long since faded for everyone in our family, including me. The local economy was tiny and lethargic, and now that I was tied to it by selling real estate full time, my earning potential was severely restricted. We were surrounded by well-established Mormon communities, of which we would never fully be a part of. And, according to Uncle Robert, we lived under constant threat of death by volcanic eruption. While we loved homeschooling our children, we also longed for them to have quality opportunities to participate in extracurricular activities like music, theater, and sports. There simply were no private Christian schools near us, so we looked north to Montana.

In the summer of 2009, we found Manhattan Christian School in Churchill, Montana, and were immediately impressed. We quickly found a great rental home near the school and decided to move right away. Living on the outskirts of Bozeman put us about an hour away from Whitehall, which meant we could attend church every Sunday; and it got us about two hours closer to Paige's parents, which was a huge benefit for her. Now that we had moved to Montana and were attending the Whitehall Church full time, the Klassens felt it was necessary for them to visit and check out the church. Needless to say, the Klassens weren't impressed.

After the Sunday service, Jack commented that he didn't hear anything different than what you'd hear at all the other worthless churches in our country. What he really meant was he didn't hear Uncle Robert. Later that afternoon, after a wonderful barbecue at Shane Wagner's home, we all relaxed on the back patio. I was on the periphery of a conversation Jack had with Shane. I got the impression Jack and Cathy weren't there to meet people and make new friends, but rather to interrogate Shane and the other Whitehall leaders and find flaws in them and their beliefs. This way they would have ammunition to convince Paige, who would then convince me, to cut off ties with the Whitehall Church. For if Paige and I were at a church listening to someone other than Uncle Robert, that was a threat to him and to the Klassens. Uncle Robert conveyed a belief that he had the market cornered on wisdom and biblical interpretation, and the Klassens believed him. To discover someone else was just as wise or knew something Uncle Robert didn't—and, thus, Uncle Robert wasn't as special as they thought—would have been unfathomable for Jack and Cathy.

With their microscope of self-righteous skepticism operating at full power and aimed at Shane and the others, Jack and Cathy were ready to pounce on any of their transgressions, real or imagined. At one point in the afternoon, as we were all milling about and preparing for the evening barbecue with the congregation, Shane needed to head back into town to pick up something at the church building, which was an easy five-minute drive from his house. Shane asked Cathy, who happened to be standing nearby, if she wanted to come along with him and she agreed. The two of them drove off, looking happy. They went to the church, picked up whatever Shane needed, then drove back to the home. When they arrived back at the house, everything seemed fine. However, Paige and I later found out that Cathy felt Shane had kidnapped her. She was so incensed about it that she emailed Paige, stating her demand that Shane apologize. In the same email Cathy complained that Shane hugged her goodbye, against her wishes, at the end of the weekend as she and Jack were about to leave. I was standing there as Paige, Shane, Shane's wife Donna, Jack, Cathy, and I all hugged each other goodbye. Shane probably thought nothing of it. But Cathy was furious.

I share all this not to nitpick anyone's behavior but, rather, to point out the severe condemnation and judgment aimed at the Whitehall congregation. No one is perfect and those attending that church had their rough edges, just like we all do. But the venom directed at Shane and the rest of the Whitehall Church was egregious. When Paige asked me how I planned to deal with Shane on these issues, I told her I thought her mother's accusations were ludicrous and never said a word to Shane about it. I can't imagine that went over very well with Paige, or her parents, but she never spoke to me about it again.

ONE OF THE MOST fascinating things about the Whitehall Church was their involvement in election sermons. The idea was to hold a Christian sermon at the State Capitol either on election day or around the day newly elected state legislators were sworn in. An election sermon might seem unconstitutional to many 21st century Americans, but not so to 18th century Americans. The practice was common in early America. Churchgoers would listen as the pastor reminded everyone about the Christian principles upon which our great nation was founded and their Christian duty to elect virtuous and wise public servants. That last sentence may also sound grating and unfathomable to many modern Americans, which is sad, but also why I was thrilled to learn about the election sermons and see them brought back. When it came time to plan the 2010 election sermon at the State Capital in Helena, I thought it would be great to have Uncle Robert come.

I hoped Uncle Robert and the Whitehall Church leaders would hit it off and form a dynamic duo of Christian leadership and action, one that might possibly spur a real revival in Montana, if not all of America. I often felt very alone around Uncle Robert and the Klassens. It seemed I was the only one who had reservations about him and asked tough questions. By combining the forces of Uncle Robert and the Whitehall Church, I hoped for a bit of iron sharpening iron, as it says in the Bible ("*As iron sharpens iron, so one person sharpens another.*" Proverbs 27:17). By discussing and studying the Bible together, the Whitehall Church and I could perhaps chip away at some of the more bizarre beliefs of Uncle Robert, and in turn, Uncle Robert could impart some of his Biblical wisdom to smooth out the rough edges of the Whitehall congregation that had caused so much alarm in Paige's parents. Looking back, I realize it was incredibly naive of me to think Uncle Robert would allow anyone to "sharpen" him, for he didn't need to be sharpened. In his mind, and the mind of the Klassens, he was the sharpest man alive, most likely the sharpest man to ever live, and if there was going to be any iron swinging around, it was most certainly going to be Uncle Robert pounding everyone else into submission.

Because of my background in broadcasting and public speaking, Shane asked me to emcee the election sermon and two-day conference that followed. Uncle Robert accepted our invitation and came along with Paige's parents. Peter Marshall, who wrote the book *The Light and the Glory* was brought in to give the sermon and be the featured speaker during the conference. He probably knew very little about the Whitehall Church and wasn't a good fit. By the end of the conference, which was attended by roughly one hundred people, I could tell there was tension between Marshall and most, if not all, of the Whitehall Church leadership.

There was tension elsewhere that weekend. Friday night, after the election sermon, we all went out to eat at a local restaurant. Uncle Robert, along with the Klassens, sat next to Tim Martin, one of the pastors at the Whitehall Church. Tim was Shane's son-in-law. Despite making a living as a humble window washer, Tim was very bright and well-read when it came to biblical doctrine. He had recently published a lengthy and well-researched book on covenant theology titled *Beyond Creation Science*. Uncle Robert, along with Paige and I, had read the book. During the meal, Tim and Uncle Robert debated over the points made in Tim's book as well as Uncle Robert's view on Jews and Gentiles. Sitting next to them, Jack hung on every word. At one point, Uncle Robert brought up parenting and how some parents are total failures: all they do is give birth to another being, like an animal, or a sperm donor. Tim, acknowledging agreement, said even cockroaches can have offspring. At that comment, Jack nodded solemnly and turned his head away from the conversation. As he reflected on Tim's comment, he became emotional, his eyes watery. Watching him, I could tell he clearly felt that was him; he was the kind of father who could be compared to a cockroach. Over the years, Jack had made several remarks about his abject failure as a father, and, at that time, he had no relationship whatsoever with three of his five children. I felt awful for him and wondered when he would be able to move beyond those feelings of guilt and regret. He had been talking with Uncle Robert for years, ostensibly to learn and grow from his advice and instruction. So why could he not move on, leave the regret behind and do something about it, like reach out to his three estranged children and work toward becoming the father he wanted to be? Was it because he simply couldn't move on, or because Uncle Robert didn't want him to move on, wouldn't let him move on? I was almost certain it was the latter.

I had my own bout of anxiety that weekend as well. One day, we had a question and answer session with the audience and a panel of speakers on stage that included the featured speaker, Peter Marshall, and two of the Whitehall Church pastors. As emcee for the weekend, I was also the moderator of this Q&A session. Standing there on stage in front of the audience, I was terrified that Uncle Robert or Jack would turn the meeting into a circus by asking an inflammatory question about Jews and Gentiles or who knows what else. But as the moderator, it was my job to make sure the event didn't turn into a circus. In my mind, I had to balance moderating the event and meeting the expectations of the audience with meeting the expectations of my wife. I knew that anything less than full and unwavering support for whatever Uncle Robert did or said in that moment, or any other moment, would open me up to certain and swift condemnation from Paige. If Uncle Robert and Peter Marshall or the Whitehall leaders were going to cross swords and do a little iron sharpening, I certainly didn't want to get caught in the middle and end up bludgeoned right there on that stage.

Looking back, I shouldn't have placed the success or failure of that meeting on my shoulders. If Uncle Robert stood up and started challenging Peter Marshall and, indeed, did turn it into a free-for-all, so what? It wouldn't have been my fault. But I also felt a strange duty to protect Uncle Robert and Jack from themselves. At the time, I had a very small but growing sense of admiration and respect for Uncle Robert based on how well read he was and his knowledge in certain areas. However, I still recognized he was slightly crazy and off-putting and, if given enough rope, could easily hang himself in the eyes of anyone listening to him. And because I was so invested in making the connection between Uncle Robert and the Whitehall Church work, I was determined to prevent that from happening.

Conversely, Uncle Robert had nothing invested in that moment. If, in his mind, he stood up and shared the truth like a beacon of light and no one believed him, so be it. It wasn't his fault he found himself amongst a herd of swine. He couldn't care less about his relationship with the Whitehall Church members. In fact, the pattern that I observed was complete and utter apathy on the part of Uncle Robert to create meaningful relationships with anyone outside our tight circle.

This may have been the reason why there was never any small talk or chit chat when Uncle Robert was around. Uncle Robert was never interested in mere conversation because he was never interested in getting to know you or simply be a friend. He wanted to control you. And if he couldn't control you, then he didn't care about you.

Thankfully, the Q&A session didn't turn into a circus, but beneath my suit and tie, my white undershirt was soaked with sweat.

LATER THAT WEEKEND, Uncle Robert called a special meeting to discuss Tim's book. This was classic Uncle Robert. I could tell he was seething at having to sit and listen while Peter Marshall, for whom he had little to no respect, led the conference agenda. He wanted everyone listening to him. So, late one night, we met in the lobby at our hotel. It was Uncle Robert, me, the Klassens, Tim Martin, and one or two others in the Whitehall Church. Paige wasn't there as she was putting the kids to bed in our hotel room. As usual in these settings, Uncle Robert held court. He peppered Tim with questions about his book and his beliefs on the Bible. Uncle Robert held no position of esteem in Tim's eyes, so Tim wasn't nervous or anxious for his approval. Nevertheless, he squirmed at a few of Uncle Robert's questions, and I found myself surprisingly happy at the sight of it. I'd been in that position numerous times, and seeing someone else uncomfortable in the hot spotlight of Uncle Robert's probing questions was a delight.

The reason Uncle Robert called the meeting was to browbeat Tim over his treatment of the identity of Jews and Gentiles in his book. Tim's book was long, around 500 pages, with extensive footnotes, and it took him years to write. We sent a copy to Uncle Robert who read it prior to the election sermon. There were only a few pages that touched on the issue of race identity, but this was Uncle Robert's most important issue, one he was extremely passionate about. Get this wrong and you were condemned by him as a Pharisee, a non-sheep or non-believer. Similar to their meeting at the restaurant a night earlier, Uncle Robert laid out his theories, and Tim wasn't convinced. And because of Tim's failure to correctly deal with Jews and Gentiles on those few pages, Uncle Robert thought the entire book was a travesty and that Tim should immediately stop all sales, do a recall, and undertake a massive rewrite to not only fix the offending pages, but whatever else Uncle Robert found wrong with it.

I didn't get the impression that Uncle Robert had made it clear to Tim during that meeting that he should recall and fix his book, but that's exactly how Uncle Robert and the Klassens remembered it. Tim never ended up seeing eye to eye with Uncle Robert; he never fixed his book according to Uncle Robert's wishes and never went through with a recall. This was seen as brazen and disrespectful toward Uncle Robert and, thus, condemned Tim in the eyes of Uncle Robert, Paige's parents, and Paige as well. When the weekend ended, it wasn't a total failure, but there certainly wasn't a spark of kinship and shared purpose between Uncle Robert and the Whitehall Church that I had hoped for. Unfortunately, from there, things only got worse.

LESS THAN A year later, Peter Marshall died at the age of 70. I knew very little of the man so initially I had no idea what caused his death. But Paige knew. She told me she expected it because, at the end of the conference, Uncle Robert had told her Marshall was nearing the end of his life. Uncle Robert was so disgusted with Marshall's entrenched viewpoints and unwillingness to consider the validity of his ideas that he knew Marshall's energy and life were quickly leaving him. After a quick internet search, I discovered Marshall died from a massive heart attack while exercising at a gym. This only served to further enhance Uncle Robert's stature in Paige's eyes. Me, I thought it was kind of creepy. I had visions of Uncle Robert gleefully sticking needles into a tiny doll made to look like Peter Marshall while Paige and Jack lingered close by in reverential awe.

The venom and hatred that Uncle Robert and Paige's parents displayed toward the Whitehall Church was unfortunately taught to our children. Many years later, my children, who knew nothing about the theological differences amongst the adults and were only parroting the hateful words they'd heard, would literally hold their breath as we drove through Whitehall on Interstate 90, so as not to breath in the surrounding air that was polluted by the foul and wicked members of the Whitehall Church.

CHAPTER 14
PAIGE'S FORTIETH BIRTHDAY PARTY

———◉◉◉———

OUR FINAL CHILD was born in February of 2011. Zoe came in the middle of the night after another relatively quick labor and delivery. Unlike Alex's birth, where, for most of the labor, it was just Paige and I, several ladies were there to help: a midwife, her assistant, and a doula. When the appointed time seemed close, one of them went upstairs, roused Naomi, and brought her down to watch. It was a beautiful moment and wonderful delivery, free of the drama and stress that had accompanied the births of our older children.

We now had five children, the same size family that both Paige and I grew up in. My quiver was full, but my bank accounts were not. Perhaps our greatest struggle wasn't parenting five children but, in fact, feeding and clothing them. Now earning a living selling real estate, the Great Recession that started in 2008 clobbered us. Our move from Idaho to Montana only exacerbated the problem. For about a year after the move I tried to develop a new clientele in Montana and hang on to my business in Idaho (Young Real Estate). It proved to be logistically and financially foolish. The drive from Ashton, Idaho to Bozeman, Montana, while stunningly beautiful, was also one hundred forty-five miles long, crossed the Continental Divide, and was prone to whiteout conditions due to high elevation snowstorms. I simply couldn't afford to live in Montana, run a business in Idaho, and drive back and forth between the two each week. By 2010, the real estate market had finally tanked in tiny Fremont County, Idaho, as it already had everywhere else. Not much was selling, and we were incredibly fortunate to sell our Ashton home when we did. The real estate market in the Bozeman area wasn't much better as nearly a third of all home sales in 2011 were either short sales or a bank owned property. Listening to nails scratch a chalkboard was more pleasing than working in that real estate environment.

To put it bluntly, we were broke. Things got very tight in our household. To get by, we cut corners, ate most of our meals at home, ate vegetables from our garden and venison from the deer I hunted, carried credit card debt, worked odd jobs, held a garage sale, and sold non-essential things on eBay or Craigslist. For over thirty years, I had held onto my ticket from the lone World Series game I'd ever been to, Game Six of the 1977 Series between my beloved L.A. Dodgers and the despised New York Yankees. The Yankees won the game and the series as Reggie Jackson hit three home runs that night. I sat in the outfield bleachers with my father and brothers. Back then fans still were allowed to run onto the field after a series-clinching win. The Bronx in the 1970s wasn't exactly the safest place to be after dark, so we left the game early and listened to the final innings on the car radio as we drove home. Now, broke and in need of cash, I sold that ticket on eBay. I also sold my titanium road bike and some of the antique collectables I inherited from my grandparents. It was a time of survival, and we did what we had to to survive

The three things that did the most to plug the holes and kept our family afloat during these years were the proceeds from the sale of our Ashton home, the liquidation of all our savings, and the generosity of my parents, who sent us money regularly. I was fortunate enough to grow up in a home where we had everything we needed. We lived in a large house in an affluent neighborhood. We took family vacations every year and college tuitions were paid for. My father made a good living as an actuary, and money, at least from my vantage point as a child, was never an issue. Paige, on the other hand, grew up experiencing great fluctuations in her family's fortunes. Some years, her father earned enough to provide for all their needs with money left over for birthday and Christmas gifts and the occasional dinner out. Other years, they experienced abject poverty. They, too, had to be creative to survive and Paige learned, at an early age, how to live and be happy with very few material comforts. But now she was experiencing poverty again and I felt miserable for putting her and the children through this lean time. Money, or the lack thereof, didn't cause the breakup of our marriage, but it didn't help either. Would we have experienced the same bitter dissolution of our family if I were rich and we lived in a big home, drove fancy cars, ate dinners out, and I could afford to dress Paige in the finest fashions of the day? Probably, because Uncle Robert's destructive presence was so powerful, not even vast wealth and creature comforts could have overcome it.

WITH PAIGE'S FORTIETH birthday approaching in the summer of 2012, I had to get creative with my present to her. I simply couldn't afford to rent out a hotel ballroom and feed a hundred guests or book an exotic trip for the two of us to some Caribbean island. But when the opportunity to take care of our friends' ranch was offered to us, a free location to host a large party was dropped in my lap. Located in a valley shadowed by the majestic Tobacco Root Mountains west of Bozeman, the ranch was several hundred acres in size and bisected by creeks and canals that were lined with huge cottonwoods. The owners would be off to Europe for a few weeks and needed someone to tend the cattle, chickens, pigs, dogs, and cats. It wasn't a high-end dude ranch that you would advertise in a glossy brochure, but it was more than adequate for what I wanted to do.

It was to be a surprise birthday party, so I didn't tell the youngest three children. Why burden them with the task of keeping it secret from their mother? I invited several friends and neighbors from our local community, the entire Whitehall Church, as well as my parents, Paige's parents, her older brother Jeff, and, of course, Uncle Robert. Party planning isn't my forte, but things were going incredibly smooth right up to the morning of the event. The late June weather was perfect—sunny and warm without a hint of rain or humidity. The guests would all be showing up in less than two hours. The food and beverages were taken care of, and Paige was still completely in the dark. Then I got a call on my cell phone from Paige's parents. They, along with Jeff, Uncle Robert, and his sidekick, Michael Erving, were staying at a small hotel in nearby Three Forks. About a week earlier I had emailed them, as well as my parents, detailed instructions on what to do and how I wanted the day to unfold. In order to keep the whole event a surprise, timing and execution were crucial.

Now, less than two hours before I hoped to surprise Paige, I put the phone to my ear and heard, "So, what's the plan?"

My reaction? I'll describe it this way. There is a funny scene in the movie *Napoleon Dynamite* where Uncle Rico, a lovable but goofy guy says, "I'll bet I could throw a football over them mountains," as he points toward some distant peaks. At that moment, I was so angry, I felt like taking my cell phone and throwing it over the nearby Tobacco Roots. Apparently, Paige's parents, as well as Jeff and Uncle Robert, either hadn't received my emailed instructions or hadn't bothered to read them. Either way, I had to quickly get them up to speed with directions to the ranch and when they should arrive.

Amazingly, it got worse.

Instead of following my instructions to the remote and hard-to-find ranch, they decided to plug the address into an app on their phone and follow those directions. About an hour later, they called again. They were lost, heading up a dirt road that might, after winding through the mountains, eventually bring them to the ranch sometime in the next few days.

I'd had enough. I tersely told my mother-in-law that it would be really nice if they could make the party, but unless they followed my directions exactly, they would never get here on time. They listened and did arrive on time, barely.

Meanwhile, I drove Paige and our youngest three children a few miles down the road to the old mining town of Pony, where we spread a blanket in a park and sat down for a relaxing picnic. At the same time, all the guests arrived at the ranch and quickly set up for the party. After an hour or so at the park, we drove back to the ranch. Before heading up the long driveway that led to the ranch house, I asked Paige to put on a blindfold. We drove up to the house, got out, and with Paige holding onto Zoe and me holding Paige's arm, we walked toward the hundred or so guests who were silently waiting. Once close enough, I took off the blindfold and everyone yelled "Happy birthday!" Her initial reaction was shock, but the emotion of the moment, seeing all the guests, her parents and Uncle Robert, soon overwhelmed her and she buried her face into my chest and started crying. I knew it was a good cry.

THIS DAY, IN many respects, was a microcosm of life with Paige, her parents, and Uncle Robert. Many people had worked hard over the previous days and weeks to make it a memorable event. Paige was completely surprised and, with friends and family gathered around her, she was showered with love and appreciation. But there was simply no chance that the day would unfold like any other normal birthday party. Instead, the day would take several bizarre twists and turns that, upon reflection, nearly overshadowed Paige's actual birthday.

I had arranged for several people to stand up and say a few words about Paige once the food and drinks were served and the cake was cut. My mother, Paige's mother, and Jeff all spoke briefly and uneventfully. When it was Jack's turn to stand up in front of the gathering and speak about his oldest daughter, the only daughter he had a relationship with, instead of using his time to talk about Paige, he urged everyone to listen carefully to Uncle Robert, who was to speak next. I was embarrassed listening to him as he hardly mentioned Paige. It was a call to worship at the altar of Uncle Robert that was so inappropriate and obsequious, I couldn't wait for Jack to sit down and be quiet.

Uncle Robert did speak, and like his talk at our wedding, I can't recall a single word he said. Not that very many people were listening anyway. Summer in Montana is fire season. It's common for the skies in July and August to be filled with smoke from forest fires. Humidity is low and the spring rains have long since disappeared. At some point during the celebration a massive fire started right before our eyes on the steep wooded flanks of the Tobacco Roots. At first a tendril of smoke lifted toward the sky, then the fire spread, then it erupted. We had a front row seat to the unfolding disaster. Towering flames angrily devoured huge pine trees like they were tiny hors d'oeuvres. Although it seemed like we could reach out and touch the flames, the fire was actually well over five miles away, so there was no immediate danger. Many, including most of those from Whitehall, were too distracted by the fire to listen to the speakers. Despite Jack's pleas, I doubt Uncle Robert's short speech had an impact on anyone. The fire ended up engulfing huge portions of the mountain range and took weeks to finally extinguish. It was one of many fires in what became a particularly bad fire season for Montana.

Later in the afternoon, after the guests had left, the only people who remained, aside from my family, were Paige's out of town contingent—her parents, Jeff, Uncle Robert, and Michael Erving. We spotted a helicopter in the distance and surmised it was dispatched by some government agency to survey the fire and assess what to do. The fire gathered momentum, and it was sobering to watch it burn down the forest. But, thankfully, Uncle Robert shared with us the solution to the problem. According to him, all forest fires could quickly and easily be stopped dead in their tracks if only the federal government would have the courage and wisdom to listen to him. Fires need oxygen. Deprive a fire of oxygen and it will go out. Once a forest fire was spotted, his idea was to immediately dispatch military jets and have those jets drop bombs on the fire. If located quickly, the fires would still be small and one bomb could momentarily suck the oxygen from the fire and, theoretically, put it out.

One doesn't need much imagination to come up with several reasons why his idea was both idiotic and horrifically dangerous: errant bombs, crater scarred mountainsides, terrorized citizenry, blown-up firefighters, etc. I kept my thoughts to myself regarding bombing forest fires, but with other matters Uncle Robert spoke about frequently, I asked a lot of questions. Too many it turns out. That night we gathered inside the ranch house for a mini-conference. Uncle Robert used the time to coldly rebuke me for continuing to ask for clarification on his beliefs regarding the identities of Jews and Gentiles. He bluntly told me to no longer ask him questions on this topic. His final word was delivered verbally to the group as well as in a nine-page report he typed for me and brought to the party. Copies of this report, which featured blistering attacks on me and my limited intellect, highly critical comments on Congressman and Presidential candidate Ron Paul, the John Birch Society, and members of the Whitehall Church, were distributed to Jack, Jeff, Paige, Michael, and me. It also included several pages of discussion on Jews, Gentiles, Hebrews, Talmudic conspiracies regarding the Federal Reserve, and Communism.

By 2012, I was, unfortunately, accustomed to being on the receiving end of Uncle Robert's verbal and written assaults. What made this attack so infuriating was the timing. This day was supposed to be a celebration of Paige. We were supposed to joyfully focus on Paige and how thankful we were for her. Instead, Uncle Robert launched an angry diatribe directed at me and completely ruined whatever celebratory mood remained of the day. I can't help but think that part of his motivation for berating me that night was to put me in my place, which was beneath him. Without trying to pat myself on the back too much, I had planned a darn good birthday party, and, that afternoon, Paige had been gushing in her praise and thankfulness for me. Did it bother Uncle Robert to hear Paige talk about me that way? Did he need to reassert his control and dominance of me and Paige and our marriage by denigrating me? As he wound down his dismissive remarks toward me, I could see disgust tightening the features of Paige's face, disgust for her husband because, no matter what else I did, if Uncle Robert disapproved of me, then so did she.

Even with everything that I've already written about that day, I still haven't covered what was, to me, the most bizarre feature. The strangest thing about Paige's fortieth birthday celebration wasn't her parents having no idea what the plan for the day was, or Jack's call to worship at the feet of Uncle Robert, or Uncle Robert's idea to put out fires by dropping bombs from airplanes, nor the tongue lashing he gave me because I asked too many questions about Jews. The oddest thing was the birthday letter. The letter was a trifold birthday announcement brought to the party by Paige's parents with several copies made and passed out to the guests. Displayed were several pictures of Paige and a story. When I first saw it during the party, I read it quickly, but at night, right before bed, I read it again. I never verified who wrote it; the writing sounded like Jack, but the story had Uncle Robert's imprint all over it.

"Once upon a time ... in a faraway kingdom, lived a beautiful young princess ... who was held captive by a wicked overlord. Because she had grown up under the overlord's control, she was unaware of how completely she was dominated. As she matured, the princess gradually became aware of how imprisoned she was by the constant pressure to always do things perfectly or else the overlord would be displeased with her. Alas, she was never good enough. The princess tried very hard to escape, but no matter what she did, she was powerless. One day, the princess lost all hope of meeting the demands. It was impossible. In despair she gave up trying. That very same day, a handsome prince visited her village and saved her from the overlord's power. She did not have to try to do everything perfectly any longer to be loved. Then she looked up. The sky looked bluer than it ever had. She looked at her face. It was relaxed. She was no longer worried when the overlord yelled in her ear that she was doing things wrong. From that day on, her life was full of joy and power to love and laugh and live life fully. She was very, very supremely happy."

It was a strange story, but it clearly had a deeper meaning, and I knew what the writer was trying to get at. The young princess was dominated by her mind, thoughts, and ego, which was represented by the wicked overlord. When she finally gave up trying to save herself, the Lord, as represented by the handsome prince, entered her life and saved her. And now that the Lord reigned in her life, she was no longer a slave to sin or the wicked overlord. I knew what Jack, or another writer, was getting at because I had become used to the odd way in which Uncle Robert communicated (which, of course, was the way Jack tried to communicate). But I wondered what other people thought of the story. Did they understand the story's attempted Gospel application? Did they think Paige was the princess? Since I was her husband, was I the Prince? Who was the wicked overlord? And why did the sky look bluer than it ever had?

Perhaps on that day when I read the letter, it wasn't as odd sounding as Uncle Robert's preposterous idea of dropping bombs on forest fires. But years later, when I stumbled across it and understood better the dynamics between Paige, her parents, and Uncle Robert, it took on much greater significance, and I realized just how remarkably bizarre it was. And ironic. Without meaning to be, part of it was an incredibly accurate description of Paige's relationship with Uncle Robert. She had grown up under Uncle Robert's control and her thoughts and beliefs were completely dominated by him. But unlike the princess in the story, Paige was oblivious to this. The last thing she would do is connect the wicked overlord with Uncle Robert and take steps to escape his control. Also oblivious was whoever wrote it, which I'm convinced was either Jack or Cathy (with final approval and editing provided by Uncle Robert). Thus, hiding in plain sight for all to read was the fact that Paige wasn't free but rather still imprisoned, no matter how blue the Montana skies were. And instead of distancing herself from Uncle Robert, Paige seemed to be moving closer to him with each passing day, which also meant moving further and further away from me.

CHAPTER 15
SURROGACY AND THE WEDDING BAND

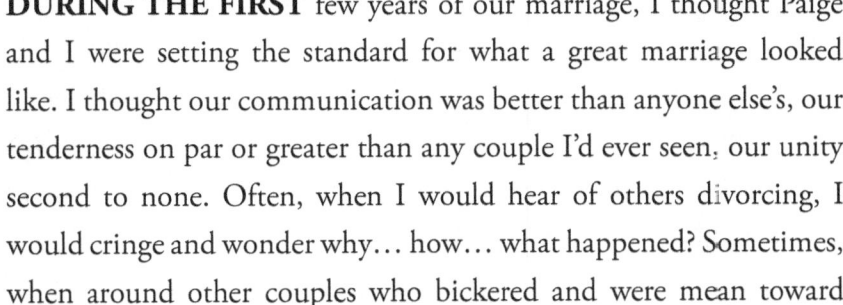

DURING THE FIRST few years of our marriage, I thought Paige and I were setting the standard for what a great marriage looked like. I thought our communication was better than anyone else's, our tenderness on par or greater than any couple I'd ever seen, our unity second to none. Often, when I would hear of others divorcing, I would cringe and wonder why… how… what happened? Sometimes, when around other couples who bickered and were mean toward each other, I would inwardly roll my eyes then pat myself on the back for how extraordinary my marriage was, how much better we were, how much better *I* was. Separation, strife, arguing—divorce—would never afflict our marriage.

However, after over a dozen years of married life, I knew our relationship lacked the magic and passion it once had. We didn't communicate as well as we used to, and I was clearly not as united with Paige as she was with Uncle Robert. As an eternal optimist I believed wholeheartedly we could be that couple again; we could be that close, that united in mind and spirit, our goals perfectly aligned as they were during the Inkom years.

However, with every new rift and disagreement Paige and I had, almost always the result of something Uncle Robert said or did, the foundation of that belief was chipped away. Questions crowded into my heart and mind. Did she always feel this way and I just didn't know it? Was Uncle Robert always this important in her life, and I was simply oblivious? I always knew Uncle Robert lurked somewhere, his thoughts and beliefs permeating our lives like the proverbial leaven in the loaf, but the extent to which he was now dominating not only Paige's parents' lives, but Paige's life as well, was becoming increasingly alarming.

It was clear that the glory days of Inkom were a long distant memory. And, at times, the breach between us was so blunt and raw that it shocked me and sent a shiver of fear down my spine. As a sports broadcaster I did a lot of research online getting ready to call the games assigned to me. One day, I happened across an online article on an attractive woman who had been a star college basketball player the same time I played in college. I made a positive comment about her to Paige, and she said, "Maybe you should have married her." I was stunned. She said it so matter-of-factly, without sarcasm, that it conveyed the feeling that had I indeed married this other woman, Paige would have been fine with it. And, as I had done so many times before, I failed to follow up and ask what she really meant. Did she really mean she would have been okay with that? I didn't ask because I was afraid that's exactly what she would say.

One night, instead of swallowing the question I so desperately wanted to ask, I asked. Lately, I had sensed such strong resentment and disrespect from her, I had to find out if it was true or just my imagination. The answer was as obvious as the nose on my face, but I still asked, holding out hope that, somehow, I was misreading her and that, yes, she still respected, adored, and honored me.

Just after we had turned the lights out and were lying in bed, still awake, I asked her if she respected me like she did Uncle Robert and her father and older brother. Her reply was swift and blunt: "No."

Once again, I was stunned and lay wide awake, unable to sleep, terrified by the failure of my marriage and wondering what that meant for the future. While she slept soundly, I crept out of bed and walked down the quiet country roads that surrounded the home we rented. For several hours, under a beautiful moonlit night sky, I cried and walked alone trying to grasp the crushing reality of Paige's true feeling towards me. That my wife didn't respect my opinions and looked to other men for guidance and direction was devastating.

I blamed myself for the state of our relationship, but not because I was truly humble or felt a prompting from the Lord to feel this way. Rather, my fawning and fearful belief in Paige's infallibility, buttressed by her imposing self-confidence, fueled my self-doubts. Instead of being angry at Paige for not respecting me, I focused on the fact that I was jealous of her profound respect for the other men in her life. I decided to do something about it. I called all three to apologize.

Her father, Jack, and brother, Jeff, couldn't have been more gracious and kind in their responses. They immediately forgave me and complimented my willingness to tackle the issue of my jealousy head on. My phone call to Uncle Robert was much different. He was angry, combative, and defensive. He interpreted the call and my jealousy of his position in Paige's life as a challenge and threat. His defense soon turned to offense. Who was I to question his role in her life? So, what if she respected him and not me? Hadn't he known Paige for longer than me? He spoke as if he occupied a lofty position in her life that I could never dream of attaining; as far as he was concerned, I was some Johnny-come-lately.

Calling Jack and Jeff felt good, their responses a relief. The call with Uncle Robert left me with the same feeling I often had when communicating with him—a queasy mixture of confusion and discomfort. His responses were so utterly unpredictable, I never knew how he'd react or what he would say. As a result, I was always nervous communicating with him. Would this call turn out well or would it be another uncomfortable near disaster that put me further out of step in the dance of life that Uncle Robert and Paige were enjoying? I knew Paige wanted me to call and email him more often, and I knew since they talked so much, she would know exactly when I had or hadn't called him. In her mind, all my shortcomings could easily be rectified if I would simply spend more time listening to him. As a result, I felt tremendous pressure to call Uncle Robert, but I didn't want to call him because I didn't like him, didn't trust him, and, deep down, didn't want anything to do with him. So, I hesitated, rationalized, and procrastinated, which made it that much harder when I finally did summon the courage to call him. And call him I did, repeatedly, because somewhere in my subconscious, I knew my marriage would continue to decline and never recover unless I embraced him.

I was in a horrible predicament, and, as a result developed coping mechanisms. After years of listening to Uncle Robert and asking him questions, only to be more confused, I came up with an analogy that, to me, aptly described his communication style. If asking someone a question could be equated with asking someone to give you a chocolate chip cookie, then Uncle Robert's response was never to simply place the cookie in your hand, but to pour sugar, flour, butter, and chocolate chips into your hand. The result was a big mess. But if you were patient and diligently considered the cookie ingredients, his words of wisdom, you not only ended up with a chocolate chip cookie, you also had the knowledge of how to make one yourself. Framing things within this analogy enabled me to agree with Paige and her parents that Uncle Robert was the expert in everything. It was clear they believed that. However, as I looked at the figurative gooey mess of cookie ingredients in my hand, it was hard to consider Uncle Robert the expert on anything. The cognitive dissonance of loving Paige, who believed so fervently in Uncle Robert, while I struggled to believe anything he said, was so severe that I had to come up with a solution to rid my mind of the tension. Thus, I arrived at the chocolate chip cookie analogy.

And make no mistake, in the eyes of Paige and her parents, Uncle Robert was *the* expert on all subjects (recall the incident with Thomas's teeth and the dentist). It seemed he had an opinion on everything, and those opinions were absolutely and unequivocally above doubt or reproach. While I have many stories of Uncle Robert spouting idiotic ideas, only to have them swallowed hook, line, and sinker by Paige and her parents, only one example is needed to drive home the point. At one of our conferences in Idaho, Uncle Robert encouraged us to behave like the conies in Proverbs 30:26, which says, *"The rock badgers are a feeble folk, yet make their houses in the crags."* These humble creatures were wise to build their homes in the rocks and Uncle Robert said we should do likewise because of the risk of worldwide nuclear war. If we built our homes into mountains or hillsides of rock, then we would have a better chance of surviving a nuclear blast. The threat of nuclear destruction was similar to the threat of an imminent eruption of the giant volcano beneath Yellowstone National Park that Uncle Robert had warned us about years prior. With the Yellowstone threat, we could move away from the area, but with the ability of nuclear weapons to be sent anywhere on earth, there was no option of moving away. We had to take action where we lived. Forget about looking for a place with a two car garage or large master bath, we needed to find a really big piece of rock that only Fred Flintstone would fall in love with.

Being a real estate broker, I constantly looked at properties and always kept an eye out for something that I'd like to buy for our family. One time, I found a beautiful piece of land that had lots of great survivalist features. The parcel was nearly one hundred acres in size and could easily support both livestock and a massive garden, had fresh water from an adjacent creek, was near the forest for hunting, and was private yet not too far from the essential services (hospital, airport, etc.) of a large town like Bozeman. I thought it was nearly perfect, but it didn't have a mountain or large hillside to build a home into like Uncle Robert suggested. When I described the property to Paige, she was angry that I would dare think this property was suitable for us, since it didn't have the required hillside/mountain. My years of experience as a broker analyzing rural properties like this in Idaho and Montana meant nothing. Uncle Robert's word meant everything.

WITH UNCLE ROBERT occupying such a prominent place in Paige's heart and mind, it's no wonder he also claimed a fair amount of her affection too. One day, while working in the yard of our Bozeman home, I absentmindedly put my hand into the pocket of an old grungy jacket and pulled out a wedding band. It was my old wedding band, and I hadn't seen it in years. I had lost it at some point while living in Inkom. I figured I took it off one night before playing a city league basketball game in nearby Pocatello and simply misplaced it. After a long and fruitless search, I decided to buy a new wedding band and assumed I would never see the original one again. After many years and many moves, it was a miracle the ring hadn't fallen out of the pocket, or I hadn't thrown out the old jacket. The ring looked just like the one I was currently wearing, but it brought on a wave of nostalgia. This was the ring Paige put on my finger the day of our wedding so many years ago. It reminded me of our earlier days, better days filled with laughter and joy. I was thrilled to find it and immediately showed it to Paige. She too was happy I found it, although perhaps not as excited as I was.

Now I had two wedding bands and, obviously, could only wear one at a time. Not long after finding it, Paige informed me that Uncle Robert had also lost his wedding band and was currently without one. The implication was clear, and she barely had to ask. I didn't want to, but we sent my original wedding band to Uncle Robert. Paige was very pleased with my decision, but I found it unseemly. It wasn't so much my wedding band as it was *ours*, and instead of keeping it, whether on my finger or in a desk drawer, she wanted to give it to another man. Not only did it demonstrate where Paige's true affections lay but it was also another example of my weakness and doing what I felt was necessary to appease my wife, rather than being honest and telling her my true feelings. Let Uncle Robert get his own new wedding band; better yet, let his wife, the one who held a steady job, buy him a new one. It hurt that my wife was eager to give my wedding band to another man. But I swallowed the hurt and the anger and tried my best to simply let it go.

AS IT TURNS out, the story of the wedding band was nothing compared to the surprise request Paige presented to me in late 2014. It was between Thanksgiving and Christmas; Paige and I were out on a date while our children stayed home. We had instituted a weekend schedule that called for Friday night to be our date night while Saturday was family night. This Friday date night, we went to a local coffee shop, and Paige got all decked out—fancy clothes, makeup, the works. She looked great. After we sat down with our coffee, she told me of her burning desire to have another child. Previously, we had talked on occasion about having another child, hopefully a boy, and naming him Matthew. Despite our dire financial situation and our plates already being full with five wonderful children, I was all for it. But this child Paige was now speaking of wasn't for me or for us, but for another man. She expressed anguish over the fact that Uncle Robert didn't have a male grandson to carry on his bloodline. His two boys, Thad and Devin, had so far failed to provide a male heir for Uncle Robert, and as they approached their forties, it didn't look like it would ever happen. Thad and his wife gave birth to a daughter and adopted two other children, one a boy, but not blood related to Uncle Robert. Devin and his wife also had a daughter, and she had had a son prior to their marriage, but again, this grandson was of no blood relation to Uncle Robert. To Paige, it was of the utmost importance that Uncle Robert's bloodline be preserved through a male grandson. So, on that night, our date night, Paige, my wife of over seventeen years, the woman I loved and adored, the mother of my five children with whom I hoped to one day have a sixth child, asked me to let her become pregnant with Thad Booty's son so she could be a surrogate mother and finally provide a male grandson for Uncle Robert and preserve his precious bloodline. This time I wasn't just stunned, I was furious.

I wanted to scream no, "Hell no!" I wanted to scream so loud that all the coffee cups in the place would shatter. But I didn't scream. I did, however, make it abundantly clear that I was against it and then started asking lots of questions. How would she do this, have sex with Thad? No, she answered, through in-vitro fertilization. What if she had a girl, would she try again with Thad for a boy? Yes, as many times as necessary, in fact. Did she think this was safe, given the fact she was over forty? Yes. Had she considered the impact this decision would have on me and our children? Yes. It was yes to everything, but I was a million miles away from a yes. The nauseatingly uncomfortable prospect of Paige giving birth to Uncle Robert's grandson had me obsessed with no. My many questions and obvious lack of support for the idea made Paige angry.

There was now no pretending the elephant wasn't in the room. Paige and Uncle Robert (who loved the surrogacy idea) were on one page and I was on another. As far as I knew, the only people she told about her desire to be a surrogate were Uncle Robert and me. I was very much against the idea and simply couldn't muster any support for it even though I tried. Without me on board, Paige wasn't going to go through with it. She and Uncle Robert both realized that without unity between Paige and me on this issue, following through would have the potential for disastrous results. My first call to Uncle Robert to discuss the topic didn't go well. He too was angry with me. Why would I stand in the way of uniting the two families, meaning, I thought, the Youngs and the Bootys. What he probably meant was uniting the Klassens and the Bootys, something the Klassens and Bootys had dreamt about for years. Paige and Rebecca weren't that far apart in age from Thad and Devin and, as parents are apt to do when their children are young, visions of a marriage uniting one of Uncle Robert's sons to one of Jack Klassen's daughters was not only suggested but encouraged. Alas, it never happened; but now, thanks to Paige's brilliant idea, the tie that would forever bind the two families could finally be consummated.

There was one small problem. I stood in the way. I did research on surrogacy and culled online articles about the dangers and pitfalls that could occur, especially when trying to do it after the age of forty. I brought up all the logical and rational reasons I could think of as to why we shouldn't go through with this. Neither Paige nor I had ever met Thad's wife. Would she be okay with it? I had only met Thad once and hardly knew him. They lived in Hawaii and we lived in Montana. How would we get the baby to them? Who would pay for all the logistics and medical expenses? Was it even legal for Paige to do this after the age of forty? But all the logical and rational reasons against it had zero impact on Paige. In her mind, if it were meant to be, then the Lord would provide a way. An admirable position indeed, but what wasn't admirable or biblical was another twist to the story.

As it became clear to Paige that I was dead set against the idea and it would be hard to convince me otherwise, she shared a shocking revelation; she had taken a vow before the Lord that she wouldn't have another child with me without first offering the option of surrogacy to Thad Booty. I was stunned and hurt that Paige would make such a vow against me. She was, in essence, saying she valued Uncle Robert and his bloodline, his place in the Body of Christ, his future, his plans—basically everything about him—more than me. As I struggled to accept the fact that my wife made this vow behind my back, she continued to pour salt in the wound. When we discussed the idea again a few days later she bluntly stated that Thad Booty was vastly more mature than me and any child born to him versus another child unfortunate enough to have me as their father would have a much better life, become a much stronger Christian, and have a much greater impact for the Kingdom here on earth. She repeated this several times, as if it were a settled fact that everyone agreed with and there was simply nothing I could do about it. I was immature, Thad Booty was mature, and that was that. I didn't argue and fight back because I didn't want to argue and fight with my wife. I loved her and wanted her to love me. I wanted her to respect me and admire me, not consistently put me down and live a life of frustrated resignation because she had married the wrong guy. I felt small and

138

unwanted and probably acted that way.

The incredible irony is that the main reason Paige didn't simply steamroll me and be a surrogate anyway, or at least offer the prospect to Thad, was the reluctant, yet firm opposition from Uncle Robert. While Uncle Robert would have loved to see Paige give birth to a son for Thad, a grandson for him, he was deeply concerned with Paige's decision to make a vow before the Lord that was not only done in secret but also clearly in opposition to me, her husband. He pointed out to Paige the unbiblical nature of what she had done, and made the point so convincingly, she backed down from her ultimatum and even apologized to me for making the vow. Nevertheless, in the end, she listened to Uncle Robert, not me.

Stung by my refusal to go along with the plan, as well as Uncle Robert's rebuke of her for making the vow, she maintained a cold and dismissive assessment of me as a father and husband. In an odd way, she actually stuck to her vow because there was no way she was going allow herself to get pregnant by me, not then, and as it turns out, not ever again.

The surrogacy issue became a wedge that had sunk deep and was pushing Paige and me further and further apart. We never got down to the root of the issue, we never uncovered her *why*. I never pressed her to explain why a child born to Thad Booty was so much better off than one born to me. Why did she think Thad Booty was so much more mature than me? Why was I such a bad father? Why was having a son with me not good for the Kingdom? Why did she secretly take a vow before the Lord against me? Why was it so important to preserve Uncle Robert's bloodline?

But I wasn't good at asking her questions, especially those kinds of questions, probably because I was afraid of the answers. And afraid of her.

After that, the surrogacy issue didn't come up again for several months, not until after the June 2015 conference. And that conference changed everything.

II
THE NIGHTMARE
2015 - 2017

CHAPTER 16

ABIGAIL AND NABAL

—◉◉◉—

THE BIBLICAL STORY of Abigail can be found in 1 Samuel Chapter 25 and takes place in the ancient Israelite town of Carmel. Abigail is said to be beautiful and intelligent, but unfortunately her wealthy husband, Nabal, was foolish, surly, and mean. At the time, David, the future King of Israel, was trying to stay away from the current King of Israel, Saul, who was trying to kill him. While on the run, David hears that Nabal is shearing his many thousand sheep, and David sends his subordinates to ask for help. Even though Nabal is reminded that David and his men have protected and treated Nabal's servants and flock kindly, Nabal gives a rude and insulting response. At this, David is ready to kill Nabal and all the men in his household. But Abigail, who heard what happened, quickly intervenes and intercepts David, who, along with four hundred of his men, is on his way to exact revenge. Bowing down to David, Abigail humbly offers him large quantities of provisions and begs him not to avenge himself by shedding blood. She calls her husband wicked and foolish and acknowledges the Lord will indeed one day make David ruler over Israel. David is pleased and impressed by Abigail's good judgment; he accepts her gifts, grants her request, and tells her to go in peace.

When she arrives home safely, Abigail finds her husband drunk and decides to wait for him to sober up before she tells him what happened with David, which she does the next morning. Upon hearing the news, Nabal's heart fails him, and ten days later the Lord strikes him dead. After that, David asks Abigail to be his wife, and she accepts. It's a remarkable short story with clearly defined characters. The integrity and honor of David is matched by the courage and intellect of Abigail, while the foolish and ungrateful Nabal gets what he deserves, his brief appearance in the Bible coming to an inglorious end.

In early 2015, with my rejection of her proposal to provide Uncle Robert with a male grandson fresh in her mind, Paige told me that she felt like Abigail. She referred to herself as Abigail more than once, usually after some kind of incident involving me and Uncle Robert: a poorly asked question on my part, something I said that contradicted him, etc. Paige said she often felt like she had to cover for me and protect me from making a fool of myself. Even though, at that point in my life, I had read the entire Bible several times, I had to look up the story of Abigail to refresh my memory. When I reread the story, I was dumbfounded, for it was clear that if Paige felt she was Abigail, then, clearly, I was Nabal. And it didn't take much thought to figure out that Uncle Robert represented David in this story. Did Paige really think I was surly and mean? Did she view my repeated questions to Uncle Robert about Jews and Gentiles and America's Sovereign National Credit as a sign of disrespect? Was I a fool, as the name Nabal means, because I didn't accept everything Uncle Robert said without question or reservation? You can probably guess by now that I didn't ask Paige these questions.

THE ABIGAIL COMPARISON was another stinging comment that hurt deeply, but it was nowhere near as painful as the words Paige shared with me on my birthday in March 2015. Friends of ours had built a tiny cabin on their property that they rented out for extra income. Paige would often clean the cabin so we could have some extra income too. And, occasionally, in addition to what they paid Paige to clean, our friends would let us use the cabin for a night. So, we took advantage of their generosity on my birthday and spent the night at the cabin. It was extremely rare for Paige and me to spend the night away from our children, but the cabin was close by, and, with cell phones we were always within reach. The birthday card Paige gave me was made by her and filled with kind words … until the last line where she wrote I was a "man that lives in my [her] life." Hardly believing what I read, I read it again and again. She didn't end her birthday card to me, her husband of almost eighteen years, addressing me as the love of her life or her best friend or amazing husband or any other similar description of love and affection that I hoped for. Instead, I was simply a man that lived in her life. Awkwardly I thanked her for the card but said nothing until the next morning.

After breakfast, I timidly brought up what she wrote, worried she might actually confirm that, yes, she saw me as nothing more than a man that lived in her life. And that was exactly what she said. At times, that really was all she saw me as, just another man. When I pressed and asked why she felt this way, she reiterated similar themes she'd been complaining about for some time—I was difficult to talk to, focused on the lack in our lives rather than the abundance, not a risk taker, incredibly immature, and, worst of all, I was a Pharisee.

Being called a Pharisee was far more demeaning and carried far more significance and weight than simply being called a hypocrite. Being a Pharisee meant I was someone who said all the right things and claimed to follow God, but in my heart, I was far from Him. Being a Pharisee meant I was concerned about the cleanliness of the outside of the cup but didn't care about the inside, where cleanliness really mattered. It meant I talked the talk but didn't walk the walk. It meant I cared more about the traditions of man than the words of Christ. Saying someone was a Pharisee was akin to questioning someone's faith and salvation rather than coming right out and saying you didn't think that person was a Christian. Not only did Paige think I was a Pharisee, she also thought our whole family was, and, for that reason she was all the more convinced not to have Matthew with me. Only Uncle Robert was capable of leading Paige to such a dark conclusion. Rather than utilizing his incredible power and control over Paige's heart and mind to promote growth in the fruits of the Spirit like love and joy and peace, Uncle Robert nurtured an oppressive atmosphere of condemnation, judgment, and regret. This atmosphere, this dark cloud, manifested itself when Paige claimed our entire family were Pharisees; it manifested itself with Jack Klassen every time his shoulders sagged or his eyes misted over at the thought of being a dad on par with a cockroach; it manifested itself when Paige claimed the Lord nearly killed David in her womb because of her lack of support for Uncle Robert when he was being slandered by Rebecca; and it manifested itself in many other ways.

"A man that lives in my life." I couldn't stop those seven words from running through my mind, over and over, mocking me, haunting me. But, ever the optimist, I thought this would be the low point in my life and in our marriage; it could never get worse than this. I was confident our marriage would rebound and grow stronger from this point, rising from the ashes like the phoenix. I envisioned a victorious future where we would fall madly in love again and, together, look back on this moment and thank the Lord for giving us a strong and vibrant marriage. I kept the card for about a year or so as a memento to remind me where we came from, sure the words would seem outlandish to Paige once she fell in love with me again. At that point, we'd throw it out together and celebrate our unity and shared love. But things didn't get better, and when Paige didn't fall madly in love with me, I finally threw the card out.

A WEEK AFTER my birthday, Paige requested that Uncle Robert be our marriage counselor. I swallowed hard but agreed. Despite all the things that had taken place over the past few months, I still didn't think we needed a marriage counselor, and certainly didn't want Uncle Robert doing the counseling. Uncle Robert lived a thousand miles away, literally. What good was he going to do living that far away? Of course, that kind of reasoning was simply my mind trying desperately to grasp onto a logical reason, any reason really, that would cover for the real reason I didn't want him as our marriage counselor: I didn't trust him and resented the position he held in Paige's life. I was also quite certain any other marriage counselor on the face of the earth, one working with full knowledge of Uncle Robert's grip on Paige, would tell us that the first thing we needed to do to strengthen our marriage was get rid of Uncle Robert.

Our first meeting with Uncle Robert as our official marriage counselor took place a few weeks later. He and his sidekick, Michael Erving, whom we all called Brother Michael, were driving through the area and made a side trip to come see us in Bozeman. I never really knew where Uncle Robert was going on his travels or for what reason, other than having a vague understanding that he was working to spread the Gospel. That is to say, I have no idea if he drove to Montana specifically to see us. Regardless, the meeting went well, all things considered. He asked that we not be like our parents and was especially concerned that Paige not turn into her mother. It was the kind of blunt and tactless comment that, had anyone else said it,

147

would probably have elicited an angry reaction from Paige. But it was the kind of thing Uncle Robert said and did frequently. Had Paige's mother, Cathy, been sitting at the table with us, he still would have said it. And she probably would have agreed with it.

The most alarming thing shared at the meeting was when Uncle Robert told Paige she hadn't made a mistake years earlier. He didn't explain what mistake he was talking about, but the look he shared with Paige made it clear that they had discussed this supposed mistake many times before. She was emotional and tearing up when he looked her in the eyes and said it. Since this was a meeting about our marriage, I couldn't help but assume the mistake they were referring to was the mistake of her marrying me. Once again, I didn't ask for a number of reasons: I assumed I knew what the mistake was, I assumed they would have thought it a stupid question because the answer was so obvious, and I didn't want to let Uncle Robert know I was unaware of what Paige was thinking. I didn't want to give him that satisfaction. Not only did I not think Paige and I needed marriage counseling, but I also deeply resented having Uncle Robert in a position of authority over me and my marriage. I didn't see him like Paige did. I didn't need his approval like she did, and I certainly didn't want his opinion to be the prevailing opinion in our marriage.

At the start of the meeting, I was reminded why I was so uncomfortable around him, and why Paige was so subservient to him. About twenty miles out, Uncle Robert called Paige for driving directions to our house. He had never been to our home, and we lived in a rural area, so directions had to include landmarks like "cross the river" or "just past the golf course." And that is what Paige did, but Uncle Robert and Brother Michael still managed to drive past the turnoff for our house not once, but twice. When he finally arrived, Uncle Robert showed Paige the notes he took from the directions she gave him over the phone. Paige told Uncle Robert to look for our street a few miles past the river and gave him an approximate distance of four to six miles. In actuality the distance is shorter, around two miles, so Uncle Robert placed all the blame for him and Brother Michael twice missing the turnoff on Paige. She mildly protested at first but then let it go and accepted Uncle Robert's version of the mistake. My first thought was, *This guy is such a jackass. Can't he ever admit he's wrong and accept responsibility for something, especially something as trivial as this?* The answer was obviously no. The express purpose of him driving to our home was to share his expertise, his brilliance, his unparalleled intellect. The last thing he was going to do was humbly accept the fact that Paige was right and he was wrong. He *always* had to be right and relished pointing out others' mistakes, real or imagined.

UNCLE ROBERT'S ABILITY to cultivate an aura of invincibility and perfection in the mind of Paige can be seen in the story she recounted to me once. She recalled seeing Uncle Robert, upset over something regarding his car, kick one of the tires in anger. Paige admitted this little incident helped her see that Uncle Robert was in fact human and imperfect like the rest of us. Over the years, I often challenged his infallibility with as much delicacy as possible, in the hope of helping Paige see him as a mere mortal. I'd like to think my little challenges helped, but the story with the kicked tire took place well before Paige met me. What was unsaid but implied by her little story was that at one point in her life she *did* see Uncle Robert as nearly perfect. And what was also implied was that the worst thing Paige had ever seen Uncle Robert do was innocently kick a car tire.

It had become clear that Paige and her parents sensed my reservations about Uncle Robert. She shared the tire kicking story with me because she wanted Uncle Robert more relatable so I would hopefully have an easier time trusting him. Jack did something similar while the two of us were driving in my truck when our family still lived in Ashton, Idaho. Out of the blue, he said he didn't believe everything Uncle Robert said just because it came from him. Uncle Robert hadn't been the topic of our conversation, but obviously it had been on Jack's mind and was bugging him so much he felt compelled to tell me. I simply nodded and listened, but the way he brought it up, the awkwardness and timing of it, made me think he probably *did* believe everything Uncle Robert said. I wondered: did it bother Jack that I thought he believed everything Uncle Robert said or, in fact, was it more bothersome to Jack that he knew he believed everything that came from the mouth of Uncle Robert? Either way, the comment came and went, our conversation moved on to something else and Jack never said anything remotely like it ever again.

The most obvious, and perhaps disturbing, example of Uncle Robert's belief in his infallibility has to do with the story of the little lamb he killed. As a young boy growing up in Syria, Uncle Robert loved playing with his slingshot. His father had given him strict instructions on how to use it safely, but, one time, he failed to heed his father's word. Out in the fields by himself, Uncle Robert let fly a rock that headed for a short rise. Just after letting go of the sling that sent the rock hurtling through the air at deadly speed, a lamb appeared and lifted his head into view. The rock hit the lamb in the head and killed the poor animal. It was a tragic accident brought about by Uncle Robert's disobedience to his father's word. I recall him telling the story more than once during our Conferences. A hush would fall over the room as he brought us back to that seminal moment, and when the story was done, all the adults would sit in solemn, almost tearful reflection.

To me, it was clear Uncle Robert was insinuating that the killing of the lamb was his first and only sin. Ever. Years later, I brought this up with my children and one replied, "Dad, he told us this was the only time he ever sinned."

Uncle Robert's one moment of humility—admitting sin—was couched in obvious and jaw-dropping arrogance. Yes, Uncle Robert was mortal like us, but his only sin was remembered like 9/11, or Pearl Harbor, or the crucifixion. On the Heavenly scoreboard, I and everyone else were racking up sins like Cy Young won baseball games; Jesus Christ threw a perfect game and Uncle Robert was close behind, tossing a one hitter. He and Christ were on a whole other level of righteousness and saintliness. And that's exactly how he wanted us to see him.

THE NEXT STORY is a wonderful example of foreshadowing. You, the reader, will see what is coming a mile away, but, unfortunately in 2015 I wasn't able to see past my nose. By then I was years into the long and painful journey of walking on eggshells trying to please a dissatisfied wife, and in my desperation to please Paige, I became blind to the added weight I was carrying. Forget walking on eggshells; I couldn't step on a cinderblock without crushing it. The story started with me reading the Bible to our children after dinner one night. Once I was done reading Matthew Chapter 26 (which tells the story of Peter the disciple disowning Christ) Paige made a curious comment about the Disciple Peter. She said Peter didn't become a Christian until after he had denied Christ three times and wept over his sin.

Peter not a Christian until the night before Christ was crucified? It just didn't sound right. The next day I had to travel to a broadcasting event, so after studying some of Matthew, I emailed Paige from the road, asking for clarification. I pointed out that earlier in the Gospel of Matthew, Chapter 16, Peter tells Jesus that He is *"the Christ, the Son of the Living God."* Then Christ says this:

> *"Blessed are you, Simon son of Jonah, for this was not revealed to you by man, but by my Father in heaven. And I tell you that you are Peter, and on this rock I will build my church, and the gates of Hades will not overcome it."* Matthew 16: 17-18 NIV

Without getting into a deep discussion about election and predestination, that statement from Christ sure seemed like strong evidence that the Apostle Peter was indeed a Christian.

These days things go viral on social media when someone posts a photo or video that is captivating or unique, and before long millions of people have looked at it. Similarly, my question about the timing of the Apostle Peter's salvation went viral in our little group of Uncle Robert followers. Emails bounced back and forth between me, Paige, and Uncle Robert, with Paige's parents included as always, but silently watching and reading from the sidelines. Paige responded to my query by writing that Peter experienced a *"full conversion once he saw that his idea of who God is was wrong and he saw his own weakness of conviction."* In other words, when Peter answered Christ's question correctly and called him the *"Son of the living God,"* and Christ told Peter his answer was given to him by God the Father, Paige believed Peter still had the wrong idea of God. Peter still had to do more, learn more, say more in order to be saved, or, in Paige's words, come to a "full conversion" or come to a "full knowledge" of the Lord or adopt a "Kingdom perspective." For Paige, part of the stumbling block of seeing Peter the disciple as a Christian at this point in the Gospel narrative was what happens later in Chapter 16. When Jesus tells his disciples he is going to be crucified, Peter rebukes him and says, *"This shall never happen to you!"* Again, Christ's response is direct and to the point. He looked at Peter and said, *"Get behind me, Satan! You are a stumbling block to me." Matthew 16: 23*

The Apostle Peter had a clumsy habit of sticking his foot in his mouth: for instance when he arrogantly tried to justify himself by asking Christ how many times he needed to forgive his neighbor, or when he vowed he would never deny Christ, and this instance in Chapter 16 when he tried to rebuke Christ. Peter was a lot like you and me; sometimes, we say stupid things we wish we hadn't. But being a Christian means you're saved thanks to the free gift of grace given by God, not by the eloquence of your words. And as Christ said, this free gift is revealed to us not by man, but *"by my Father in heaven."*

If the Apostle Peter's declaration that Jesus was *"the Christ, the Son of the living God"* was still not enough evidence for Paige to believe he was a Christian, what then did he lack? What was Peter missing? With God already revealing His truth to Peter, could it be that in order to experience the "full conversion" Paige thought he lacked, Peter was still missing something that needed to be revealed by someone like Uncle Robert?

And for those of you way ahead of me, you're probably saying to yourself, "Yes, but *which* Peter?"

CHAPTER 17
THE 2015 CONFERENCE: SAVED BY BOOTY

PRIOR TO OUR 2015 conference, Uncle Robert asked everyone to come prepared to share their testimony. The plan was to take occasional breaks from Uncle Robert's long monologues and listen to each other's testimony. By testimony, he meant the story of how we became a Christian and what the Lord has done for us. Sharing your testimony is a popular and, often, very effective way of sharing the message of Jesus Christ. There is a well-known story in the Gospel of Luke when Jesus healed a demon possessed man. This man had so many demons in him, they called themselves "Legion." Jesus sent the demons out of the man and into a nearby herd of pigs, which promptly ran down the hill into the lake and drowned. The man who had been healed of the demons was obviously thankful and begged Jesus to let him follow him. But Jesus told him no, he had something more important for him to do: *"'Return home and tell how much God has done for you.' So the man went away and told all over town how much Jesus had done for him." Luke 8:39*

What has God done for me? Do you ever ask yourself that question? Your answer is your testimony. I have shared my testimony numerous times, even in several foreign countries. I spent part of two summers in college playing basketball for a Christian organization called Athletes in Action (AIA). In the summer of 1988, the team I was on traveled to Brazil where we played and shared our faith in and around the cities of Sao Paulo and Rio de Janeiro. The next year, I traveled with AIA to Communist Poland (roughly three months before the Berlin Wall fell down) and then to Greece. The idea behind these AIA trips was to gather a large audience to watch a good basketball game, then, at halftime, while the audience sat there waiting for the second half, we would walk onto the court, grab a microphone and interpreter, and share our faith, our testimony, in Jesus Christ. AIA teams have been traveling to Eastern Europe and former Soviet Bloc countries for decades, but in 1989, traveling behind the Iron Curtain to share Christianity was still a dicey proposition. Our team wasn't the first AIA team to travel to Poland, but we were the first to speak publicly about our faith. We found out right before our fourth and final game against the Polish National team that we would be allowed to speak to the audience. We drew straws to see who would get to speak. I drew one of the long straws and, although I didn't get to share my testimony, I still got to say a few words to the audience. Sadly, we later found out that our interpreter had watered down the Christian message shared by one of my teammates. He was probably terrified of the Polish authorities coming down hard on him if he didn't.

I was always jealous of testimonies that were filled with emotion and drama. Mine seemed so bland in comparison. Jack Klassen's testimony had changed over the years, and now, it was filled with anguish and triumph, mostly centered on the role Uncle Robert played in bringing him to Christ after decades of *thinking* he was saved. He had shared it at an earlier conference, which ended up with Jack sobbing over all the pain he had supposedly caused them both by not listening to Uncle Robert earlier. It was a bizarrely awkward scene. Jack, while sharing his testimony, was so overcome with emotion, he got up, walked across the living room to where Uncle Robert was seated on his chair, knelt down, grabbed hold of Uncle Robert's hand and cried, while Uncle Robert sat solemnly and soaked in Jack's submissiveness.

That wasn't the only odd moment surrounding a testimony in the Klassen's home. During one of my first visits to Hayden, Paige, her parents, their friend, George Bookman, and I were sitting at the dining room table chatting after dinner. Jack shared his testimony—his pre-Uncle Robert-dominated testimony—one he would later come to see as false. Then Cathy shared her testimony or, at least, something she said was her testimony. I don't recall her mentioning anything about being saved, or having new life in Christ, or victory over sin, nothing like you might hear other Christians sharing. Instead, she went on and on about this "little piece of shit." She repeated the phrase several times, and as best as I could decipher, she still had this "little piece of shit" in her life, which was perhaps some unconfessed sin or area of her life she was unwilling to surrender to the Lord. And even though it was just a "*little* piece of shit," it was obviously a big deal to her. Well, if that were a testimony, sitting at that table, at that moment, I wanted nothing to do with testimonies. So even though I was still auditioning for the position of son-in-law, when Jack asked me to share my testimony, I declined. Cathy's "little piece of shit" testimony would years later be cleaned up by Uncle Robert as he apparently saved her by exorcising the demon that shouted like a horse as it left her.

THE DRAMA AND emotion I was looking for in my testimony had nothing to do with horse noises or a "little piece of shit" or

157

kneeling at the feet of Uncle Robert. What I felt I was missing was a Road to Damascus type moment like Saul had. My testimony goes back to when I was a teenager and I accepted the Lord as my Savior while at summer basketball camp. The week-long camp was held at Camp-of-the-Woods, a Christian family resort center on the shores of bucolic Lake Pleasant in Speculator, New York. Each year, the camp director, Norm Sonju, who was also general manager of the Dallas Mavericks at the time, would gather a few of the Maverick players and some Christian coaches he knew and have them teach young boys how to play basketball while also teaching them the love of Christ. Each night, after the drills and games had ended, we gathered as a group for a time of Bible study and worship. The invitation to receive Jesus Christ as personal Lord and Savior was often given in settings like this. I had heard it before, but on that particular night, I repeated the prayer silently in my heart and mind. I knew I was a sinner, I needed to be saved, and I needed to receive Christ's forgiveness. My understanding of Christianity was very basic and elementary, but, I believe, also fundamentally strong. I was a believer. I had faith. Isn't that what the thief on the cross had, faith? Had the thief on the cross attended Bible studies, sung worship songs, tithed, joined a church, prayed the "sinner's prayer," or had the Gospel message thoroughly explained to him by someone like Uncle Robert? No, he simply saw Jesus on the Cross and believed. Then he died, and later that day, he saw Jesus in paradise. And there I was, eyes closed, sitting in the old field house at Camp-of-the-Woods, surrounded by other basketball-loving boys my age, realizing for the first time that I truly believed in Christ.

Afterwards, I didn't tell anyone. I prayed the prayer because I was sincere, not because I was trying to gain attention, impress anyone, or fit in with everyone else. I believed the message of Christ because

I knew it was the truth. I knew it was the truth because the Lord drew me to Him. So, there was nothing to brag about. And I didn't say anything because I was shy and introverted. Plus, growing up the youngest of five boys in a competitive home environment where sarcasm flourished, I was very reticent when it came to sharing my most personal and private beliefs. After leaving the field house, I went to my cabin to grab a coat and head to the Teepee. The Teepee was the gathering place where burgers and fries, pizza and root beer floats were served along with good conversation and camaraderie. It was very dark as I walked alone along the path that paralleled the lake shore, the only light coming from the Teepee a hundred yards off in the distance. Out of the dark emerged a camp counselor who came up alongside me and we walked together to the Teepee. I knew him, but not well; he was one of the counselors at the basketball camp but not my counselor. Within short order, he asked me if I was a Christian. I replied that I was. He then asked if I had accepted the Lord that night at our camp fellowship meeting. I quickly and reflexively replied no. I immediately regretted it and wished I had told him the truth, but I was caught off guard by his question and uncomfortable being the topic of our conversation. I wasn't uncomfortable with my faith, but uncomfortable with this man I didn't know well asking me such personal questions. I was also too shy and insecure and socially inept to correct the situation. I remained quiet and we continued walking to the Teepee.

And that was it. I didn't experience some dramatic Road-to-Damascus moment. I experienced an awkward Path to the Teepee along the shore of a small lake in upstate New York. And that awkward moment haunted me for years, decades in fact. Over the intervening years, I repeatedly asked the Lord into my life, wondering and worrying that I hadn't done it right the first time or, worse, had somehow negated my faith and response to the Lord's calling by lying about the timing of it that night with the camp counselor. I had heard of other men who, doubting the efficacy of their prayers, would repeatedly ask the Lord into their life, or surrender their life to the Lord, or give their life to the Lord—whatever term you want to give to the moment you believe in the Lord and receive His gift of salvation. I am convinced the Lord chose me before He laid the foundations for this world. I also know I received salvation and eternal life in that moment as a thirteen-year-old, and that my doubts and subsequent attempts at doing it better or saying it better were not only unnecessary but clear evidence of why I needed to be saved by a loving and patient Savior.

WHEN IT CAME time for me to share my testimony at our 2015 conference in Idaho, I was well aware of my audience and shamelessly tailored it for their approval. Sitting in Uncle Robert's chair at the front of the living room with everyone watching me, I was nervous. Listening were all five of my children, ages four to seventeen, Uncle Robert, his sidekick Michael, Paige, her brother Jeff, and their parents. Everyone was either a committed devotee of Uncle Robert or simply too young to know what to think of him. I don't recall exactly what I said, but I know it included several bits of jargon Uncle Robert would approve. It wasn't my testimony at all, but rather, something I hoped would appease the adults in the room. It didn't work. Uncle Robert had said at the start of the conference that if we wanted to ask questions after a testimony was shared, go ahead. So far, no one had. But right after I finished speaking Paige raised her hand. She asked if I saw myself "On the hook or in the boat?"

Her question was in reference to another analogy that Uncle

Robert had recently shared. I came to learn that when Uncle Robert shared an analogy or parable with Paige and her parents, it carried the same weight as a biblical parable. In other words, it was Gospel. "On the hook or in the boat" was simply the latest and greatest from him, and it sounded really good. The idea was if you're truly saved you're in the boat of the fisherman, Jesus Christ. You're safe and secure, rescued from the dangerous waves of life. If you're on the hook you're still in the water, struggling, fighting, resisting like a fish; you're not saved, not a Christian. The hook is Christ calling you, pricking your conscience, making you aware of your need for Him. And when you stop resisting His call and give up, like a fish finally does once it's out of strength, you get reeled into the safety of the boat. Again, this all sounds fine, but you won't find it in the Bible. By asking the question, Paige was clearly stating she didn't think I was in the boat but, rather, still on the hook.

My response was that I was in the boat, but I could tell that Paige, and perhaps others, didn't believe it. I was the outlier at the conferences, having become a Christian before meeting Uncle Robert and, thus, without his aid and assistance. The other adults there, all who felt they owed a significant debt of gratitude to Uncle Robert for leading them to Christ, may have wondered whether or not my faith was not only genuine but even possible. Was it possible to become a Christian without the guidance and direction of Uncle Robert? My testimony probably set off alarms warning them that I wasn't a true Christian but, rather, a false one, a goat, a Pharisee, a wolf in sheep's clothing.

Later, Paige and I went for a walk around the neighborhood, just the two of us. I brought up the question she asked me after my testimony, knowing full well she doubted me. She never directly said she didn't think I was a Christian but nibbled around the edges with loaded questions. She said she had never heard me tell our children, "The Lord saved me from myself," which was another Uncle Robert saying. While I think it's an accurate one, Paige always made me feel that if you had never heard one of Uncle Robert's sayings, then you weren't privy to its truth until *after* he shared it with you. In other words, if you had never heard the saying, "The Lord saved me from myself," then the Lord had *not* yet saved you from yourself. So, when Paige said she had never heard me say that phrase, I stopped walking, turned and faced her, put my hands on her shoulders, and, in a clear and loving voice, told her that the Lord had indeed saved me from myself. At that moment, I couldn't have been more confident of that fact. Paige, on the other hand, was not.

The conference continued and Uncle Robert continued to weave incredible tales of hyenas and sperm donors and sex into the biblical narrative of characters like Adam, Eve, King David, and Abraham. In one very telling admission, Uncle Robert claimed that Jeff was his "firstborn." Clearly, he meant firstborn in the Lord, as in the first of our little clan whom he led to the Lord. Nonetheless, it was a stunning and boldly arrogant assertion, especially with Jeff's real father and mother, Jack and Cathy, sitting there listening. Obviously, they didn't dispute Uncle Robert's claim.

Many years later, while researching cults, I found out this is classic behavior of cult leaders: blur the lines of the nuclear family and you blur the lines of authority and attachment, making it easier to ascend to the position of father over everyone. This had already been accomplished in Jack, as demonstrated in numerous ways: telling Paige her true father was Uncle Robert, submissively kneeling down to Uncle Robert at a previous conference, and, as of late, addressing Uncle Robert as Dad. And with Jeff being Uncle Robert's *first*born, the implication was that he had more spiritual children. I should reiterate that Robert Booty looks nothing like any member of the extended Klassen or Young family. That's because he isn't blood-related to any of us. Both families are very tall and lean with traditional Northern European looks: blond hair, blue eyes, paler skin, etc. Robert Booty was short, overweight, with dark hair, dark eyes, olive complexion, bulbous nose and a round face. While obvious to any adult that Uncle Robert wasn't related to any of us, recognition of this sort isn't always obvious to a child. Thus, for my young children who were already calling him *Uncle* Robert, hearing him call Jeff his firstborn son and hearing their grandfather, Jack, call him Dad probably blurred the lines of family even more.

A day later, Paige was the last one to give her testimony. (Uncle Robert never gave his. I was very curious and wanted to hear it, but no one mentioned it and he never offered it. I got the distinct impression that were I to ask him to share his testimony, it would be perceived as an insult. As if when God was laying the foundation of the world, it was assumed Uncle Robert was right by His side pulling out his measuring tape. And I wouldn't ask God to tell His testimony so I shouldn't dare ask Uncle Robert to either.) It was a beautiful, warm summer evening, so we went out to the back deck and sat down in a semi-circle to listen with Uncle Robert in the middle, always in the seat of honor. Before Paige started her testimony, Jeff played Celine Dion's *"Because You Loved Me"* on his laptop computer while Paige sung along. It's a song of devotion and thanks to a beloved mentor, friend, even lover perhaps. And she sang it to Uncle Robert. The chorus goes like this:

> *"You were my strength when I was weak,*
> *You were my voice when I couldn't speak,*
> *You were my eyes when I couldn't see,*
> *You saw the best there was in me.*

Lifted me up when I couldn't reach,
you gave me faith because you believed,
I'm everything I am because you loved me."

I was so accustomed to Paige's admiration and love for Uncle Robert, that, in that moment, I didn't see anything wrong with it. I didn't see the profound disrespect and dismissiveness that was being heaped on me by my wife singing a love song to another man while my children and I sat nearby. Nor did I find it odd that Paige professed her faith in the family guru right before sharing her testimony of what the *Lord* had done for her. With everyone's eyes and ears glued to Paige, she sang a portion of the song, then gave her testimony. It was, in some ways, similar to Jack's speech at her fortieth birthday party; it was less about Paige and how she became a Christian and more about Uncle Robert.

Uncle Robert sat there and soaked it in as only he could. I couldn't imagine another Christian in a position of leadership— pastor, teacher, or mentor—not objecting to Paige's testimony. A true Christian mentor would immediately tell Paige, with loving patience, *There is way too much of me in your testimony and not enough of Jesus Christ.* A true Christian mentor would have been bothered by what Paige shared and made it clear he wasn't her savior.

Not Uncle Robert. He basked in the glow of Paige's fawning praise. Sadly, this was all lost on me in that moment. What bothered me was that she wasn't singing about me. All the attributes that I wanted her to see in me, she saw in another man. In fact, she barely mentioned me in her testimony. Her testimony, the song—it was all very powerful, a perfect final testimony for our little group of Uncle Robert followers.

Paige's doubts about my testimony, followed by the supreme confidence she displayed in her testimony, caused my doubts to kick into overdrive. Desperate for her to see me as a Christian, I was tormented by anxiety and confusion. Was there really something I was missing? Had I failed to discover an elemental truth about Christianity all these years? Did Paige and Uncle Robert, these two fascinating, intelligent, confident believers, really know something I didn't? Not only that, did they know something that every other Christian I knew was unaware of? And if not, then why was Paige, after all these years, still doubting my faith?

Just as the first glimpses of lavender peeking over the eastern horizon mark the dawning of a new day, it dawned on me that perhaps the only person who could convince Paige I was a Christian was Uncle Robert. After so many years of wanting him to leave me and Paige alone, I now found myself urgently wanting something from him. If he were convinced of my salvation, then Paige would be too. But was he? Later that same evening (after Paige's testimony) Paige, Uncle Robert, and I talked about salvation and Paige's lingering doubts about me. During that little discussion, it became clear that Uncle Robert had his own doubts regarding me. It wasn't so much what he said, but, rather, what he left unsaid. Just like that ball or rock terrified my young mind as it grew in my dreams, Uncle Robert's inability or unwillingness to declare me a Christian made sleep that night nearly impossible.

THE NEXT MORNING, Paige and I went for another walk. It was the last day of the conference, and Uncle Robert wanted to head home to California. I wanted an answer before he left; I wanted to hear him say, definitively, either I was a Christian or I was not. On this walk Paige asked me three questions, trying to lead me to the obvious conclusion that I wasn't a Christian: Did I truly love her and the children like a Christian husband and father should? Did I truly love the Word of God? And did I truly love my neighbor as myself? I had been conditioned by her and Uncle Robert to believe that if I wasn't doing those things perfectly, then I wasn't really doing them at all. So, I waffled in my responses, and, rather than continue the exhausting fight to convince her of my salvation, my belief, my faith, I simply caved. Tears flowed as I looked her in the eyes and told her, based on the answers to her questions, I must not be a Christian.

I can see now that the answers to her three questions don't uncover whether or not you're a Christian, but rather this: *Are you a Christian walking closely with the Lord and maturing in your faith?* I may never have been able to love her and our children the way she thought a Christian husband and father should. By the 2015 conference I had read the entire Bible cover to cover four times, but in the eyes of Paige, I would never love the Word of God like Uncle Robert did. And how does one prove to a skeptic he loves his neighbor as himself? Even if I could answer all those questions with Uncle Robert-like credentials, it wouldn't have meant a thing when it came to my salvation. Salvation is a free gift, pure and simple, and the moment you try and demonstrate why you're worthy of it is the moment you become just like the rich young ruler in the Bible who incorrectly thought he could somehow earn salvation through his actions. But I was beaten down, vulnerable, and weak. Instead of using this opportunity to help me grow in my Christian walk and encourage me in my faith, Paige encouraged me to doubt it. And Uncle Robert was only too willing to pile on.

We went inside and asked to speak to Uncle Robert. I looked into Paige's eyes as we sat waiting for him to come in and talk with us. Paige looked back at me with loving amazement and hope, and I was so happy because I thought this would mark the end of her doubt and the end of our problems. In that moment, it felt more like finding the long-lost answer to a blissful marriage versus believing in the Lord for the first time. When Uncle Robert came into the room, we closed the door and told him what had just transpired on our walk. I had been convinced by Paige that I needed to be saved and that's all the evidence he needed. We then gathered all the adults in the living room while the kids played outside on the front lawn. Uncle Robert spoke for a bit, giving the gathering the appropriate solemnity. I confessed my numerous sins to everyone there, he led me in praying a sinner's prayer, and, just like that, I was saved. Immediately afterwards, everyone hugged and shed tears of joy. Paige embraced her mother and cried like she'd been through a major ordeal. Watching them comfort each other I realized *I* was the major ordeal, and in that moment the seed was planted for future doubt. Because right then, this thought popped into my mind: *Why was Paige getting comforted?* Surely, I wasn't that bad?

I WANTED TO be baptized that day. I wanted all of us to pack into our cars and drive to Lake Coeur d'Alene and have Uncle Robert baptize me with everyone standing on the beach watching, just like he had done for Paige a few years prior. That baptism had washed away Paige's sin of allowing the Pocatello pastor to baptize her in 1996 before she was truly ready, before she was truly a Christian. Now it would be my turn; Uncle Robert would baptize me into the true faith, the one that really mattered, the one Paige believed in. The only problem was Uncle Robert was antsy to get on the road and get home. So, we decided to postpone the baptism.

In hindsight, I am incredibly thankful I didn't get baptized that day. I didn't need to. I'd been baptized at the age of twenty-three while living in Colorado, years before I met Paige or Uncle Robert. I publicly and honestly professed my faith in Christ. Did my life dramatically change that day? Not that I recall. But I was baptized because I wanted to, and I wanted to be obedient to the Lord.

THE ELATION OF finally figuring it out and supposedly knowing for certain I was saved didn't last long. Before the day was over, the doubts came back with a vengeance. I had been a believer in Jesus Christ since I was a teenager, so what was *new*? If salvation is a free gift, why did it seem like I had to *earn* it? Did I really have to gain all this understanding of the Word of God *before* I could be saved? Were my baptism and countless professions of faith all somehow *lies*? I shared my doubts with Uncle Robert over the phone in the days following, and he tried to assure me I wasn't saved as a teenager and I did, in fact, need to go through this recent conversion. I wanted to believe him, but the doubts were far worse than anything I experienced before the conference. More than anything, I wanted the doubts to go away. I wanted to be confident in my faith and sure of my testimony. But confidence and assurance were elusive.

On the opposite end of the spectrum was Paige, whose confidence seemed limitless. Unlike Jack, Cathy, and me, Paige didn't need Uncle Robert to pick up the pieces of a fraudulent confession of faith. She didn't have to change her story or repeatedly update her testimony over the years. If the proverbial wise man built his house upon a rock, then Paige had built her home on top of El Capitan, the largest granite monolith on earth. And like a small and inconsequential rock climber standing at the base of El Capitan, shadowed and humbled by the mile high rock as he looks up toward the peak, I stood in awe of Paige. She had scaled the mountain the right way, the first time, and made it look easy. At least, that's what I thought at the time.

Uncle Robert thought I should tell my family my new testimony in person, but since my parents and brothers lived all over the country, I decided to put it in writing. Uncle Robert suggested I include the Bible verses he shared in our conference that led me to see I wasn't truly saved. But there weren't any. There were certainly several parables of condemnation and judgment that Uncle Robert pulled out of the Bible with dubious accuracy, the kind that produced severe self-loathing in Jack: but what convinced me I wasn't saved were the doubts of Paige. So, I wrote the letter and sprinkled it with several bootlicking references to the patience, love, wisdom, and sheer heroism of Paige and Uncle Robert.

A few days later, it was time to tell our children. Paige and I gathered all five of our children in our living room. She and I sat in chairs facing them and I told them what happened at the conference, how I thought I was truly saved, truly a Christian, but was not. I was very emotional, tears streaked my face; Paige was stoic. The children all had their own unique reactions: sad, confused, embarrassed, indifferent, contemplative. It was eerily reminiscent of the time in our basement in Inkom, Idaho when Jack sat stoically next to Cathy as she confessed to never being a Christian until her recent conversion at the hands of Uncle Robert. And with that confession, Cathy also had to confess never truly loving Jack and never truly loving Paige or any of her siblings because, without Christ, she couldn't truly love anyone but herself. The same logic, with all the same implications for everything I had ever done, said, or written, would now apply to me.

CHAPTER 18

FALLOUT

---◦◉◦---

BY THE TIME the 2015 conference rolled around I was forty-seven years old. I had lived a good life—grew up in a loving Christian home, graduated high school then college, traveled the world, played basketball in front of thousands, appeared on network TV, been relatively successful in two separate careers, made lots of friends, married a beautiful woman, and fathered five wonderful children. But that was all tainted now, for during every one of those events I was a nonbeliever. Not a single one of those memories could be looked upon with satisfaction or pride. I was lost, and now, thanks to Uncle Robert and Paige helping me find my way, I needed to lose those memories. Like a brainwashed Chinese Communist in the 1960s trying to rewrite history, I proceeded to throw out hundreds of old photographs I had kept. Snapshots of a gangly kid growing up in New Jersey, scenes with me and my buddies in college, photos taken in Colorado and Idaho and Brazil and Poland and Greece—all gone. Life was starting over, this being year one. My history, life prior to the conference of 2015, needed to be rewritten. Just like an economist has to adjust historical prices and wages to compensate for the ravages of inflation, so too I needed to adjust all my historical relationships and memories to compensate for not having listened to Paige

171

and Uncle Robert earlier. It was a confusing and lonely task.

Because I had shared so little about Uncle Robert and his views with anyone outside of our small group of followers, I found it hard to share my new testimony with other friends and family. On the one hand, I was certain few would understand it, and some might not even believe it. And on the other hand, I wasn't so sure I completely believed it myself. Even though I was trusting Uncle Robert more and more, there was always a nagging question lingering in the deep recesses of my mind. Did the Klassen family guru really know what he was talking about, or was he a fraud? Making matters worse was Paige's reaction to my newfound faith, which wasn't a warm and welcoming embrace, but more of a hands-on-hips "it's about time" posture. And with time running out on her biological clock, I knew I needed to confront the surrogacy issue again.

PRIOR TO MOVING out West in 1991, I had lived my whole life on the East Coast, sheltered from the wonders of wide-open plains and purple mountain majesties. When I decided to move to Colorado in May of 1991, I bought an old green station wagon adorned with fake wood paneling and left New Jersey and the East Coast behind. Along the drive, I suffered several flat tires, yawned my way through the Midwest, then rolled into Colorado on a beautiful sunny day. In the far distance, I saw what I thought were low hanging clouds. Then I realized they were, in fact, the Rocky Mountains. I was changed forever. Ever since then, I've had a love affair with the mountains of the West. I can scarcely drive to the grocery store without gawking at the mountains surrounding Bozeman. On long car drives, my children dismiss me as an insufferable romantic because I wax poetically about each and every mountain range that comes into view. And that's okay. They've grown up out West where seeing mountains is a common sight, just like the grocery store. But not for me. The sweeping vistas, the wide-open spaces, the towering peaks will never get old and I'll always be inspired by them.

One of my favorite vistas can be seen from the back deck of a cabin owned by friends of ours. The cozy, hand-hewn log cabin sits on the banks of Harrison Reservoir and has jaw-dropping views of the impressive Tobacco Root Mountains, the same mountains to suffer the wildfire during Paige's fortieth birthday celebration years earlier. It is a secluded location, tucked into a valley where all you see is water, fields, mountains, and sky. In July 2015, our friends offered Paige and me the use of the cabin to celebrate our wedding anniversary. It was a wonderful retreat, and Paige and I enjoyed the time to get away.

One afternoon we took a long walk along the rolling hills overlooking the lake, enjoying the views, the sunshine, the solitude. Near the end of it, I finally worked up the courage to tell Paige that if she still wanted to be a surrogate so Uncle Robert could have a grandson, I wouldn't stand in the way. It was still not something I wanted, but I felt I owed it to Paige to allow her to offer this gift to Thad, Uncle Robert's son. I knew she still wanted to. It seemed her devotion to Uncle Robert was stronger than ever, so why wouldn't she? And in her commitment to help me finally become a Christian, she displayed a certain devotion to me, one that compelled me to thank her by giving her the opportunity to fulfill this deep desire of hers. She listened politely as I made the offer, thanked me, then asked if this was something I truly wanted. I told her no, and it was clear that unless I truly wanted it to happen, rather than just being okay with it, she wasn't going to proceed. And that was the last we ever seriously discussed it.

Just the thought of seeing Paige pregnant with Uncle Robert's grandson made my skin crawl, yet the conference of 2015 marked an unmistakable shift in my attitude toward him. Ever since hearing about the Klassen's family guru, I had been skeptical and wary of Uncle Robert. But after that conference, my attitude toward him softened, and thus began a period when I began to trust and even rely on him like never before. I was still uncomfortable around him and always nervous when speaking with him. But it was different now. I started to see what Paige and her parents saw in him. I saw a patient mentor, an unconventional yet brilliant leader who wasn't afraid to say difficult and challenging things when needed. Mostly, it was his ability (which he passed on to Paige) to criticize and condemn sin when necessary that made him stand apart from all other Christian mentors I'd had over the years. And if I was truly a newborn babe in Christ, as I was slowly becoming more comfortable admitting, then just as surely all those other Christian men who played the role of mentor in my life had failed miserably. They had failed because they weren't observant enough or bold enough or cared enough to confront me over my hypocritical behavior and therefore expose me as a fraud and nonbeliever. Thus, the intense criticism that Paige and Uncle Robert had directed toward the pastors and leaders at the various churches we attended now spilled over to these Christian men who had played a special role in my life. History had to be rewritten, and these men were no longer allowed to be heroes in my life.

One of these men, according to Paige, was Norm Sonju. Norm, as I mentioned earlier, ran the basketball camp at Camp-of-the-Woods in upstate New York. Norm had been the general manager for the NBA's Dallas Mavericks during the 80s and 90s and the Buffalo Braves (now L.A. Clippers) before that in the 70s. He was incredibly well connected in the two worlds that really mattered to me: basketball and Christianity. He was also a very kind and generous man.

Thus, when I asked him if he would read my novel, *The Blue Team*, and endorse it, he readily agreed. However, to get to this point in the story of how my first novel came to be, I need to take you back a few years.

THE BLUE TEAM started out as a nonfiction account of the life of an anonymous division one basketball player. Not the guy in the highlight reel dunking, but rather the guy getting dunked on. That was me. I started writing it during my senior year at George Washington University in 1991. But other than a few of my teammates, who would, no doubt, get a kick out of the funny stories, I didn't think the story would be that interesting or have much of an impact on the reader. So, I turned it into a novel and then would write off and on for most of the 90s. I sent early versions of the story for people to read and critique and got the proverbial "Don't quit your day job" kind of responses. Around the time my broadcasting career took a nosedive and I shifted into real estate, I sent the manuscript to Ric LaCivita, my former TV producer, friend, and mentor. Ric, who was a great storyteller, said every great novel is about something more than just plot and characters. There is always an underlining theme or message or moral to the story—love, revenge, faith, patriotism, etc. When he asked what my novel was *really* about, I didn't have an answer. So, I put the project aside again and focused on real estate. Also, around this time, my exposure to Uncle Robert increased. At his conferences or in email exchanges, he would often talk about the Lord saving us from ourselves and how our mind, our ego, was our worst enemy. This sounded familiar to what I would sometimes hear from successful athletes during my broadcasting career: their greatest adversary was their own mind, and their greatest challenge wasn't defeating the other team or other competitors but, rather, their doubts. And through the Lord saving us from ourselves (in essence renewing our minds) the Christian athlete would be able to banish all doubt and fear and have the peace of mind to make the game-winning shot.

Thus the message of *The Blue Team* was discovered. With that, the on again off again hope that I would one day write a book turned into a determined commitment to see the project through. Over the years, Paige had read several versions of *The Blue Team*. She was never effusive in her praise of it, but she did show a lot of patience in allowing me the time to write and chase my dream of publishing the story. I started working with a very good editor, and, in the fall of 2014, I spent a few days at my friends' cabin on the Harrison Reservoir working on the manuscript. With no cell phone service, no internet, and those incredible mountain views to inspire me, I got a lot of work done and started to see the light at the end of the tunnel.

In addition to weaving Christian principles into the basketball narrative, I ended up writing a love story between two of the main characters. This was a surprise to me; it wasn't something I set out to do, it simply happened. In *The Blue Team*, the characters Thomas Conner and Jenae Swanson developed a genuine love for each other that I modeled after my own marriage. Jenae was an athletic, kind, intelligent, Christian woman, and when I wrote of her, I thought of Paige. A friend of mine who read an early version of the book said I had succeeded in writing a love story *to* my wife without writing a love story *about* my wife. I don't think Paige ever saw it that way.

By the spring of 2015, I was ready to have the book published. Before I did, Paige strongly encouraged me to have her father and Uncle Robert read it. I obliged and emailed them copies, which they immediately panned, not the actual story, but the Christian message. I spoke at length with Jack one evening while waiting for a connecting flight in the Salt Lake City airport. I was headed off to another broadcasting assignment but couldn't wait to know why he thought my book wasn't a Christian book. He was adamant I not publish it until I made major changes, and if I did publish it without these substantial changes, I would forever regret it. He felt the story made a mockery of Christianity and wasn't a true representation of what it meant to be Christian. He also said he and Uncle Robert had discussed my book and were in agreement. When I asked for specific details, Jack had a hard time giving me any, other than the main character in the book, loosely based on me, wasn't truly saved but rather fooling everyone into thinking he was a Christian. Sound familiar? It should, because this criticism of my book came a few months before the infamous conference in June 2015 when I allowed Paige and Uncle Robert to convince me I wasn't saved.

What came next, what *had* to come next, was obvious. I had to change the book. I will admit that there were a few controversial scenes I removed from the text that did make the story better. But when it came to the core of the book, who the main character, Thomas Conner, was and what he believed in, I had a hard time going along with Jack and Uncle Robert's suggestions. Changing Thomas Conner's story revived the doubts about my own story. Requiring Thomas to do certain things and gain a deep understanding of Christianity *before* he could be saved implied a salvation through works and completely destroyed the foundational Christian belief that salvation is a gift from God and comes through faith in Jesus Christ alone. It dawned on me that what Jack and Uncle Robert (and Paige who immediately agreed with their critique once she heard it) were requiring of Thomas Conner was what they really wanted from me. And that really bothered me.

By January of 2016, I already had a glowing endorsement of

my book from Norm Sonju, as well as from my former coach at George Washington University, Mike Jarvis. My plan was to launch the book in March during college basketball's March Madness. Yet two months away from publishing my long-treasured book, I was having major doubts about its entire premise and it drove me crazy. I finally called Uncle Robert to talk to him about it. In regard to my salvation, he said he never meant to take away what I experienced as a teenager at the basketball camp when I accepted the Lord, but rather impress upon me that I was in essence "orphaned" all those years with no one to guide and nurture me in the Lord, until, of course, I met him. It was another astonishing statement with far reaching ramifications: first, it was an insult to all the Christian men in my life (my father, Norm Sonju, other Christian coaches and mentors, etc.) who supposedly didn't do anything to guide me in my faith; second, and more importantly, it insinuated that God the Father wasn't up to the task of being an effective father to me either. The Bible is clear: when we believe in Jesus Christ, we become adopted sons and enjoy the incredible privilege of calling God our "Abba," or Father. But in Uncle Robert's mind, I had no true father; I was "orphaned" until he came into my life. It took me years to connect these dots, but, thankfully, the Lord opened my eyes to this truth.

My immediate take away from the phone conversation with Uncle Robert was that I was, in fact, saved as a teenager, and, thus, so was Thomas in my story. With this monkey of doubt off my back, I could now proceed with my book as written, which is what I did.

I PUBLISHED *THE Blue Team* in March 2016 and at the end of the month traveled to the Final Four in Houston, TX to promote it. Upon my return, Paige and I actually enjoyed, from my vantage point, a brief period of tenderness and unity. It didn't last long. Paige started traveling frequently to promote her doTERRA essential oils business. In May, she traveled to California where she stayed with Uncle Robert and Aunt Staci, and they introduced her to several friends who could potentially become clients. Upon her return the predictable happened: she was upset with me over something she and Uncle Robert discussed while she was staying with him. This time, it was the issue of tithing. Tithing is a biblical concept that goes something like this: everything comes from God, all of it. Literally, from the air we breathe, the planet we live on, to the clothing we wear, it's all a gift. To demonstrate obedience and a grateful heart, the Lord asks us to give back the first 10% of everything we earn. Whether your tithing is to your local church, a missionary organization, or some other person or entity in need, the important point is you give, and give with a thankful heart. The topic is discussed at length in the Bible, so this is a grossly simplified overview, but, hopefully this conveys the general idea. Over the years of our marriage, our tithing was at times sporadic and rarely 10%. In the beginning, our tithing usually went to various Christian organizations like Prison Fellowship or our local church, and some went to Uncle Robert. As time passed, more of it went to Uncle Robert, until, eventually, it all did.

Remember that conversation I had with Jack Klassen in my pickup truck when out of the blue, he said he didn't believe everything Uncle Robert told him? Well, in that same conversation, tithing came up, and Jack objected to me sending some of our tithe to the Whitehall church. He was adamant that we send all our tithe money to Uncle Robert. He couldn't articulate why we needed to do this, but he was absolutely convinced we should. "Uncle Robert can explain it," he said. Yeah, I'll bet he could. Years later, in the spring of 2015, we were still struggling financially. We were broke, and Uncle Robert knew it, so out of what I believe was sincere generosity on his part, he suggested we simply take the tithe money we would have sent him and keep it for ourselves as a tithe from him. At this point, we were tithing exclusively to Uncle Robert, and not once over the years did he ever send us a check or give us cash as a tithe. The idea seemed nonsensical to me, but I went along, and we stopped sending him tithe checks. In Uncle Robert's mind, and in Paige's, he was tithing to us, but as far as I could tell, neither one of us was doing anything. All tithing just stopped.

This went on for about a year or so until I read a book on tithing that, ironically, Uncle Robert suggested I read. Based on that book (and a little bit of common sense) it seemed clear to me that Paige and I weren't tithing. I told Paige as much and said we should resume. She was livid. To her Uncle Robert was once again demonstrating his brilliance and generosity by allowing us to tithe to him, and he in return was tithing back to us, all at the same time. For me to suggest nobody was tithing was an unconscionable insult to Uncle Robert. On her trip to California in the Spring of 2016 they spoke about this. Of course, Uncle Robert was deeply insulted, and Paige returned home to Montana ready to take my scalp.

I somehow managed to make the situation worse with a simple email to Uncle Robert. I asked him a question about the Bible and kept it short and to the point. Instead of bogging him down with unnecessary small talk I got right to it and asked my question. Uncle Robert also brought this up with Paige on her visit and was, once again, highly offended. It wasn't so much my question, but the lack of context and appropriate fawning praise for his intelligence that my email lacked. He said he wanted me to provide him with my thoughts on the question. What did I think? What did I understand? Without that, it would be hard for him to answer me.

What I knew to be the case from prior experience was this: if I gave him nothing but the question, all he had left to do was answer it. However, if I also provided my understanding of the issue, then he had sufficient information to dive into an elaborate and rude dismantling of my mental and moral deficiencies prior to answering the actual question. So, during the same late-night talk in which Paige blistered me for not recognizing the fact that Uncle Robert was tithing to us, I was also ripped apart for not properly asking Uncle Robert a question. She must have thought of me as Nabal on steroids.

CHAPTER 19
My Last Conference

———◦◉◦———

IN JUNE 2016, our family made the annual migration to Hayden, Idaho for our Conference. That year, Uncle Robert gave us the assignment of reading the book *A God Who Hates,* which I did right before the start of the conference. The author, Wafa Sultan, like Uncle Robert, grew up in Syria and emigrated to America. Her book is fascinating and provides a penetrating look into the mind of an Arab Muslim and why the Middle East was the perfect breeding ground for Islam. Hundreds of years ago the typical Arab would wake up every morning knowing that this day could be his last thanks to a death caused by lack of food, lack of water, or a rival tribe's murderous raid. Life was harsh and filled with fear. A harsh, angry god was recognizable and familiar.

Uncle Robert was raised in Syria, which was once the cradle of Christianity, but in the 20th century, was dominated by Islam. As I read Sultan's book, I discovered two uncomfortable truths. First, the aggressive, confrontational, and manipulative communication style Sultan attributed to Arab Muslims was also a good description of Uncle Robert's mode of communicating. He never shied away from a difficult or uncomfortable topic, was never wrong, dominated conversations, hated having to listen to others talk, was quick to cast blame, and even quicker to pronounce judgment. Second, Arabs and Middle Eastern Muslims proclaim a god who is stern and quick to condemn, attributes that Uncle Robert often focused on. The more I thought about Sultan's conclusions, drawn from her thirty years of living in Syria, the more I realized the same harsh and hateful environment she described influenced the way Uncle Robert presented the Gospel of Jesus Christ.

I knew Uncle Robert was the most important person in Paige's life, and, as much as that bothered me, I also knew he wasn't going away. Subconsciously, I knew I had two choices: either I continue to resist Uncle Robert and hope that he was somehow removed from our lives, or I accept him and all that he stood for and hope to one day see him as a brilliant leader like Paige did. After all, if I was going to have this family guru running my family, marriage, and my life, I wanted him to be smart and intelligent, someone I could believe in and support. I didn't want to fear him and his words. I didn't want to worry that he would continue spouting ridiculous nonsense every time he opened his mouth.

Realizing that Uncle Robert promoted a Gospel laced with hatred and judgment wasn't the only thing making me uncomfortable as I read Sultan's book. I also realized that Paige was starting to sound a lot like Uncle Robert. In the last year or so, she had doubted my faith, compared me to the foolish Nabal, said I was merely a "man that lived in her life," repeatedly affirmed she didn't respect me or trust me like she did Uncle Robert, and was quick to dismiss other Christian men we came in contact with. As I reflected on this, my jaw nearly hit the floor when I read Sultan's analysis of Muslim relationships. She writes,

> *The human mind is programmed to feel inferiority*
> *or mastery in accordance with the status of each party.*

When two parties meet, each of them recognizes in some imperceptible way which of them is the stronger. The weaker party discards all his cards, while the stronger takes control and begins to impose his conditions. In Muslim society very few relationships are founded upon mutual respect. Even at the level of personal friendship, each party is well aware of the other's weaknesses and strengths. When two people meet, each recognizes by a simple process of calculation which of them is the stronger, and each will naturally incline to play the role of either the master or the slave.... However small the difference between the two parties may be, one will always dominate while the other submits, with no half measures.

Paige and I may have shared a mutual respect early on in our marriage, but lately, it was clear she was stronger and dominant, whereas I was weaker and submissive. If someone asked the both of us an important question on a topic like politics, religion, or childrearing, she never glanced over at me to see if I wanted to answer and never deferred to me. Rather, she always answered first, giving her opinion, which, if it wasn't mine too, it needed to be. If she could see me as the drunken fool, Nabal, or simply a "man that lived in her life," then it seemed clear she had less invested in our marriage relationship and could envision a life without me. Conversely, I was desperate to strengthen our marriage, heal the wounds and divisions that had separated us, and have us draw closer than ever before. She had little to lose; I, on the other hand, worried about losing everything.

In a rare display of courage and boldness, I brought this up with Paige about a week before we headed to the conference in Idaho. I told her it seemed she had assumed a dominant role in our relationship because she was less concerned about the health of it. Our relationship didn't seem that important to her. This, of course, made it easy for her to say all the things she'd been saying. Without hesitation, she agreed. Unfortunately, my boldness ended with her answer. I failed to ask her why she didn't care. Did she feel this way because she simply didn't love me anymore, or did she need someone to dominate to release the tension and frustration of being so thoroughly dominated by Uncle Robert? I didn't know then and I don't know now. Perhaps it was a bit of both.

It turns out that we hardly talked about the book *A God Who Hates* at the conference. But I do remember a call with Uncle Robert sometime during that year where he relayed a story to me that was similar in nature. It was about a sinister Muslim man he knew who lived in the Middle East. The man was married, but remarkably cruel to his wife. For years, she put up with his barbaric treatment, and, at one point, he banished her to sleep outside on the hard ground. Not content with this humiliation, the husband added further insult to injury by pelting her with small pebbles. Then, like a plump Superman, Uncle Robert entered this dark narrative, swooping in to save the day. Miraculously, he was able to persuade the man to see his wickedness, at which time, the man apologized to his angelic and long-suffering wife. Uncle Robert said, in his mind, that story was an apt description of my marriage with Paige, that she had suffered at my hands just like the poor Muslim woman sleeping outside. So desperate was I for a happy marriage with Paige, I didn't even utter a single word of objection.

OF THE MANY topics discussed by Uncle Robert at the Conference of 2016, only one stood out. A little context is in order. In the summer of 2016, the dominant focus in America was the presidential race between Donald Trump and Hillary Clinton. Uncle Robert was a huge fan of Trump, mostly because he despised Clinton. According to Uncle Robert, a Clinton presidency would almost certainly spell the end of the American Republic and ignite World War III. If she became president, we would almost certainly need that house built into the mountainside.

With all of my young children in the room listening, Uncle Robert emphasized to us the significance and depth of Clinton's wickedness as only Uncle Robert could. His metaphor of choice was the hyena. The spotted hyena, also known as the laughing hyena, lives in Africa in packs or clans where the female is dominant over the male. One possible reason for this could be the presence in the female of a pseudo-penis, or, at least, in Uncle Robert's mind, it was a possibility. The pseudo-penis of the female hyena looks a lot like the penis of the male hyena, sometimes even bigger. In the world of the hyena, the females walk around with bigger penises than the guys, and the poor, timid male hyenas lick the genital area of the females as a sign of submission. And, of course, the biggest and baddest female hyena of them all was none other than Hillary Clinton. Uncle Robert assured us that with her fake penis hanging out for all to see, a President Clinton would strut around the world stage forcing subservient male leaders in other countries to figuratively lick her groin.

Two of my children were under the age of ten at the time of this conference. Thankfully, they don't remember much of that sick and perverted monologue from Uncle Robert. This was perhaps the quintessential example of Uncle Robert getting away with something that, had another adult male attempted to do, both Paige and I would have intervened immediately. I shake my head when I think back to this moment and wonder why I didn't tell him to stop or at the very least pull my children out of the room. Paige had no problem standing up for our children when another male leader did or said something inappropriate—recall her storming out the church service in Ashton, Idaho when the young pastor brought up the choking game. But, when it came to Uncle Robert, his word and judgment were unassailable. And that included the topic of sex. In addition to hyena penises and pseudo-penises, Uncle Robert spent a good deal of time on the sex between Adam and Eve and the consequences for the human race. In other one-on-one conversations over the years, he enlightened Paige on his endurance in bed, what physical acts between couples were okay and what was off limits, and other elements of sex that you would think a married woman should be discussing with another woman, not another man who wasn't her husband. But the privacy that I assume other married couples have was something we never enjoyed. When it came to Uncle Robert, Paige told him everything. And when it comes to the inappropriateness of this issue, I place the blame squarely on the shoulders of Robert Booty. He was the one who cultivated this very one-sided relationship with Paige from the moment she was born. She didn't always know what she was doing, but *he* did.

PAIGE, HER PARENTS, and Uncle Robert took several trips to the "office" during that conference. I even tagged along for one of them. Casinos have never been my thing, but it was interesting observing them in that environment. They were all having fun but, at the same time, taking it very seriously. This was work, serious stuff with serious money to be made. I thought it was seriously nuts, but I kept that thought to myself. At one point in the evening, Paige ran out of gambling money, something I suspect happened just about every night at the "office." Uncle Robert came to her rescue and handed her a crisp $20 bill to go blow … I mean waste … I mean gamble ... oh, whatever.

The look on her face when he handed her the money was one of pure joy, thankfulness, and surprise. I couldn't remember the last time she looked at me like that, and I was jealous. Extremely jealous. The smallest gestures and words from Uncle Robert produced such profound joy and awe in Paige and her parents. I just didn't understand it.

A little later, once she had spent the $20 given to her by Uncle Robert, I peeled off a $20 bill, handed it to her, and asked that she give me the same look she gave Uncle Robert. At first, she looked at me confused then attempted to duplicate the face she displayed to Uncle Robert ... but it wasn't the same. It was forced, and we both knew it. She asked that I not do that again. Let the joy and thankfulness come naturally, she said. She was right, but, lately joy, and thankfulness seldom crossed her face when looking at me.

ON THE LAST night of the conference, Paige asked me to have a talk with Uncle Robert and her parents. We put the children to bed and the five of us met at the dining room table. Jack and Cathy sat next to each other at the head of the table, while Paige and Uncle Robert occupied one side of the table. I sat opposite them. The roles were so obvious, I was surprised we didn't all dress the part: Paige was the prosecutor, Uncle Robert the judge, Jack and Cathy the jury, and I was the defendant. The first order of business was Paige's concern that I had stated, thanks in large part to my January phone call with Uncle Robert, that I would change my testimony from the previous June. In essence, she still didn't think I was saved. After receiving a sufficient tongue lashing from Uncle Robert on that subject, he looked at Paige and asked her if she wanted to address another subject, the one she frequently complained to him about. Reluctantly she said yes. That topic was our physical intimacy. All that needs to be shared here is that she didn't really love me at that point, so intimacy with me wasn't something she enjoyed. The discussion was frank and open. To say I was mortified to have this discussion in front of Uncle Robert and Paige's parents is a gross understatement. I was utterly and completely humiliated, and when the meeting ended, I felt as worthless as a dish rag. As we all stood to leave and go to bed, Paige smiled and gave Uncle Robert a big hug.

With these last two conferences (2015 and 2016) the Klassen home in Hayden started to feel like the scene of a crime, with my mind and soul outlined in chalk on the living room carpet. As the summer of 2016 wore on, things got much worse.

CHAPTER 20
THE BUTTE AMBUSH

THE HUMILIATING MEETING at the conference in June did nothing to help my relationship with Paige. A few weeks after the conference, I disregarded one of Uncle Robert's suggestions for our relationship, which somehow graduated to a command in Paige's mind, and she became irate. She said I was the least trustworthy person on earth and that if before we were married, she knew ten percent of what she knew about me now, she never would have married me. Not long after that, she warned me to stop trying to put a wedge between her and Uncle Robert. At the time, I actually felt a small pang of guilt and apologized. Now, I marvel at her brazenness and complete lack of awareness. Did she not realize she was a Christian woman warning her Christian husband to stop trying to put a wedge between her and another man? Did she not realize Uncle Robert was creating a wedge between a husband and his wife? Did this not set off *any* alarm bells in her mind? And why did I not make the wedge as wide as the Grand Canyon by confronting Uncle Robert and telling him to butt out of my marriage? I didn't because the mind control that Uncle Robert exercised over Paige was having an effect on me. Tragic as it was, at that moment, I saw Uncle Robert not as the cause of my troubles but the answer to them.

191

The verbal attacks continued. As a real estate broker I was busy trying to make a living, and summer was usually my busiest time. I was gone from home a lot and not around our children very much. One night, after a long day away from home, I walked into our bedroom and told Paige I missed spending time with the kids. She calmly told me she was glad I was gone so much and not spending time with the children because when I did, they were negatively affected by me and would start acting fake. Something inside of me snapped at the sanctimoniousness of her words. I shouted at her, "They're my children too!" and stormed out of the room. It was the first time I had ever raised my voice at her in anger. I had never been more upset with her than in that moment. I don't remember discussing the incident after that, but I would imagine at some point I apologized for raising my voice at her. A day later, it was Paige's turn to get angry.

Thomas went out with his friends to watch a movie, and when he came back home, he shared his misgivings about the movie they saw. He didn't think it was appropriate and regretted seeing it. He sent a text to his friends sharing his views. It was very tactfully and well-written and I told him I was proud of the way he dealt with the situation. I doubt many eighteen-year-olds would have had the maturity to handle it that well. Paige also read the text and thought it could have been written better. As soon as she shared her critique, I could see Thomas's shoulders sag, the confidence in his eyes dim, the wind stolen from his sails. Pretty soon, Paige and I were standing behind him, looking over his shoulders at his cell phone, reading the text again. I said I thought it was great and congratulated Thomas for taking a stand. A moment later, Paige asked to talk with me in private. We retreated to our bedroom and the moment the door closed behind her, she coolly told me she was on to me. She thought I cut her off and made her look bad and that I did it on purpose as part of a broader plot to turn the children against her and make them love me more. She then threatened me: if I ever did something like that again, she would gather all the children together and "expose" me and my agenda to the children and make the truth known. I was speechless. The notion that I was trying to turn the children against her so they would love me more was so outlandish and absurd, I didn't know how to respond. I'm sure I came up with some kind of tepid protest, but don't recall it because it didn't matter. If Paige truly thought that I was trying to turn the children against her, based on my support of a text Thomas wrote, then it wouldn't matter what I said to deny it.

I felt very alone, cut off from the outside world, held in suspicion by the mistrustful little world I had trapped myself in. I couldn't talk openly and honestly about our relationship with Paige because she was convinced I was the problem. If I dared point the finger at Uncle Robert, things would have gotten much worse between Paige and me. I couldn't talk about what was going on between Paige and me with our children because they were too young to understand, and, more importantly, it also would have been inappropriate to do so. Nor did I share any of this with my friends or relatives. No one outside of our little group of Uncle Robert followers had any idea what was going on. None of our friends in Montana or my family knew about the "office" or America's Sovereign National Credit or hyena penises or any of the other bizarre thoughts and ideas that came out of the mouth of Uncle Robert. If I started sharing with an outsider the challenges Paige and I were facing in our marriage, I would inevitably have to open the floodgates to all this craziness. And that wasn't allowed. To our little group, it wasn't that Uncle Robert was, in reality, just plain kooky; rather it was that the rest of the world wasn't ready to hear and understand his brilliance. Until they were, we had to protect him. We had to protect the leader of our little church at all costs. And it was clear that Paige started to see me as a threat, a cancerous tumor that needed to be irradiated before it spread.

IN EARLY AUGUST, Paige asked that I reserve a certain upcoming day so she and I could drive to Butte to rendezvous with Uncle Robert and her parents for a short meeting. She didn't say what the meeting was about, but I had a gut feeling they were planning something for me, and I had an inkling it might look a lot like the meeting at the June conference in Hayden. When the day came, Paige and I drove to Butte and met her parents, had lunch with them, then drove across town to a dumpy motel near the highway where we met Uncle Robert and his ubiquitous sidekick, Michael Erving. We helped carry Uncle Robert's and Michael's bags into their dark and dingy motel room then crammed ourselves in as well. It was a beautiful sunny afternoon outside, but the room felt like an oppressive and depressing grotto. I sat on the edge of one bed with Paige close by while her parents sat on the other bed. Uncle Robert sat in a chair facing all of us, presiding over the gathering as always, with Michael plopped on the floor like an obedient dog at his master's feet. There wasn't much chitchat; there never was with Uncle Robert in the room. He dove right into the agenda for the gathering by asking Paige if she thought I was a Christian. As I turned and looked over my shoulder, her icy blue eyes met mine with a deadly seriousness that was underscored by her firm, "No." No one else said anything, but it was clear to me that everyone in the room agreed with her. Any hope I had left that this might be a fairly short and painless meeting went out the window. I had been ambushed.

The roles were a little bit different now than at the June meeting. Paige's parents, along with Michael, were still the jury, but Paige was now the star witness, and Uncle Robert was both the prosecutor and the judge. I, of course, was the treasonous defendant about to be drawn and quartered. Point by point, sin by sin, Uncle Robert asked me questions about my past and made statements to dismantle me, humiliate me, and present to all gathered a worthless, sinful, scumbag of a human being. Me. I was in tears as I sat on the bed listening to him rip me apart. At one point, he asked me how many women I had been physically involved with before I met Paige. I was ashamed to admit it was more than a handful. But I had confessed all of that to the Lord and to Paige before I married her. I had asked for and received forgiveness from both. Who was Uncle Robert to bring up these sins twenty years later? I had been totally and completely faithful to Paige our entire marriage (which wasn't something Paige's father and older brother, two men she adored and respected far more than I, could claim in their respective marriages). Uncle Robert then arrogantly claimed it was as if I had already left the marriage. In essence, I had, by my actions and thoughts, left Paige years ago.

When he said that, I thought it was absurd and insulting but didn't dare say anything. However, to Paige and the rest there, *nothing* Uncle Robert said was absurd. In all of their minds, he had just brought before our church a legitimate accusation, and I didn't refute it. He then dramatically waved his fat little hand toward the door and asked if I wanted to leave. And if I did want to leave, since I had in my heart and mind already left Paige years ago, then I was free to go and might as well go right now. You could hear the proverbial pin drop. Again, it was such an absurd and asinine question, that it took me a second to realize Uncle Robert (and everyone else) was waiting for me to respond. I said no, I didn't want to leave.

But Uncle Robert wasn't done, not by a long shot. As if to punctuate the lunacy of me leaving Paige, he said he would walk a thousand miles on his hands and knees to be with Paige. That's quite a remarkable statement coming from someone who was our Christian marriage counselor. The fact that this statement, coming from a bald, corpulent septuagenarian, didn't seem creepy was a testament to the incredible mind control he had over me. Not only that, I was completely missing the forest for the trees: Uncle Robert claimed to be our pastor and marriage counselor; he determined when we were saved; he dispensed advice on everything from intimacy within our marriage to how to discipline our children; we tithed to him exclusively; we looked to him for guidance on every important topic; and his word was unassailable. Yet here he was, in one breath, asking if I wanted to leave Paige, then seconds later bragging he would walk on his hands and knees to be with her. That was a despicable forest.

As he went on, I knew the only resolution to this meeting was me surrendering again, and being saved *again*. After being sufficiently demolished, the church that was gathered in that drab and somber room must have felt I was now ready to finally do it right. After faking it as a teenager, faking it a year ago—faking it my whole life— the assembled little church of Uncle Robert deemed me worthy to be saved by Jesus Christ. So, Uncle Robert prayed, then I prayed, and that was that. There were no celebratory hugs this time around. It was much more subdued, as if everyone there was annoyed at having to go through this a second time and, perhaps, a little miffed that I had pulled a fast one on them at last year's conference. We hung around for another hour then Paige and I left. I was silent in the car almost the entire way home.

If this story of the Butte ambush sounds sick to you, it's because it is. Everyone in that room was sick in their mind, including me. If I had been thinking clearly and not allowed myself to be brainwashed by a narcissistic little man, Paige and I would never have been in

196

that motel room. I would have done a better job of protecting Paige and our children and waved Uncle Robert and all his cultish desires right out of our lives. I should have done that at the beginning of our marriage, but I didn't. It was the summer of 2016, nearly twenty years after first meeting Paige. Twenty years of hearing how incredible, brilliant, loving and wise Uncle Robert was. Twenty years with Paige, the love of my life, who was now clearly pulling away from me because I wasn't adhering to her standard for me, the Uncle Robert standard. My wife and children didn't question Uncle Robert. My in-laws didn't question Uncle Robert. I was the only one who did question him in our little cult. By doing so, I was turning up the heat. Not on him, but on me. I was the frog in the pot of hot water … and the water was starting to boil.

STRANGELY, I ENJOYED incredible peace of mind for a few weeks after that event. I wasn't struggling with doubt, and I wasn't questioning my faith. For a short while, Paige actually believed me. I know because of what she said to me after I found the body of one of my real estate clients in his garden shed. This client, RJ, had been suffering with chronic physical pain for years and simply had had enough. He hadn't been seen for a few days and was usually meticulous about walking his dog at the same time every morning and afternoon. Since I had his house listed for sale, I had a key to get in. I went by the house and couldn't find him. Seeing me on the front porch the neighbor called my cell and asked if he could come over so we could both check on RJ. He did, and when we went inside, RJ's beloved dog was there but there was no sign of RJ. Then we found his note. Then I remembered the backyard shed. And that's where we found him.

When I told Paige, she pondered the news for a brief moment, brow deeply furrowed, then said, "First you committed suicide, then RJ did."

If you read that last sentence more than once and are still a bit confused, let me explain.

One of Uncle Robert's sayings was that if someone were so despondent that they wanted to give up and end their life, rather than literally killing themselves by suicide, they should figuratively do it on the cross. In other words, they could give up their current life and get a brand new one without physically killing themselves. They just had to give their life over to the Lord who was crucified for us so that we might live. Paul talks about it in Romans: *"For we know that our old self was crucified with him so that the body ruled by sin might be done away with, that we should no longer be slaves to sin."* *Romans 6:6*

When the Lord saves us, our old self is crucified or done away with, and we become new creations. Again, Paul writes: *"Therefore, if anyone is in Christ, the new creation has come: the old has gone, the new is here!" 2 Corinthians 5:17*

This is perhaps the classic example of Uncle Robert taking a biblical truth and putting his own dark and odd spin on it. Even more, it is another example of Paige parroting his words with very little, if any, filter, context or love. When she compared what happened to me in the Butte hotel room with RJ taking his life in his garden shed, I turned sharply to look at her, figuring she was making a tactless joke. She wasn't. She was serious. How could she compare me, with my back against the wall, being bullied mercilessly, and yet still choosing life and love, with RJ and the unthinkably scary places his mind took him to the night he ended his life? I couldn't imagine going back to February 1997 when Paige first told me she'd surrendered her life to the Lord with Uncle Robert and comparing it with that of a recent suicide.

That Paige compared what happened to me in Butte with RJ's tragic suicide was indeed tactless, but it also showed she believed I had indeed finally been saved. That belief turned out to be short-lived.

IN EARLY SEPTEMBER, we decided at the last minute, that, rather than the two of us going to the upcoming doTERRA convention in Salt Lake City, Utah, I should stay behind with the children. Paige had been excited about going ever since she returned home from the convention the year before. She had purchased tickets for both of us months ago, but without a good babysitter lined up, we both thought it best I stay home. Rather than just throw the ticket out, she offered it to Uncle Robert, and of course, he immediately agreed to join her. Before she left, she sent me a kind email thanking me for taking care of the children and allowing her to "*fulfill this part of my destiny.*"

With Uncle Robert going, it was no longer just a trip where Paige could learn how to grow her essential oils business. Now, it was more. With him around, it was always something more. The two of them decided they would try and get an audience with the president of doTERRA, David Stirling, right before the convention officially kicked off. I would imagine that a day before the start of an annual convention, the president of a fast-growing multi-level marketing company like doTERRA would be slightly busy. Determined to do her part and secure an influential audience for Uncle Robert, Paige sent President Stirling an email, portions of which are below:

> *Dear President Stirling,*
>
> *I am contacting you on a very important matter that is close to my heart when it comes to the impact we each can have with our time, attention and resources. I*

have shaken your hand, given you a hug and looked into
your heart and I see a man of vision, purpose, integrity
and honor. I am convinced that you are the man that
would want to hear what I have to say on behalf of our
nation and our world. Would you be willing to set aside
15 minutes somewhere in your busy schedule to give me
an audience? I would come with my trusted friend and
Father in the Lord whom I have known all my life so
he can help me articulate what is on my heart to share.

Surprisingly, President Stirling agreed to meet. I heard about the meeting when Paige returned home. She spoke of it with reverential seriousness but didn't share a lot of details of what was said, other than Uncle Robert was brilliant in presenting his message, and President Stirling seemed receptive. Receptive to what, I can only imagine. Casinos are churches? Watch out for female hyenas? I later learned that one of the most ubiquitous traits of a cult leader is a grandiose sense of self and mission. Having shared his pearls of wisdom with yet another influential person, Uncle Robert could certainly check the box marked "grandiose sense of self." But when Paige returned home from Salt Lake City, I wasn't thinking about cults nor, at that time, did I see Uncle Robert as a cult leader. I was, however, well aware of the pattern that had emerged over the past few years: whenever Paige spent significant time with Uncle Robert, she returned home cold, angry, and judgmental toward me. So I braced for the storm.

A few days later, the storm hit, and I discovered what Paige was angry about this time. She and Uncle Robert stayed in the same hotel room while in Salt Lake City, the one she and I were supposed to share. I had an idea she was going to do this before she left and never said a word, nor did I say anything about it when she returned.

I never once thought anything sexual happened between her and Uncle Robert. That's still true today. But that wasn't good enough for Paige.

She angrily accused me of harboring sinful thoughts about her and Uncle Robert. She was convinced I thought something happened between the two of them. I vigorously denied it, but Paige was beyond being swayed at this point. There was simply nothing I could do or say to pacify her. The irony here is palpable. Here was a man who professed to be more spiritual and enlightened than the rest of the world, a man who was quick to condemn and judge others, sharing a hotel room with a gorgeous married woman half his age while his wife was back home in California. And here I was, staying at home with our five children, never once even entertaining thoughts of having an affair with another woman during my entire marriage, yet I was the one accused of doing evil. Even if nothing inappropriate happened between Paige and Uncle Robert what kind of message did their sharing a hotel room convey to others? *"Abstain from the appearance of evil..." 1 Thessalonians 5:22*

I don't know what Uncle Robert said to her, but something changed in Paige when she came back from the doTERRA conference. As painful as it was, I was used to the anger and accusations she would heap on me after spending time with Uncle Robert. But this was different. She was cold and cruel in a way I'd never seen before. When she ripped me for thinking bad thoughts about her and Uncle Robert sharing a hotel room in Salt Lake City, she was just getting warmed up. Her assumption that I had harbored ill thoughts about her and Uncle Robert was proof I was still not saved. Despite what I went through at the conference in June 2015 and the recent Butte ambush in August, she was convinced I had still not fully surrendered, not recognized my total depravity, not completed any number of other Uncle Robert phrases necessary for salvation. In the Bible, Christ says repent and believe the Gospel. But that was never good enough for me. The bar for my salvation was continually being raised, and no matter what I said or did, it simply wasn't enough for Paige to be convinced. Not only did Paige not see any fruit of the spirit in my life or evidence of a true change in heart, she said ever since Butte, I had acted like a zombie, like someone on drugs. We sat in my office at home as she furiously heaped extra portions of her condemnation on me. Weak, confused, and beaten down, I cried like a child being scolded by an angry mother.

By the last day of September 2016, I was ready for some good news. I kept waiting for this terrible year to turn around. I kept hoping, every day, for something good to happen, something that would stop the downhill slide in our marriage and turn back the clock to the days of Inkom, the days of love, joy, and happiness. Days when I was sure I loved the Lord and He loved me. Days when I felt loved by my wife. I planned to go deer hunting the next morning. I loved hunting. I loved getting up early and sitting quietly in my tree stand, watching the sun rise over the Bridger mountains, watching the wildlife: the deer, fox, and eagle. And I loved the thrill of seeing a buck wander toward me. It was a great hunting spot with lots of deer coming in and out of the area, but I still never knew what was going to come my way.

And sometimes, it is a good thing we don't know what's coming.

CHAPTER 21
THE RECONCILIATION PERIOD

I WENT OUT hunting the chilly morning of October 1, 2016 at my usual spot, in a tree stand anchored to a sturdy cottonwood a hundred yards west of the Gallatin River. I saw a number of whitetail does ready for the taking, but something inside of me told me not to shoot a doe. It was as if they somehow represented Paige and I had already hurt her enough. I felt I should leave them alone and shoot a buck, for the buck represented the old Peter who still needed to die. But no good bucks came my way, and I ended up not taking a shot that morning. As I left the woods I realized the old Peter was already dead. He no longer needed to be killed, since he'd been crucified on the cross with Christ and risen with him as well. This type of absurd overthinking and overanalyzing every event in my life, from the trivial to the impactful, was becoming more common. Paige and Uncle Robert had been in the habit of doing it to me for so long that I started doing it to myself. It seemed their goal was to unearth every single thought or deed in my life that, once exposed, would humiliate and rebuke me, once again casting doubt on my salvation. Since I was desperate for their approval, I started to tell them about every thought that was less than pure, thinking my brutal honesty would help matters. It didn't.

When I got home, I asked Paige if we could go on a walk together. Even though our walks were no longer relaxing for me, I wanted to tell her about my hunting experience. It was mid-morning by this time, the sun was out, and the day had warmed considerably, perfect for a stroll along the country road we lived on. We were quiet for a few minutes, each of us absorbed in our own inner monologues, then I told her about my thoughts in the tree stand. She asked a question or two then chastised me for my wrong interpretation on the significance of the deer. She switched gears and said she had something she wanted to share. She told me she wanted us to have a reconciliation period and during this time we would act as if we were two unmarried people. We would have no intimacy, sleep in separate bedrooms, and make the children aware of what we were doing. If during this reconciliation period things improved between us, then we could stay married. If not, we would go our separate ways and live apart from each other. She said her body and mind were wearing out from having to fight my ego and old self all these years. She felt she was physically deteriorating from the effort and the Lord told her she needed to do something about it. She also brought up the analogy used at the 2016 Conference, the one about being on the hook or in the boat, but seemed to modify its meaning with a new wrinkle. She said I was a fish that had been on the hook all these years, struggling and fighting with her as *she* held the line rather than the Lord.

She didn't shout, nor did she show much emotion; rather, her words were delivered with dispassionate detachment. But I became emotional. Devastated, shocked, and terrified, I could barely stand. I couldn't imagine life without Paige because I never thought I'd have to. Would I be able to survive without her? As soon as we got done with our walk, I called Uncle Robert. By this time, I too was calling him regularly for advice and encouragement. Paige had been having lengthy calls with him nearly every day for years. Uncle Robert was probably spending hours a day counseling all of us if you coupled our calls with the calls he received from Jack and Jeff. It didn't occur to me then to ask why all of us seeking counseling from him were living such messed up lives. The times in my life when I was the most anxious, confused, scared, hurt, or vulnerable were also the times I was in regular communication with Uncle Robert. This wasn't a coincidence. But on that day, October 1st, I needed help, and, sadly, I thought he was the only person I could turn to. Surprisingly, Uncle Robert said we should stay in the same bedroom while we worked it out and not tell the children or anyone else. Paige obeyed Uncle Robert's suggestions, which I'm sure, to her, were more like commands. So, we stayed in the same bedroom and didn't tell anyone, not even our children, what was going on.

Looking back on this day, the question that's so perplexing is why I didn't seek help from anyone else. Why did I think Uncle Robert was the only person I could talk to? And would things have turned out differently if I had let someone else know about our troubles? Answers are hard to come by, but I'm confident that had I reached out to somebody else and sought their help, it would have been seen by Paige and Uncle Robert as an extreme act of betrayal, defiance, and wickedness. Seeking direction from someone else automatically meant I was rejecting Uncle Robert's advice, and that was one of the worst sins I could commit. From their standpoint, bringing another voice, another viewpoint, into our marriage would have been akin to inviting a rattlesnake to live in our house. By this time, all outside voices weren't welcome. I'm sure Paige felt completely comfortable with Uncle Robert being the only voice of wisdom and reason in her life. He was safe and secure; his words formed the cocoon within which she lived. But I felt isolated, cut off from the rest of the world.

Whenever someone said, "How's it going?" or "How are you?," I could never answer truthfully. I prevaricated, always hiding the pain and suffering I was going through. And this isolation, this cutting off from the outside world, is another common trait of cults.

The other question that begs an answer is, what did we do about reconciling our marriage? The short answer is nothing. Paige and I never sat down and discussed reconciling. I never asked her what she needed or wanted in order to reconcile our marriage, nor did she ever explain to me anything specific that she needed in order for us to stay together. While we both talked with Uncle Robert on the phone for hours on end, I don't ever recall him discussing specific points or issues in our marriage that needed to be addressed. Rather, the same tired complaints about me and my faith, or lack thereof, kept coming up. We stayed in the same bedroom but didn't talk much and hardly ever hugged or expressed affection for each other. She continued to be harsh and judgmental toward me, and I became even more timid and insecure around her. It felt like they were ganging up on me, like our marriage counselor and my wife were on one team, and I was on the other. I was the enemy, and I was losing badly. The words being used by Paige and Uncle Robert served to widen the gap between them and me. Uncle Robert said Paige was an angel that was sent here to help save me and serve me, but I had rejected her all these years. How he thought I had rejected her he never fully explained. Paige talked often about fulfilling the destiny the Lord had for each of us. Given the tenuous nature of our marriage and her lack of desire at reconciling, did she really think the Lord's destiny for her was to divorce her husband? And then there were the words I never heard. There were days when Paige would talk with Uncle Robert for hours. While Uncle Robert or I would almost always share with Paige much of what we discussed, she shared with me very little of her conversations with Uncle Robert. And under no circumstance was I ever allowed to ask what they talked about. What they discussed was private and none of my business, and if Paige thought I needed to hear anything from their conversation, she'd tell me. What kind of "marriage counselor" would cultivate such a poisonous atmosphere of secrecy in a marriage he was trying to help save?

DURING OUR RECONCILIATION period, which lasted the rest of the year, Paige took several trips to Northern Idaho and Southern California, ostensibly to build her doTERRA business. I would imagine she also wanted to get away from me and be with those she really trusted, Uncle Robert and her parents. Whenever she left, I wrote her a note to take with her, which were becoming increasingly submissive and sycophantic. It seemed every sentence was bloated with hosannas for her and Uncle Robert. Rather than enjoying these letters, Paige was tired of them. One night, the two of us sat down with Naomi to talk over a disciplinary issue she was having. Paige did nearly all the talking as I sat and watched and admired. Afterwards, I wrote Paige another note.

> *Paige, It was wonderful to see you love Naomi and help her see the truth. She is so blessed to have you as her mother. Thank you for loving her, loving all the children, and loving me. I hope you had a fantastic meeting tonight! You are a hard worker and great at what you do. Love, Peter*

At the bottom of the page, she wrote the following and gave the letter back to me: *"Peter, I asked you to please speak directly in person when you have something to say. I am giving you your note back. I do not want your disrespectful praise."*

That sums up the progress we made at reconciling.

207

DURING THIS TIME, I read *The Untethered Soul* by Michael Singer. Just like *A God Who Hates*, this book was suggested by Uncle Robert, which meant Paige read it too. Over the years, Uncle Robert had us read other similar self-help books by authors like Wayne Dyer and Eckhart Tolle. I enjoyed Singer's other book, *The Surrender Experiment*, but found *The Untethered Soul* deeply disturbing. One day, I read an especially difficult section that seemed to indicate I had to let Paige and my family go in order to grow emotionally and spiritually. But I didn't want to do that. I was Paige's husband and the father of our children. I made a vow to Paige to love her and be her husband all the days of my life. And no matter what, I would always be the father of my children. If letting them go meant no longer serving in the role of husband and father, then I wanted absolutely nothing to do with it. Perhaps I was confusing letting go with giving the ones I loved freedom and space. It is also possible in my weakened and manipulated state of mind that I was very needy, and letting go felt like more isolation, more rejection, and more suffering.

Paige walked in the room and saw me sitting up in bed, crying my eyes out. I shared with her my struggles with the book, and she seemed utterly disgusted with me. To her, my refusal to let go was seen as a need for total control over her and the children. She talked about another portion of the book, an analogy the author gave of a caged tiger. Without knowing it, we allow ourselves to be caged in tight confinement most of our lives, cut off from our natural and healthy environment, just like the tiger in the zoo. But when we awaken spiritually, we realize we are caged and thus can do something about it. Paige said she felt like she was the tiger, and I was the cage, causing her to suffer all these years in a confining and miserable marriage. With those words, it felt like she reached over, cut out my heart and stomped on it. This was my wife, the love of my life, telling me this after nearly twenty years of marriage. How? Why?

To be clear, there were no shouting matches between us, no cussing the other person out. Nor was there any physical abuse of any kind. I never laid a finger on Paige in anger, ever. And neither of us slept around. We were physically faithful the entire time we were together. But just as there are nonsexual ways to be intimate with someone who isn't your spouse, as Paige was with Uncle Robert, there are also ways to be cruel without shouting or swearing. And on occasion, Paige knew how to cut like a knife. One of those times came that Thanksgiving while we were at Paige's parents' home.

The kids were in bed and the adults, Paige, her parents, Jeff, and I were getting ready to watch a video in the living room. Paige was sitting in one of two reclining seats that made up a nice, comfortable leather couch. I came and sat down next to her in the adjoining seat. She immediately sat up straight and asked if one of her parents wanted to take her seat, under the pretense of giving them a more comfortable place to sit. They declined. Then she practically begged Jeff to switch with her and take her seat. He too declined. There I sat, silently and painfully witnessing this blatant and cruel display of disdain for me. It was so egregious and ugly, her parents and brother must have been embarrassed. That image of her, sitting up straight on the couch, face contorted in disgust, trying her best to embarrass and humiliate me, stood in such stark contrast with the loving and warm Paige I used to know.

Near the end of our Thanksgiving stay in Hayden, it was arranged between Thomas, Paige, and Uncle Robert that Thomas would stay at Uncle Robert's home in California at the end of our upcoming trip to see my parents. Our plan was to drive to see my parents in Central California for Christmas. On our way back home, we would swing by Uncle Robert's place and drop off Thomas, who would stay a week and then fly home to Montana. Staying at Uncle Robert's was like a spiritual retreat that Jack and Cathy did for a few weeks most summers. Jeff also traveled there often to sit at the foot of the wisest man we knew and learn from him. It was something Paige had done several times in the past few years, always without me. Thus, it was only natural for Thomas to express a desire to do so as well, and he was quickly accommodated. The only problem was I had wanted to go there myself for some time but hadn't summoned the courage to ask. I figured if I could spend a week with Uncle Robert, all my questions, doubts, misconceptions, and everything else that was holding me back from being the husband, father, and child of God I desired to be would be done away with. But unbeknownst to me, Thomas had beaten me to the punch. If I asked to go now, I knew Paige would view it as motivated by ulterior and sinister motives. Sure enough, when we arrived home from our Thanksgiving visit and I asked Paige about the possibility of getting away in December to see Uncle Robert, she became irate. She thought I wanted to make my pilgrimage to Uncle Robert's in early December simply to upstage Thomas and do it before he did. No amount of pleading would change her mind, and I never went.

In my journal on November 29, 2016, two days after telling Paige I wanted to go visit Uncle Robert at his home in California, I have this written: *"Incredibly difficult day as Paige helped me truly see how wicked I've been!"* I can't recall what it was that she showed me, but the next day's journal entry is this: *"Finally! True surrender! The Lord gave me courage to believe and trust! I needed to see I was not fully surrendering: I was holding onto Paige and the children; my idea of myself as a husband and father."*

Yes, even after the 2015 Conference in Idaho and the 2016 Butte ambush, not to mention my experience at Camp-of-the-Woods as a teenager and my baptism at age twenty-three, I really thought that I *still* needed to be saved. Or perhaps more correctly, I was *convinced* I still needed to be saved. This time, Paige and I were sitting in our home office with the voice of Uncle Robert filling the room via the speaker on my cell phone. It was a similar drill as the previous two times with Uncle Robert, but a few words were changed here and there. The impetus, however, behind this third attempt with Uncle Robert was the exact same as the previous two: Paige still didn't think I was saved. The reason why my latest attempt at being saved, the one in Butte, didn't work according to Paige was because I was bargaining with God and not truly surrendering. She claimed I wasn't willing to surrender her and our children, I only wanted to become a Christian on my terms. I was, in essence, negotiating with God: I'll believe in you only if you let me keep my wife and children. Both Paige and Uncle Robert made it clear that this latest attempt at salvation would also fail should it become clear to *them* that I had indeed only believed so I could hold onto my marriage. If you're wondering where the joy and victory was in all this, so was I.

A few days later, I drove to Northern Idaho to call a football game for ESPN3. It wasn't exactly a marquee matchup—Georgia State at the University of Idaho—but it was still ESPN, and, since I was only calling a few games a year as a side gig, I was looking forward to going. Rather than stay at a local hotel, I stayed with Paige's parents at their home in Hayden. I didn't mention anything to them about the conversation I'd just had with Paige and Uncle Robert. It was already my third time at bat with Uncle Robert and I figured I didn't need to make another elaborate announcement. I was a Christian. I was saved. So were they. I didn't feel any different, so I didn't say anything. Later on, Uncle Robert spoke with Jack and Cathy and asked them if, while I was there, I had shared with them my big news about finally becoming saved. They reported back that I had not, which, of course, was seen as a huge red flag to Uncle Robert.

It was very hard to focus on the game at the University of Idaho. When I said the game wasn't a marquee matchup, I wasn't kidding. Idaho Vandal football and the word marquee hadn't been worthy of sharing the same sentence in a very long time. Other broadcasters weren't beating down the door to do their games, but I loved calling them. I loved the drive there from my home outside of Bozeman, I liked the small town of Moscow, and I loved being able to say I called games for ESPN. By this time, I had called about a dozen games at Idaho, so I knew most of the crew pretty well. It was like a reunion; we gypsies in the sports broadcasting world would hop on planes or drive in cars, traveling all over the country, so we could see each other a few times a year and get paid doing what we loved. But this day my mind was everywhere else except inside Idaho's stadium, the half empty Kibbie Dome. I couldn't keep the thoughts of whether or not Paige was going to leave me out of my mind. To help me focus on the game and not worry about it, I wrote down on my games notes a verse in the gospel of John that was particularly helpful to me at that time: *"If you remain in me and my words remain in you, ask whatever you wish, and it will be given you." John 15:7*

I read that verse over and over, and yes, I asked in my heart for the Lord to save my marriage and keep my family intact. I called the game and was able to stay focused through much of it, but, at times, my mind sabotaged my efforts and I'd be lost for a play or two. I don't think anyone listening noticed, but it certainly wasn't my best effort.

After the game I drove through the inky black night on the remote, winding two lane highway to the dot on the map called Worley, Idaho and met Jack and Cathy at their favorite "office," better known as the Coeur d'Alene Casino. We played the slots for a bit, and I managed to walk away with around $18 more than I spent. I was so excited. When I got home to Bozeman the next day, I presented the money to Paige, as a pagan might toss gifts into the mouth of a volcano in the hopes of appeasing the gods that lived within it, and then thanked her for encouraging me to go to the casinos.

THE ENTIRE YOUNG clan, my parents, my four brothers, and their families, traveled from all over the country to be together the summer of 2016 at Camp-of-the-Woods to celebrate my mother's eightieth birthday. We all had a fantastic time being together as well as celebrating and honoring my mother. Since we had all been together so recently, not everyone made the trip to California for Christmas at my parents' beautiful home that overlooked a golf course. Still, several families were present, which made for a wonderful atmosphere. This type of gathering hadn't happened with Paige's family since prior to 2000. Since then, Rebecca, Lance, Phil, and their families had been completely shunned. The Klassen family had been replaced with the smaller and exclusive family of Uncle Robert. Despite being surrounded by my loving family, I was miserable. No one knew what was going on between Paige and me, and for much of our time in California, she was aloof, off by herself working on her doTERRA business. Since it was absent in my marriage relationship, I was more keenly aware of the tender touches, affectionate words, and loving smiles shared between my parents as well as my brothers and their wives. I wondered if Paige and I would ever again enjoy that kind of lovingkindness.

I didn't dare tell anyone in my family about our marriage troubles. If I did and Paige found out, she would have only become more irate with me and moved even closer into the arms of Uncle Robert.

And while the tension between Paige and me was probably obvious to all, nobody said anything to me, which was both a relief and a disappointment.

Ever since I was a child, our family kept up a Christmas tradition where, before opening presents, everyone shared what the Lord taught them the past year, or what they learned, or a favorite Bible verse, etc. Inexplicably, Paige came to disdain this tradition and told our children it wasn't true sharing but rather a show where all the grandchildren felt pressured to say something that would hopefully please Grammy Young. Simply put, if it wasn't an Uncle Robert tradition, then it had no merit and was worthy of derision. Before gathering with the other families for this time of sharing, we met with just our children. Paige told them they didn't have to say anything if they didn't want to. I was flabbergasted but didn't object. I think the younger children took that to mean mommy didn't want them to say anything, so they didn't. When it came time for Paige to share, she quoted the verse in the Gospel of John that says, "*The truth will set you free.*" It was an oblique reference that made it seem like she had gained tremendous insight this past year regarding her faith that had set her free. To me, it meant she finally saw the truth in me and our marriage and hoped to be free of both soon. Since no one else knew what was going on in our marriage, no one picked up on her comment. When it was my turn to share, I was an emotional wreck. I didn't want to come right out and tell everyone, *Hey, remember that letter I sent you back in 2015 about finally being saved? Well, Paige and Uncle Robert helped me see that was all a lie, but this year, I really did it right. Well, actually the second time I tried this year I finally got it right. I think...*

A few days after Christmas, we left my parents' house near the California coast and drove home. On the way, we stopped by Uncle

Robert's home in Calimesa and dropped Thomas off so he could stay a week. My mind swam in a sea of contradictions and emotions; as always nervous to be in the presence of Uncle Robert yet, simultaneously, desperate for his approval; scared of doing the littlest thing that might offend Paige yet craving a long-lost closeness with her; not knowing how to act around either one of them; terrified my world was crashing down around me. While there, I took a photo of a picture of Uncle Robert's parents. They were very old in the photo, which I presumed was taken in Syria. I kept the photo on my phone and would look at it frequently as I drove the rest of our family home to Montana. Uncle Robert was very fond of his father and spoke of him reverentially. This is what I had to say in my journal that day: *"Seeing photo of UR's parents, especially his dad, inspired me to be tougher, like him. Quit complaining, seek the Lord, serve others, be tough, not soft, be a man! Looking at his photo on my phone was/is incredibly calming."* Later, after we arrived home, I printed off the photo of Uncle Robert's father, cropping out his mother. When Paige saw that I had printed the photo of Uncle Robert's father rather than the two of them, she was upset. To her, my removal of Uncle Robert's mother from the picture was symbolic of me and my attempts to marginalize her in the minds of our children. Always cognizant of the fact we were in a reconciliation period, I immediately printed off the photo of both Uncle Robert's parents and put that on my wall by my bed.

I had a basketball game to call for ESPN3 in Boise on the 31st, the last day of what I hoped would close the book on the worst year of my life. 2017 couldn't possibly be worse than 2016, or so I thought. Because Paige had been spending so much time with her parents in Idaho and Uncle Robert in California, I hadn't seen much of her over the previous few weeks. I missed being with her despite all the acrimony. I missed the tenderness and the companionship we used to share. I missed my best friend. Right after we got back from our trip to California, Paige planned to go back up to her parents' home for about a week. Even though I was exhausted from all the driving and still had to get to Boise in just over twenty-four hours, I decided to drive with Paige and the kids to Northern Idaho to spend more time with her. Once at her parents' home in Hayden, I took a quick nap then turned right around and drove through Washington and Oregon and arrived in Boise around 2:00 a.m. on the day of the game. It was a great game to call. Boise State beat Colorado State on a banked-in three-pointer at the buzzer. The play made ESPN's top ten list that night.

When I got home to Montana, with Paige and the little children still in northern Idaho, I found our ten-year-old dog, Larry, in rough shape due to a nasty infection. I called Uncle Robert and asked him for suggestions on what I could do for Larry. Uncle Robert wasn't a veterinarian, and the entire time I knew him, never owned a dog. But facts like that never seemed to matter. He was the expert on *everything*. So, of course, before I called the vet, I called Uncle Robert. He was certain that Larry would die soon. His reasoning? Simple: Larry, being a dog, existed for one reason only and that was to procreate. Somehow Larry would know he lacked the needed vitality to sire another litter and would, thus, lose the will to live. Uncle Robert thought I should just make him comfortable for his final days and let him die because that's where he was headed.

When Uncle Robert pronounced his death sentence for Larry, I thought back to Peter Marshall, the author and speaker at the election sermon years prior. Uncle Robert predicted Marshall would die shortly, and it turned out he did die less than a year later. I was angry at Uncle Robert for what I thought was his callous attitude toward

Larry, my beloved dog. I didn't dare share this sentiment with Paige or Uncle Robert, and as it turned out, Larry didn't die. He hung on and miraculously got better thanks to antibiotics from the vet and essential oils from Paige's doTERRA collection. His namesake, Larry Bird, was one of the most clutch performers of all time, and now, with his clock winding down, my Larry was giving an incredibly gutsy performance. And even though I was suffering from a debilitating case of undue mind control under the direction of Uncle Robert, I still found incredible satisfaction in the fact that Larry was proving him wrong by not dying.

CHAPTER 22
JANUARY 14, 2017

———◦◉◦———

ON THE MORNING of January 14, 2017, I woke up planning to get dog food for Larry before heading to Great Falls for a game I had to call that night on regional TV. Before I left, I was in the kitchen standing near the sink when Paige showed me the ratios of water and doTERRA soap concentrate to make the hand soap we used in a dispenser. I listened as she explained the process but wondered why she was showing me this. She always filled up the soap dispenser when it was empty and anything to do with doTERRA products was her domain. Not thinking much of it, I left to get the dog food but needed to get some cash first. Instead of heading east into Bozeman, I headed west toward our bank. A mile later, I turned onto Churchill Road and saw Paige's parents sitting in their car off to the side of the road. I immediately pulled over, got out and walked over to their car. They stayed in their car and smiled awkwardly as I stood at the driver side window. Having no knowledge of them visiting, I told them I was surprised to see them and asked how long they were staying. They were evasive and hesitant to answer, clearly nervous at being caught waiting just down the road from our house. I left it at "See you at home," then took off, knowing something was up. I drove to the bank, and as I waited at the drive-through to get some cash, my anxiety level skyrocketed. Was Paige planning on leaving again? Were they planning another ambush like Butte? And why all the secrecy? I got the cash and skipped the dog food. I had to get home as fast as possible and find out what was going on.

When I got back home, Paige's parents were there. Jack was playing with the kids and Cathy was sitting in a chair in the living room with her winter coat still on. I wasn't there but a minute or more when Paige asked to speak to me in the office with her father present. Cathy stood up to join us, but Paige told her to wait in the living room with the kids and she sat back down. Once the three of us were there in the office with the door closed, Paige read aloud the letter she had written.

> You say, "Without you and Uncle I have nothing" don't you have everything because of us? You have everything because you have [the] Lord, and even if we were to depart you would have everything! You say what you want but do not ask me what I want, so I will tell you.

> I have put my whole being into being a good wife and mother these past 19 years. Even though five months after Thomas was born I saw that I had made a mistake in marrying you, I stuck with it because I was counseled to do so and I believed that is what I should do. I have been encouraged to stick with it these nineteen years, but I am fully awake now and I refuse to live like this any more. I can't pretend I love you and for the sake of the children, I will no longer pretend all is good in front of them. I reject your rejection of me and who you become has no bearing on my decision. Based on my experience, I do not know what you are solid on in

your life and I will not spend my life trying to make this false union a real one. We can work together to help the children and I pray that they can become true and prepared for all the Lord has for them. For David's sake in the community, please just tell people for now that I am helping my parents a lot lately. Please keep this decision from the children until they ask questions, and then we will respond with both of us present. Please keep it from your family and friends until the children have had a chance to ask questions and understand.

I was so stunned I could hardly breath or sit still. I stood up and paced, on the verge of screaming and crying. It was a nightmare as terrifying as the one I had as a child, but my mother was nowhere to be found and the one person I looked to for comfort over the past twenty years was the very person administering the terror. Paige was firm, detached, and completely devoid of compassion. The moment had the quality of something akin to a car crash, something scary that happens so fast you don't have time to think or remember much. I don't recall what I said to her, but I knew dropping to my knees and begging her to reconsider would do no good.

After the dust settled from the initial shock and I caught my breath, I sat back down and, trembling, asked Jack what he thought of all this. He said, "I think this is the luckiest day of your life." An odd response, yes, I know, but at this point in the story, did you expect anything different? The origin for that comment obviously came straight from Uncle Robert. The idea was that when we are stopped—shown our sin or disobedience by someone who loves us— we are given a chance to correct our behavior and live in accordance with the Lord's will. So, if we stopped one of our children by pointing out their disobedience and gave them a consequence to make them turn from their sinful behavior, Uncle Robert would say it was the luckiest day of that child's life. To Jack, the luckiest day of his life was when Uncle Robert stopped him from destroying himself by convincing him he wasn't a Christian. Connecting the dots, it seems Jack thought I was *still* not a Christian and in need of experiencing the luckiest day of my life. And this was it.

The letter Paige read to me was written by her, but the spirit behind it was all Uncle Robert. From the language (*"I reject your rejection of me"*) to the secrecy (I was forbidden from talking about this with anybody), it had all the hallmarks of an Uncle Robert orchestrated event.

I was too stunned and had been so completely emasculated by Paige that I didn't protest or take a stand. I meekly left to call the game. Larry was in such bad shape, I took him with me so he'd have company. I knew Paige was moving up to Hayden and would take our three youngest children with her, so I hugged them goodbye, not thinking about when I would see them next or what was happening to them. I was only thinking about me and my marriage. The children had no idea what was going on and probably figured they were headed back to Hayden for another week so their mom could help their grandparents continue to build their doTERRA business. Before I left, I hugged Paige goodbye and told her I still loved her. She stared back with cold skepticism.

WHEN I DROVE off, I immediately called Uncle Robert and told him what had just happened. He said he knew Paige planned on having an important talk with me but didn't know she planned on leaving. He seemed to be genuinely surprised and called it a tragedy. Perhaps he hadn't directly orchestrated this event after all. He then wondered aloud if he had the authority to order Paige to go back to me. As he pondered this for a few seconds, I found myself hoping he would do it. But then he said no, he couldn't. When he asked me what I had said to Paige, I told him I was in such shock I didn't say much at all. He suggested I call her back and ask her if she would be willing to meet. I took notes as I drove, determined to say exactly what he told me to.

I hung up the phone with Uncle Robert and called Paige. I asked her if we could meet. She had already left our home with her parents and our three children in tow. I was already north of Interstate 90, well on my way to Great Falls, but when she agreed to meet, I turned around on Highway 287 and drove south as fast as my old Subaru would allow me. A few minutes later, we met in the parking lot at the Wheat Montana bakery, a local landmark by Three Forks. Paige got out of her car and so did Jack. Using Uncle Robert's words, I asked her to not give up on us but rather endure and persevere. She listened, said no, hugged me goodbye, then left.

For the next three hours I was in and out of cell range but I talked with Uncle Robert nearly the entire time. He was, in my mind, literally the *only* person on earth I could talk to at that moment. As soon as I called him and told him Paige rejected my plea to persevere, his demeanor and words did a one-hundred-eighty-degree turn just like my car had done moments before. When I told him I thought it was the Lord's will for us to stay married, he dared me to show him the evidence to back that claim. When I cried into the phone, he asked why I was crying. I told him because I loved Paige and was sad. He said love and self-pity don't go together. When I asked why she would give up now after so many years together, he replied she had given up a long time ago. On and on this went as I drove the lonely miles to Great Falls. But I craved it. I needed to hear his voice. He was the only one who knew what was going on, knew of my pain.

Paige's letter had practically forbidden me from speaking to anyone about this, so I didn't even think about calling anyone other than Uncle Robert. Finally, he said that unless I saw this as a test and something I needed to experience, then I would never grow.

The basketball game in Great Falls was a blur. I couldn't eat, couldn't concentrate, could hardly speak. It was a miracle I got through the game. I didn't tell anyone what had just happened to me. The color analyst I worked the game with was calling his first TV game ever. He was awful, but I'm sure I was too. Larry stayed in the car during the game, and I checked on him at halftime. Afterwards, we drove home in the cold and dark. When I got home around midnight, I wrote a bit in my journal. *"This test is exactly what I need! I will succeed. There is now no more fear!"* That last bit about fear couldn't have been further from the truth. I spent most of the next twelve months in a constant battle with fear. Fear kept me awake at night, prevented me from eating, caused me to lose thirty pounds, had me crying at the drop of a hat, blinded me to the obvious truth of my circumstances, and made me totally defenseless against the brutal onslaught that Paige unleashed on me. But there is one sentence in my notes from that night that stands out as rather prophetic. *"I will be stronger than ever because I am weak but He is strong and He is my life!"* After I wrote those words, I went to sleep. It would be the last good night of unassisted sleep I would have for over a year.

III
THE AWAKENING 2017 AND ON

CHAPTER 23
SLEEPLESS IN BOZEMAN

THERE WAS ONE bit of good news. I no longer needed to hold my breath, anxiously waiting to see whether Paige would decide to leave me or stay in the marriage. She had made her decision; the waiting was over. There was irony in that, but what was far more ironic was the fact that I was exclusively talking with the one person (other than Paige and me) most responsible for the mess my family had now become. In my efforts to understand and accept Uncle Robert as my marriage counselor, spiritual advisor, and authority on just about every issue, I had allowed myself to become extremely isolated. Paige and I had left every church we attended, I had distanced myself from my relatives, and now that Paige had left me, the little circle of people I could trust and talk to shrunk even further. Couple that with Paige's written request that I not discuss her leaving me with my family, our children, and the local community, I was essentially left with no choice but to talk with Uncle Robert.

Over the next few days, I spent several hours each day on the phone with him. I would put on my large charcoal grey overcoat to ward off the January chill and wandered the streets around my home or office with the cell phone to my ear, dazed, scared, on the edge of panic. Even though Uncle Robert felt like my lifeline to sanity and I eagerly looked forward to calling him, the calls were hard to swallow. As usual, he didn't mince words. He said I needed to "respect her decision and move on," and that I shouldn't "blame Paige for waking up." He also warned me not to say I need to "let her go," because she didn't need my approval to go. Nor did he want me talking about her "return" because, in her eyes, she never really left. The entire nineteen years of marriage were a nightmare and thus there was nothing to leave. And when I dared mention that I didn't think it was the will of God for Paige and me to separate, he sternly warned me that saying that was in essence "condemning her," and thus I should never say that again.

As it became clear in that first week after Paige left me that I wasn't going to simply get over it and quietly move on, Uncle Robert started to express concern that my reaction was unwarranted. I wrote in my notes that *"Uncle Robert has serious pain to see me this way, going back to my vomit."* Translated, that meant my sadness and anxiety over losing my wife and family was proof I was once again allowing my mind and ego to run my life. According to Uncle Robert, if I were a true Christian, I wouldn't be reacting this way. During that week, Paige emailed me, and while she was glad I was being counseled by Uncle Robert, she requested I not bother him for a few days. She didn't say why, other than I wouldn't understand. I was in a near panic but told her I would honor her request. Now I had no one to talk to. I was completely alone.

A FEW DAYS later, unable to cope on my own and desperate to talk with someone, I called Paige and we spoke for about forty-five minutes. She was very sympathetic but also detached, like a school teacher talking to a hopelessly lost pupil. Later that same day, I called Jack, and we too talked at length. He encouraged me to not seek a way out (whatever that would look like) of my current situation but wait on the Lord and be thankful. After speaking with both Paige and Jack, they compared notes of their calls with me and shared those notes with Uncle Robert. They realized that in the morning, Paige had encouraged me to have the attitude of one who is overcoming, but that afternoon, all Jack heard from me were the same complaints and sadness. Now all three were alarmed and angry over my failure to overcome when I spoke with Jack. It's hard to imagine they literally thought I should get over losing my marriage and family in the space of a few hours, but I didn't know how else to interpret their newfound concern and frustration.

Irony creeps in again. Had I, in the space of a few hours or even days, been able to overcome the loss of my marriage and breakup of my family, that would, to me, be a sign of trouble. Had I been able to witness all this and not be sad or mourn would have shown severe callousness on my part. For some reason, my sadness and mourning was considered returning to my "vomit," but the Bible is filled with believers crying out to God in sorrow and mourning. In Romans 12:15 it says we should *"mourn with those who mourn."* Look at the many Psalms where David cried out in anguish and pain: *"Be merciful to me, O Lord, for I am in distress; my eyes grow weak with sorrow, my soul and body with grief. My life is consumed by anguish and my years by groaning; my strength fails because of my affliction, and my bones grow weak." Psalms 31:9-10.* That is but one of many examples from David, the King of Israel, when he wept because he was sad and lonely.

Psalms is also filled with numerous passages where David proclaims the Lord as his rock and redeemer. *"The Lord is my light and my salvation—whom shall I fear? The Lord is the stronghold of my life—of whom shall I be afraid?" Psalms 27:1.* And that was where the difference now lay. Paige, her parents, and Uncle Robert were all convinced I wasn't saved and the Lord wasn't my rock and redeemer, and thus not currently available to be my light and salvation. Furthermore, since I wasn't a Christian I couldn't call out to the Lord for relief from my pain and anguish like David could. And for some reason, I was utterly convinced they were right. Going back to Uncle Robert's "in the boat or on the hook" analogy of salvation, in my notes I wrote, *"If I truly was in the boat, the gigantic aircraft carrier or luxury liner, I would not feel, or act or behave this way."* It was insanity that I believed the evil nonsense Uncle Robert was telling me. And evil is the best word to describe Uncle Robert's attempts to convince me I wasn't saved because I was sad and distraught over the breakup of my marriage and family. The un-Christian response to what I was going through would have been apathy; the Christian response was to mourn the loss. It is clear to me now that had I not experienced sadness and mourning, then I would have been a lousy husband and father who demonstrated total disregard for his family.

MY CONVERSATIONS WITH Uncle Robert pivoted from discussing Paige and our failed marriage to my failure to believe and receive salvation. Using Paige's words as his prime ammunition, Uncle Robert claimed, *"Paige saw me as an imposter and lately I gave her more evidence I was an imposter. An imposter is worse than an unbeliever."* He continued, saying I was *"in divine court and have no defense. The prosecutor* [Paige] *is shredding me."* What was needed was for me to hit rock bottom, and Uncle Robert was convinced I wasn't there yet. He warned me again not to *"seek any external support. Support will only prevent me from hitting rock bottom."* Of course, external support was exactly what I needed, and probably what Jack was referring to when he warned me not to seek a way out of my current situation.

So, while I waited to hit rock bottom and didn't talk to anyone, I suffered. But this was all part of Uncle Robert's plan, for he said, *"I deserve to be happy, but to earn happiness, I need to pay the price."*

And pay the price I did. I was miserable. I couldn't sleep at night and had no appetite during the day. I lost nearly thirty pounds, and the lack of sleep made dealing with the anxiety and sadness that much harder. I would go on walks for hours, shuffling through the cold, bundled in my overcoat, headed nowhere, pulled by some unknown need to keep moving. As soon as I stopped or tried to sit down at work, I was overwhelmed by anxiety. Uncle Robert tried to convince me that when I really reached rock bottom, the Lord would reach down to save me and my misery would be replaced by complete and instantaneous joy. But what if I wasn't instantly joyful? Uncle Robert had warned me repeatedly not to tie my salvation to any miracle of Paige inviting me back into her life. So how could I be instantly joyful with my wife gone, my three youngest children gone, and no one to walk beside me as I dealt with this tragedy? Thus, my conundrum and hesitation. Do I dare *try* to be saved again only to not experience immediate and overwhelming joy? I wrote, *"Why is this so difficult for me? Why is surrendering so hard?"*

Aside from Uncle Robert, the only person I did talk to was the Lord. I prayed constantly. In one compartment of my mind, I *knew* I believed and couldn't fathom needing to do something else in order to be truly saved. But in other areas of my mind, I was so convinced of Paige and Uncle Robert's infallibility that I did believe I was missing something. I read the Psalms over and over, sometimes out loud. Most nights I would go to bed late, around ten to midnight, but only sleep for an hour or two. I would wake, and, unable to fall back asleep, suffer the night through until it was time to get ready to go to work. Our two oldest boys were still living with me at the time. Thomas was going to college at Montana State University and David was still in high school at Manhattan Christian School, so Paige chose not to disrupt their schooling by taking them with her to Idaho. I would pace the living room outside their bedroom, moonlight streaming in through the large windows that faced the Bridger mountains, quietly crying, glad they were still in the home with me. They still knew nothing of Paige's decision, but I would imagine they sensed something was amiss. While I never let them see me cry, nor did I even whisper a word of it to them, they must have noticed my odd behavior. And odd it was, especially when it came to sleeping pills.

I WAS DETERMINED to honor Paige's request and not tell anyone she had left the marriage. In my mind that also meant not even allowing suspicion of it. Thus, when it became apparent to me that I needed to either get help sleeping or I would eventually have to check myself into the hospital, I nervously dipped my toes into the water of sleeping aids. After about a week of sleeping one to two hours a night, I went to the grocery store and got some benign over-the-counter sleeping pills. That night I agonized over whether or not I should take them. What did taking sleeping pills say about me and my fortitude, my willingness to trust the Lord with my concerns? Was I going to trust pills or trust Jesus? And what if the boys found out I was taking sleeping pills? I was terrified of them finding out and then telling Paige and Uncle Robert. For over an hour, I paced my bedroom debating with my mind whether or not I should take them. I finally broke a pill in half and took it, but the over-the-counter stuff was so weak it didn't do anything. The next night I took the whole pill. Still nothing. Next night, two pills. Nothing.

Finally, in severe physical, emotional, mental, and spiritual pain,

I drove to the nearest urgent care facility in Bozeman to get help. Once there, I paced back and forth in the parking lot for about thirty minutes before I finally decided to go in. When the nurse asked why I couldn't sleep I was evasive. I was determined to conceal what was going on and only divulged I was having personal issues. I continued to do this with every sleep doctor I saw for the next five months even though none of them knew who I was. I got two weeks' worth of pills that actually helped a little. I thought that would be enough, but two weeks later, I showed up at the same urgent care building out of pills and still unable to sleep. I was scared of my own shadow and looked like a shell of a man, hollowed out, stooped over and bent by some unnamed tragedy of life. I would imagine many of the doctors and nurses knew; they didn't need me to spell it out.

By February, I was gaunt with anxiety and sleep deprivation. Like flower boxes beneath a window, dark bags of tears and sadness settled in under my eyes. I couldn't eat until the fear and anxiety slowly released its death grip which, thankfully, happened every day around mid-to-late afternoon. Living on one meal a day and one to two hours of sleep a night, my weight dropped to a sickly 173 pounds. I was in such poor physical shape that, one day, I nearly fainted on top of a coworker's desk at my real estate office.

ROUGHLY A WEEK after Paige left, I had another local basketball game to call on TV. My part-time sports broadcasting career was already on life support before Paige left, now I was ready to pull the plug. But nobody knew what was going on in my life, and it would raise a lot of eyebrows if I suddenly just quit calling these games. Producers, coaches, and athletic directors would certainly think something was up and start asking questions. And questions from the wrong people, as I'd learned from Uncle Robert, could lead to danger. Thirty minutes before tip-off in Helena at an NAIA game, I wasn't sure I would be able to do it. I was a nervous and anxious wreck. I spent as much time as possible roaming the frigid parking lot outside the gym, suffering in the cold Montana winter air. Anything to get away from all the happy, healthy people going about their joyful lives, oblivious to my pain and suffering. I got through the game and managed to do a decent job, partly because I worked with my usual color commentator and partly because it was a good game. As soon as the game ended, I said quick goodbyes to the crew, got in my car for the ride home, and let the tears start flowing. I knew I couldn't keep doing this. I wasn't good enough to fake the enthusiasm and interest. Not long after that game, I told my producer I needed to take some time off to focus on real estate and make more money. It was plausible enough, and he bought it.

In late January, Paige surprised me by asking if I could help her out and watch the children for about two weeks while she went on an important ministry trip with Uncle Robert. At first, I hesitated and told her I wasn't sure I had the strength to have all five children at home with me. What if they saw me crying or could sense my fear and anxiousness? I didn't want to burden them with that. Nor did I want to have to field tough questions such as, Why are you sad, Daddy? Why are we always in Idaho and you're here in Montana? How come we never see you and mommy together? However, I quickly rallied and accepted. A few days later, I drove to Hayden to pick up the children. Paige had already left to travel with Uncle Robert back East to Washington, DC. Donald Trump had just been sworn in as President and Paige went along to act as Uncle Robert's official assistant/secretary while he shared his ministry and mission with whomever would listen. Who they met with and what they did is a mystery to me, but it was always that way with Uncle Robert

234

and his trips to Washington, DC. As I look back over the years with more clarity, it strikes me that this trip they took together seems like a symbolic honeymoon for the two of them. Uncle Robert had accused me of "stealing" Paige from him and Paige had accused me of caging her in a miserable marriage. Then, shortly after declaring her freedom from me, Paige took a trip across the country where she could be alone for two weeks with the man she truly loved and respected, Uncle Robert.

While Uncle Robert and Paige were saving America from the Jews in our nation's capital, the children and I were in Montana trying to get through a bout of the flu. All the kids came down with it in some form or another. I was the only one who didn't and spent the entire time playing nurse. I loved every minute of it. I still couldn't sleep, couldn't eat, and had no one to talk to, but I had all the children with me, and that felt so good. Seeing them all at home with me probably led to high levels of denial as I held out hope this would be another momentary setback in our marriage and in a matter of weeks or months Paige would change her mind. At some point during their trip to DC, Paige called me to check on the children. We briefly discussed their health then I asked her to please let Uncle Robert know I wanted to talk with him. He was sitting right next to her in the car, and the moment I asked the question, she went silent. While in DC it was protocol for Uncle Robert to go radio silent and not talk on his cell phone. The powers that be were too dangerous and we couldn't let anyone know where he was located. But I hadn't talked with him for over a week and was desperate to speak with him. Was I or was I not a Christian? I had been brainwashed to believe only he knew, and whatever he said I would go along with. I knew immediately Paige was upset, and I regretted asking the question. Knowing this, I sent Paige an email later in the day.

*I apologize for asking you to let Uncle know I desire
to speak with him. I know that he is aware of my desire.
I am sorry and ask for your forgiveness. Please tell him I
am sorry and I ask for his forgiveness too.*

Then later in the same day, Paige replied:

*We are glad you are finally becoming more responsi-
ble and respectful. Uncle is never forgetful of his promise.*

Why Paige couldn't simply hand Uncle Robert her phone while
he was sitting in the car with her is beyond me. And why he couldn't
talk on the phone with a lowly real estate broker from Montana while
in Washington, DC without endangering his life is also beyond me.
However, such was his paranoia and heightened sense of importance.
So, I suffered and waited for Paige to return from DC and pick up
the kids.

I was terrified of her return. What would I say to her? How
would I act? When she did finally return one night in mid-February, she was all smiles and acted around me as if nothing was out of
the ordinary. I was as uncomfortable as a teenage boy walking into
school with a fresh cluster of pimples on his forehead. The kids were
all happy to see her and she brought them lots of trinkets from her
time in Washington. When it came time for bed, Paige slept in the
basement on a makeshift bed on the floor, which I would imagine
raised the eyebrows of my older two boys. She stayed at our Bozeman
house for a few days and left soon after Zoe's birthday. She spent an
hour with me one afternoon in my office confronting our situation,
calmly reciting reasons why our marriage wasn't worth saving; how
deplorable I was as a husband, father, and person; and that I should
simply forget about her and move on. Like a sponge in a strong hand,
her voice squeezed tear after tear out of me, only to replace them with
her enmity, words saturated with acrimony. I was a miserable wreck.

Physically uncomfortable from lack of sleep and emotionally on edge from having Paige there, I found it impossible to enjoy Zoe's special day. When Paige left, she took the three younger children with her again and headed north to Hayden. They still had no idea what was going on, and I still had no idea how I was going to finally become a Christian. That all changed very quickly.

CHAPTER 24
CONFESSION AND INDICTMENT

WITH THE TRIP to Washington, DC behind him, Uncle Robert was available to talk again, and our conversations became even more intense. Since he was convinced I had yet to hit rock bottom in my life, Uncle Robert took it upon himself to help me get there quicker. As recorded in my notes, he claimed in the past *"I tried to be saved for social appearances not personal and I failed because it wasn't of the Lord."* He went on, saying, *"I am bound and can't decide. I am double minded, unstable in all my ways. I am demon possessed and should acknowledge I am under the control of a legion of demons. Me and my demons are one and the same. I am Satan until Christ unties me* [like Lazarus and his burial garments]*."* Conversations like this took place nearly every day. They were awful, but where else could I turn for help? I had allowed myself to be completely cut off and isolated. The only voice in my head was from this little madman with a Middle Eastern accent telling me, *"Don't give up the horror of being without faith and life."* Without a sane voice of reason to communicate with and counteract his wickedness, I believed him.

Each morning brought new horror, and as I continued to voice my pain and anguish to him, Uncle Robert encouraged me to *"allow the crushing to continue."* So, I did. Then, just over a month after Paige had left, physically sick and exhausted from lack of sleep, emotionally drained from having to keep this terrible secret from my family and friends, mentally and spiritually vulnerable from Uncle Robert's intense brainwashing, I sat down at my computer and started typing. I wrote out a confession that was intended for Uncle Robert's eyes only. I wanted him to know I was sincere and honest in my desire to be saved. I figured I needed to spill my guts on everything I'd ever done in my life and get it all out in the open for Uncle Robert to see. This way, with full transparency, there would be no chance I wouldn't do it right the next time I tried to be saved by him. I was going to once and for all, settle this matter. And like a tortured prisoner of war who will eventually say anything to stop the abuse, I wrote whatever I thought would satisfy the devious mind of Uncle Robert. This is what I wrote:

> Heavenly Father, I've tried this many times, I've tried to be saved and accept you as my Lord and savior. But I never fully trusted you, nor did I truly love you. I was pretending, holding back every time. I have been exceedingly wicked and sinful my whole life. All my life I have failed because I tried to do it on my own.
>
> I confess that I never really loved you Lord Jesus. I never trusted you. I always held back. I always clung to something or someone else. I never put all my faith, love, and trust in you. I never fully surrendered. For the past twenty years, I've been needy and clung to Paige. I was never willing to surrender her, my marriage, and the children. I always put someone or something in-between me and you. I never wanted to do your will, I always wanted my will.
>
> I confess putting idols before you, Lord. I made

success at basketball and broadcasting and writing an idol. I made Paige into an idol. As a child, I made my mother into an idol.

I confess Lord to taking your name in vain by calling myself a Christian and living a life that is totally against your Word.

I confess Lord that I am a coward. My life has been dominated by fear. I have been a slave to fear all my life. I feared being alone. I feared obeying you fully. I feared trusting you with all my life. I feared losing Paige. I feared losing the children. I feared failure. I feared running out of money. I feared just about everything imaginable.

I confess Lord that I have been selfish and covetous and undisciplined and dishonorable: I never honored my parents nor any other authority in my life, including you, Lord.

I confess Lord bearing false witness against Uncle Robert, Dad & Mom Klassen, Paige, my parents and every authority figure in my life. I confess Lord to lying to make myself look good and make others look bad.

I confess Lord to stealing: stealing from you by holding back and not willingly sharing the blessings you showered on me; stealing Paige from her parents and Uncle Robert

I confess Lord that I never wanted to be disciplined. I never wanted to be stopped. I resisted correction and rebuke and resented both and would lie to avoid them. I confess to being hateful and murderous and resistant and arrogant toward Uncle Robert Booty and Jack Klassen. I confess trying to undermine them and Paige.

I confess to being a horrible husband and father. I consistently put my needs and desires ahead of theirs. I confess to sleeping with other women before I met Paige. I confess to using Paige to meet my desires. I confess failing to protect her from myself. I confess to resisting her and undermining her with the children; I confess resisting her correction and rebuke; I confess to thinking I knew better than her and Uncle Robert and Dad Klassen.

Lord Jesus I come to you now and ask for forgiveness of all my sins. I surrender all to you Lord. I need you more than anything else. I surrender my heart, my body, my mind, my soul. I surrender Paige and my marriage and all thoughts of being a good husband. I surrender the children and all thoughts of being a good father. I surrender everything Lord and stand before you with nothing between us.

Thank you, Lord Jesus for crucifying my mind, my old sinful, wicked self. Thank you Lord for washing me clean with your blood shed on the cross. Thank you Lord [for] burying me and resurrecting me with you. Thank you for giving me new life. Thank for giving me new birth. Thank you Lord for helping me receive the fullness of you. Thank you Lord for taking care of all my needs and giving me strength, courage, faith, and belief to fully surrender and fully trust in you.

I trust in you, Lord. I believe in you, Lord. Thank you for giving me the victory over fear and doubt. Thank you, Lord for giving me the victory over the devil, my old fleshly mind. Thank you for guiding me and teaching me and disciplining me and loving me each and every day as I deny myself, pick up my cross and follow you. Lord Jesus, help me to never doubt my salvation ever again. Help me to never go back to the old Peter, the old ways of doing. Help me to abide in you every moment. Thank you for making me a slave to you, Lord so I will never be a slave to sin again.

Thank you, Lord, for bringing Paige and Uncle Robert into my life. Without their radical intervention in my life I would never know you and the true Gospel; I would never know this moment; I would never know true life.

That's quite a bizarre letter, don't you think? Certainly, some of it is accurate, but much of it is utter nonsense. The words, the phrases, the overall tone demonstrate just how much Uncle Robert's brainwashing had damaged my ability to think clearly. Stealing Paige from Uncle Robert? Having murderous thoughts toward Uncle Robert? Bearing false witness against Uncle Robert? It sounds like an hysterical apology letter to a cult leader from a terrified follower, rather than a confessional to the Lord. Which is exactly what it was. Uncle Robert took the letter and promptly showed it to Paige and the others. What's fascinating is that Uncle Robert read the letter and *still* questioned my faith, as did Paige. Those last few paragraphs where I surrender everything and thank the Lord for giving me new life were meaningless to Uncle Robert and Paige. The letter was a nice start, but it wasn't enough. It was just a letter. To *really* be saved I had to go through the process of accepting Jesus as my Lord and Savior either on the phone or in person with Uncle Robert. Without that step, without *Uncle Robert's* direct intervention on my behalf, the letter was pointless. Trying to be saved without Uncle Robert was pointless.

Uncle Robert could have acknowledged that, while unhealthy, it's common for people to experience fear or doubt, and it's understandable to be sad and anxious when your wife leaves you and takes your three youngest children, too. Fear, sadness, doubt, and anxiousness are all human emotions that even the apostles experienced. Being a follower of Christ doesn't mean you'll be perfect, and experiencing these emotions isn't a sign you're demon possessed. A true Christian teacher would seek to edify and encourage with his words, not torment and destroy. But Uncle Robert wasn't a true Christian teacher and I believe his primary motive at that point in time was to provide theological cover for Paige's decision to leave me. Leaving a loving, faithful Christian husband after nineteen years of marriage is simply unbiblical and hard to justify. But leaving a non-Christian husband who lied about believing in the Lord all those years is much easier on the conscience. Uncle Robert's main focus was always Paige, and now that she had done something clearly unbiblical, it put him in a bind. He wasn't about to disagree with her decision to leave me—that thought quickly disappeared when we spoke on the phone the day Paige left—but he couldn't just ignore a clear biblical mandate. So, he had to come up with something else, something to grease the wheels of Paige's radical decision that would make it palatable for everyone's conscience. And that something else was to define me as the devil.

AFTER I SENT Uncle Robert my confessional letter, our talks continued with the understanding I was *still* not saved. The narrative he pushed (that I must not attach anything to my salvation, like reconciling with my wife) now included the caveat that I must also admit that the past was one big mistake. In other words, I must admit marrying Paige was a mistake, something he knew I wasn't about to do. And not only was it a mistake, he actually accused me of *abducting* her. In addition, a new theme emerged around this time. In order to be saved, I now had to provide the Lord with my "final word," at which time the Lord would provide me with His. I had never heard this before, and, like so many of Uncle Robert's well-worn phrases, you won't find it in the Bible either. The idea seemed to hatch from the conversation with the thief on the cross who, according to Uncle Robert, gave his "final word" to Jesus who then responded with His "final word" back. To me, it seemed the words Jesus spoke to the thief on the cross—"*Today you will be with Me in paradise*"—weren't His "final" words but rather the start of a long and beautiful conversation. Nevertheless, this was now the bar set before me. Fall short and I was still not a Christian. Not only that, Uncle Robert also told me I would *never* hear the Lord's final word unless I agreed with him and Paige that it wasn't the Lord's will for us to marry. You won't find that piece of blackmail in the Bible either.

IN EARLY MARCH, Paige returned to Bozeman with our three younger children for a visit, at which time, she informed me she had already let them know she left the marriage. I was devastated. In her letter to me on January 14th, she said we would wait until the children asked questions and then we would respond together. I didn't get angry with her, but I can't say the same about her responses to me. The cordiality that was present for the first month after she left was starting to wither under Paige's intense anger for anything and everything I did that displeased her. One day, I spent hours on the phone with Uncle Robert taking another turn at bat in my seemingly never-ending attempt at salvation. While Paige was inside with the children, I roamed our yard and driveway talking with Uncle Robert on the phone. When done, I was exhausted but hopeful I actually did it right this time (although I never heard any mysterious "final word" from the Lord). By the time I was done talking with Uncle Robert, it was nighttime, and I briefed Paige on our conversation, then said I was going to take a sleeping pill and try to get to sleep early. By this time I had confessed to her my insomnia and attempts to abate it with medicine. When she heard me mention taking a pill, her eyes narrowed and she barked, "Who did you just surrender your life to out there?" Incredulous, I mumbled some pathetic reply then slunk off to bed. Of course, the moment she questioned the successfulness of my recent attempt at salvation due to the fact that I wanted to take a sleeping pill, I started doubting it myself. This was now the fourth time I went through the motions of being saved with Uncle Robert and I was already doubting it.

Paige erupted with anger again a few days later when we happened to find ourselves in the kitchen at the same time. At the sink, I asked her, very timidly, when her father's surgery was set for. Last I had heard, Jack was scheduled to have oral surgery sometime in late March. She had discussed this with me prior to her leaving in January, so it wasn't a secret. I had just forgotten the exact date. I said I wanted to tell my parents so they could pray for him on the specific date. She lost it. "That's bullshit!" she exploded. I was stunned and terrified. What had I done? She could barely get the words out she was so angry. After gathering herself, she made it clear my parents and everyone like them were the problem with the world, and continuing to see them as people worthy of fellowship, people whose prayers actually reached God's ears, was a clear and present danger to her, her parents, Uncle Robert, and our children. She was aghast that I still didn't get it, that I still saw my parents as Christians and not the mortal threats she deemed them to be.

REMARKABLY, THE VOLCANO of Paige's ire was just getting warmed up. The really big eruptions were still to come. While the younger children were still in Bozeman on their visit in March, I took each of them aside for a short one-on-one talk. I wanted to share with them my perspective on what had happened between me and their mommy. I kept my remarks brief. I told them I was sorry this was happening, I took full responsibility for all of it and wished I could go back and do it all over again. I then said I loved them, and I still loved their mother. Each talk was a little different but that was the gist with all of them. Later, when Paige returned to Idaho with the children, she called me and asked what I said to them. When I got to the part about me telling them I still loved her, she asked why I said that. "Because it's true," I said. No, she replied, I never truly loved her, but only thought I did. Big difference. And now that I had told the children I still loved her, it was a big problem. If the children were led to believe Daddy still loved Mommy, then they would wonder why did Mommy leave? A good question that she didn't have a good answer to. She didn't erupt with anger right away on the phone, but her outrage soon boiled over in the form of an indictment.

In early April, Paige again drove down from Idaho with the three younger children. When she arrived, it was already dark out and she quickly assembled all five of our children and me in the living room. She didn't read the written Indictment below verbatim, but pretty close.

Indictment for Peter held on April 5, 2017

Before the children and Peter, I presented this case for two major lies to be exposed (the third lie to me on the 21st was missed in the meeting.)

March 5 - Peter claims he gave his final word. He spoke with Uncle and Uncle explained why he could not hear the Lord's final word: he had placed the condition of me coming back upon it. Uncle gave Peter the assignment of identifying all the attachments that he had to his final word and surrender and talk to Uncle. He found the attachment and prayed to them. Uncle told him he was praying the Lord's will be done, praying TO his dream, desire and hope.

March 7 - Peter claims he heard the Lord's final word but "forgot" about telling Uncle about it, even though Uncle labored much to bring him into the Kingdom. When I asked him on March 15 about his not telling about his receiving the final word with Uncle, he said he had given his final word without conditions and had some doubts for the first few days but then he asked the Lord, on March 7, to show him if he had really given his final word and he "had peace" about it.

March 18 - Uncle spent 4 hours talking with Peter and pointing out his self-deception and "Bound him in his sin" calling him a sorcerer and a devil as he will not accept that I say "it was not the will of God that we married" but says that he knows it "was God's will for us to marry." As if an unbeliever know [sic] that will of God more than a believer.

March 21 - I spoke with Peter about his telling the children that "he still loves me" when that is impossible when he never loved me, the real me. He also lied to them that he was a believer when Uncle had told him that to believe is to receive and his not receiving the final word meant he had placed conditions on salvation and given him an assignment he never completed.

The following is a point I missed sharing with the children present but it is significant because it shows the reaching extent of Peter's willingness and ability to lie, hatching a plot of total fabrication of a "perfect" counterfeit believer, exhausting his final demonic energy to mimic being "one."

Amendment to original indictment: Peter lied to me on 21st when he said he was a believer, and without conditions, after Uncle had "Bound him in his sin" and exposed his having the condition on salvation of me coming back.

She delivered this crazy and breathtaking rebuke while the children sat right next to me, stunned and silent. It must have been incredibly uncomfortable for them to listen to their mother eviscerate their father this way. As I sat listening, tears streaming down my face, I exchanged glances with the younger children. They were clearly confused and scared out of their wits, so much so they wouldn't even dream of ever crossing their mother. Claiming to be a Christian without the sanction or approval of Uncle Robert was about the worst crime one could commit, and Paige was eager to drive home this point not only to me but to the children as well. She was also determined to convince the children the blame for our failed marriage and family breakup lay exclusively with me and my severe deficiencies.

Shortly after she finished delivering her indictment, Paige took the three children with her and left. They had been in the house less than an hour. She didn't tell me where they were going or staying. This new trend of secrecy continued with every subsequent visit she made to Bozeman with the children over the next year. She taught the children to keep this detail of where they stayed, and all other details like it, hidden from me. Should I ask a question they thought their mom wouldn't like, they were instructed to answer, "Why do you need to know that?" or "What are you going to do with that information?" A few minutes after Paige left, Uncle Robert called, which marked only the second time he ever called me of his own volition rather than simply returning my call. I would imagine he felt compelled to call me after Paige had just called to tell him she delivered her indictment of me. He asked how I was doing and, surprisingly, given what just happened, I was okay. I simply wanted to sleep and we spoke only briefly. The next day I wrote in my journal that Paige *"handled the situation very well"* while giving her indictment of me and *"I was proud of her."* Equally head scratching is that in regard to Uncle Robert's call that night, I wrote that it *"made me feel incredibly loved by both him and Paige."*

The next day, Paige showed up at my office unannounced for a short visit as she made her way back to Idaho. I got to see the children for a few minutes before she took off. Emotionally triggered, I left the office, got in my car and started driving. My only known destination was somewhere that I could cry without being seen. As I left town, I passed the gas station where Paige was filling up the car. In that car were my youngest three children whom I loved and missed very much. As I passed, I wondered if I should stop and say hi, but knew I wouldn't be welcomed. It was a crushing realization. I pulled off onto an empty gravel road and bawled my eyes out. A few days later, Paige followed up her indictment with an email that said, among other things,

> *I have changed my plans for April and I will not be*
> *bringing the children over to stay the last two weeks. I*
> *want them to have some time to recover from the mental*
> *and emotional strain they have experienced from the*
> *uncertainty you have encouraged with the lies you have*

told, so I am limiting their interaction with you for awhile. I have decided that you may only speak with them in my presence.

FOR MUCH OF April and May of 2017, I didn't see the three younger children. I sent a few text messages and emails to them via Paige's phone, but later found out Paige didn't share them with the children. Things at home in Bozeman were increasingly tense with my two oldest boys, as they had completely sided with Paige and her viewpoint. We didn't talk much and certainly never touched on the topic of our family separation. Now instead of walking on eggshells around Paige, I was doing the same around my two teenage sons. After seeking help from a general practitioner at the hospital, I decided to try the local sleep center. I liked the doctor. He was from New Jersey and it seemed our shared upbringing provided a connection. But when he asked about my sleep habits, such as did I sleep in the same bed as my wife, I was evasive. Months after Paige left, I was still trying to make sure no one knew what was going on, still trying to obey her directives, even with a doctor I'd never met before. Insomnia is horrible and affects every part of your life. As I look back on this period in my life, I acknowledge the insomnia played a part in my erratic behavior and writings, but only a small part. What was really driving my behavior was the fact that I had been brainwashed by Uncle Robert and emotionally crushed by Paige. The insomnia only made me more susceptible to their mental and spiritual abuse.

Around this time, I finished another book that was recommended by Uncle Robert, *Change Your Brain, Change Your Life* by Dr. Daniel Amen. The author suggested that a large percentage of the population has had some kind of traumatic brain injury in their past and they didn't know it or had forgotten about it. It could be when we fell from a tree as a child, took a hard hit in football practice, or fell on a patch of ice in the driveway. These past injuries can be far more serious than we think and lead to brain issues down the road. Based on Paige and Uncle Robert's devastating assessments of me and how emotionally and mentally unstable I was, I became convinced after reading Dr. Amen's book that I had an undiagnosed brain injury that would explain my behavior. I told Uncle Robert about this and of my desire to get my brain tested, but he was largely dismissive of the idea and nothing came of it.

I was still in regular communication with Uncle Robert but rarely communicated with Paige. I took my fifth and final turn at bat with Uncle Robert in early May as he once again spent hours on the phone with me and walked me through the process of being saved. As I walked up and down the lonely dirt road next to my house listening to him on the phone, I took notes on a yellow legal pad so I could look back at what he said and dispel any doubts that might creep up. What we discussed and what he had me say wasn't much different than all the other times. These talks were becoming tedious for both of us. The irony is he could have ended them at any moment by simply believing in me and offering encouragement and support. Instead, he stoked the fires of my doubt and acted as a gate-keeper to God, one who repeatedly raised my bar of admission into the Kingdom. Of course, I too could have ended these talks at any moment by kicking this narcissistic cult leader out of my life. But I didn't see him that way ... yet.

WHILE ENGAGED IN one of these agonizing discussions, Uncle Robert pompously declared that the only reason I wrote *The Blue Team* was to fool him, Paige, and her parents into thinking I was a Christian. I knew this was preposterous but didn't say anything. It had been over a year since I published *The Blue Team*. After attending the 2016 Final Four in Houston, I continued to aggressively market the book throughout that spring and summer. Having poured years of effort into it, I was proud of the final product. I even thanked Uncle Robert, Jack Klassen, and Paige in the book for their roles in making it a success. But when Paige asked for the reconciliation period on October 1st, 2016, I dropped nearly all marketing efforts. With my marriage hanging by a thread, *The Blue Team* was no longer a priority. Once Paige left, and things went from bad to worse, I was emotionally unable to care about *The Blue Team*, much like I became unable to care about broadcasting games. Now that Uncle Robert had trashed the book and my motivation behind writing it, I started to withdraw from *The Blue Team*. No longer was I proud of it, but rather ashamed. Friends and family who read it loved it, but I wasn't interested in their opinion. I was only interested in what Paige and Uncle Robert thought, and they didn't think much of it.

COME MAY, I still hadn't told a single member of my family what was going on with my marriage. I hadn't talked to any of them on the phone lately because it was too hard to hide the truth. So, I avoided them, which was rather easy since they all lived so far away from me. But I'd had enough. I needed to be able to talk to others, and now that Paige was restricting my access to our children, I was becoming increasingly alarmed by everything. It was obvious this wasn't going to blow over in a few months and she'd come back home with a changed heart. I decided to call Rich Lom, an old friend from my days working TV in Idaho. Rich was a safe choice because he now lived in Kentucky and there was no way Paige or Uncle Robert would find out I told him. It was a beautiful sunny day when I called my buddy, Rich. I had spent so much time nervously walking off my anxiety during the past four months, that I had to continually seek out new neighborhoods to walk in so people wouldn't call the cops about this mysterious tall man in a dark overcoat stalking the neighborhood. So, as I wandered around this swanky golf course subdivision, with its pristine paved roads, beautifully manicured lawns, and million-dollar homes, I called Rich, who listened politely as I tried to explain what had happened with Paige and me, laying all the blame on myself and praising Paige and Uncle Robert for their many superior qualities.

Rich didn't agree with any of it. He was sorry for what I was going through but raked Paige and Uncle Robert over the coals for their behavior. He bluntly declared that what they were doing was awful and I shouldn't listen to a word they said. Stunned, I thanked Rich for his support and vowed to keep in touch. In my mind the problem clearly lay with me, not Paige and Uncle Robert, and I had somehow not accurately conveyed the issue to Rich. Plus, Rich didn't believe like we did, and he didn't understand the Scriptures like Uncle Robert did, so it wasn't surprising he reacted the way he did.

Undaunted, I tried again, but was determined to do a better job this time. I next called an old high school coach of mine who still lived in New Jersey, Coach Jim Stroker. He was a legendary Hall of Fame coach—tough, dedicated, driven, and energetic as the day is long. When he coached me in football in ninth and tenth grade, I was soft and weak and probably drove him crazy. I had hardly talked to him in the past twenty years, but I'd been following his motivational videos on social media for over a year. Walking through another new subdivision, I called Coach Stroker and we had a similar talk as the one I had with Rich. Coach Stroker practically shouted into the phone like he was chewing out a referee, blasting Paige and Uncle Robert for their outrageous behavior. He was extremely encouraging to me and it was great to talk with him. But I was now 0 for 2 in telling people about Paige leaving me and getting them to see the truth of the matter and the wisdom of Uncle Robert. I considered these two talks as practice rounds for when I called my family, because I wanted to make sure I got it right with them. This was probably what Uncle Robert and Jack Klassen had in mind when they warned me about seeking outside help. No one on the outside of our little cult would understand. Or more accurately, no one on the outside of our little cult would understand Uncle Robert, and they would, therefore, support me. And support for me would equate to judgment of Uncle Robert, and that was the real danger to avoid.

ON MAY 4TH, nearly four months after Paige left me and right after calling my two friends, I finally told my family that Paige had left and taken the children to Idaho. They were stunned, but immediately offered to help in whatever way they could. My first request was to ask them not to speak ill of Paige or Uncle Robert, but rather just focus on supporting me. As hard as it may have been, they all agreed. I simply wasn't ready to hear anything bad about them. I was still convinced they were right and I was wrong. But there were cracks starting to form in the mental prison Uncle Robert had consigned me to. Just as my family (my parents, brothers and their spouses) were stepping in to shower me with love and support, Paige and Uncle Robert were trashing the family that Paige and I created over our nearly twenty years together. It started over a small issue with Thomas, who was still living with me in Montana. Paige disagreed with how I handled the situation and, in an email, let me know in clear terms I had blown it. She then launched into a shocking attack on my position as father in the lives of our children.

The children need to see you, not as . . . want-to-be father. . . but as a true friend. Using biological determinism with all its miserable attachments did not get you anywhere. Friendship allows you to make choices and allows the children the freedom to also choose. Isn't choosing you as a father better than being arrested, indicted and sentenced by biology? The children want freedom from the prison house of biological determinism, especially when it has nothing else to offer.

This I *knew* was wrong. Paige's words were wicked and hypocritical. Just a few years earlier, she had been obsessed with Uncle Robert's biology, determined to provide him a male grandson to carry on his precious bloodline. And the hypocrisy went even further for Paige embraced all of Uncle Robert's most cherished beliefs, including the one that pits Jacob's biological descendants against the biological descendants of Esau. Despite knowing all this, I still wasn't ready to confront the words or the person behind them, for even though the email came from Paige, I knew it started with Uncle Robert. As it turned out, this email from Paige attacking my position as father was the opening salvo in what would soon become an all-out assault of epic proportions.

CHAPTER 25
CRUEL, CRUEL SUMMER

———◦◉◦———

THE TEACHINGS OF Uncle Robert and the environment he cultivated with my family and the Klassens had, for the most part, been kept secret from outsiders. My friends and extended family who had heard of Uncle Robert knew it sounded and seemed a bit odd, even though they didn't know much. But when I began to share emails that Paige and Uncle Robert had sent me with a select few people that revealed how unhealthy and sick this environment was, they rightfully became concerned. Even though Uncle Robert's mode of communication was often off-putting and confusing to me, I was at least used to reading and hearing it on a regular basis. With this familiarity, his more strident diatribes may have been hard for me to swallow, but weren't cause for alarm. That wasn't the case with others, and I was genuinely confused by this. They found Paige and Uncle Robert's words, as well as my tolerance of them, disconcerting at best. Twenty years earlier, just prior to meeting Uncle Robert at Jeff's wedding, I had tried to lovingly convey to Paige how odd she and her parents sounded when they talked about Uncle Robert. The obsequious, overly fawning praise seemed weird and hinted at trouble. Now, I was talking just like Paige and her parents and I can only imagine how odd I sounded to my family and friends.

257

Everyone who saw the emails had much the same reaction—a mixture of disgust, sadness, outrage, and alarm over the things Paige and Uncle Robert were doing and saying. Slowly, a few brave souls tried to help me see the obvious: what Paige was doing was egregious and there was something seriously wrong with Uncle Robert. How anyone could harbor such thoughts and not jeopardize their eternal soul was beyond my comprehension, so I was resistant. Uncle Robert was still my go-to authority on everything, his word still supreme in my mind. Despite this internal resistance, I started reconnecting with the outside world. My brother Steve came out and visited me in May, and my brother Kevin came out in July. I started talking regularly on the phone with them and other family members, and I even started seeing a counselor. However, I still hadn't divulged to anyone locally what was going on.

I hardly saw my three younger children after the indictment talk in April. It wasn't until July that I actually got to spend any time with them. Paige offered me a few dates to come up to Northern Idaho for a visit, with several conditions attached: I couldn't go to her parents' house in Hayden where she and the children were living; rather, we would meet in town somewhere; she would be present the entire time; and she and the children would only be available for a few hours each day. My brother Kevin flew into Bozeman and accompanied me on the trip to Idaho. But he was there secretly; I didn't dare tell Paige, fearing she would react negatively. So, while I went to spend time with the children, he stayed behind in the hotel room we rented.

It was a tense first day when I saw Paige and the children. We met on the beach at Coeur d'Alene Lake. As soon as I showed up, Paige arranged a little meeting on the hot sand, a few yards from the water's edge. She called the children out of the water and had the three of them sit down on beach towels facing me. Her parents, Jack and Cathy, showed up as well. They crept down the grassy embankment from their parked car and sat down behind the children without saying a word. They never made eye contact with me or even acknowledged me with a wave. With everyone facing me, Paige accused me of being selfish and inconsiderate of her for wanting to spend so much time with the children and for trying to buy the children's love. The accusation I was trying to buy the children's love, while patently absurd, arose from my suggestion I take the children to Silverwood, a nearby amusement park. The kids had wanted to go there for years but we never had the money, so we didn't go (except for one time when Jeff graciously paid for his family and ours to go). Now that I was having a relatively good year in real estate, I was able to offer this to the children, but Paige rejected it out of hand, citing my supposed ulterior motive.

When Paige was done delivering her judgments, one of the children addressed me in a rather rehearsed and robotic voice, expressing the feeling of never being loved by me and said it was hard to be around me. I cringed inside. I had never heard anything like this from any of the children before. Why now? What had changed? I didn't say much in defense. I had no desire to cause a scene or instigate an argument. I simply wanted to spend time with the children. As soon as the meeting was over, Jack and Cathy stood up and left, and the kids went back into the water. Later in the day, after our time at the beach had ended, I called Uncle Robert for advice on how to respond to Paige's accusations. A quick synopsis of his advice on how I should handle all of Paige's accusations during this time period went like this: she's right and you're wrong; apologize and move on.

THE 19TH OF that month marked the twentieth anniversary of

my marriage to Paige. I knew it would be an emotional and difficult day for me, and now back in Bozeman, I said as much to the two older boys the night before. Sitting at our kitchen table, I asked if it would be okay if I took them out for dinner the next day because I didn't want to be alone and would enjoy some company. One shrugged his shoulders and said, "Sure," while the other said, "I'll think about it." Early in the afternoon of the 19th, I went fly fishing for the first time in years. I used to love fly fishing, but a combination of time constraints, limited budget, and changing priorities had all but ended my time on the water. I was trying to treat myself, but, instead, I spent most of my time standing in the cold, clear water of the Gallatin River crying miserably. My wife despised me, my two oldest boys seemed on the verge of rejecting me, and my youngest three lived hundreds of miles away. I simply couldn't get those realities to stop tormenting my mind long enough to enjoy the moment. When I got home later that day, I asked the boys if they'd like to go eat with me. Both declined. Unbeknownst to me, after I had invited them to dinner the night before, they talked with Paige. She was outraged I would try to pressure the boys into "celebrating" our wedding anniversary. One at a time, the boys regurgitated Paige's hatred straight to my face, saying they didn't want to celebrate something their mom considered the worst thing to ever happen to her and the worst day of her life. Many more awful and hateful words were said to me, but they were simply repeating the bile that Paige and Uncle Robert had shared with them.

It was abundantly clear to all those who had an intimate knowledge of what had recently transpired in my family that an incredible amount of hatred and condemnation was being pumped into all five of my children by Uncle Robert and Paige. The hatred and condemnation that occasionally spewed forth from the kids was almost always directed at me. As this narrative goes on, I'll only share what I feel is necessary to demonstrate this poisoning of my children.

Minutes after the boys took their turns confronting and condemning me, I received a nasty email from Paige.

I am not going to be an editor of your nonsense anymore, nor will I be a part of your phony, hallucinated 'anniversary?' The children are all thriving in the truth and reality and I will protect their right to freedom and liberty from self and all the reproach you are piling on them. How dare you ask Thomas and David to join you in celebrating something that never was and that their mother considers the worst deception of her life! You must be totally insane and the arch deceiver you always were!

After reading that email, I spent the better part of the evening wallowing in misery as I cried and walked alone on the roads by my home. I called my brothers but there wasn't much they could say to cheer me up. What *would* you say to someone in that situation? I never said anything to the boys about celebrating our anniversary, but even if I had, Paige's response was incredibly vile and mean-spirited. Yet when I spoke with Uncle Robert about it that night, he convinced me I was in the wrong. I then emailed Paige apologizing and attempting to clarify my intent. What I had done that I needed to be sorry for, I had no idea. That was the power Uncle Robert and Paige still had over me. Paige could write or say something absurdly cruel to me and Uncle Robert could still convince me that I deserved it. With Uncle Robert defending her every move, and me not defending myself at all, it's no wonder Paige continued to lash out and act so outrageously. She didn't have anyone in her life to step in and tell her she was acting inappropriately. Sadly, even if she did, the voices of Uncle Robert and her father would probably have drowned out any other dissenting voice.

In case you're wondering what Paige meant when she wrote in her email that she wasn't *"going to be an editor of your nonsense anymore,"* she was referring to letters I had written the children. Frustrated that I couldn't spend time with the children, Uncle Robert suggested I write them letters and consider my time away from them a good thing. In fact, he said the best thing I could do for my youngest three children was be as physically far away from them as possible. Presumably, this would give them a chance to recover from being in the presence of me, an insane arch-deceiver, sorcerer, and devil of a man who had previously imprisoned the children with biological determinism. Some examples of what I wrote the children in my letters are below.

To Alex: *"You are growing up in so many ways. It gives me great pleasure to see the way you obey your mother and listen to her instruction, and to know she is raising and training you to grow in the fear of the Lord."*

To Zoe: *"My heart was filled with joy as I witnessed over those four days the closeness between you and your mother as she nurtures and raises you in the instruction and discipline of the Lord."*

To Naomi: *"There is no better person than your mother to help you be a true woman. I am so proud of you."*

A bit over the top, you think? I should note that I rewrote my letters to the children to include a sufficient amount of praise for Paige so that she and Uncle Robert would consider the letters worthy to share. In my previous attempt to write the children letters, which, under Uncle Robert's direction I sent to Paige for her approval and/ or editing, she had this to say about them:

> *Peter,*
>
> *Your letter to Alex conveys a false impression that*

he is autonomous of his mother in "what he is learning from the Lord". As if he is learning from the air, mentioning me as an afterthought and only in the context of what "he" can do for me as if I am in need of him giving me what I "deserve" according to your approval. You are maintaining the fallacy of the impression that you are still in control as if you ever were, except through the sly means and stealth of self. If you were to really try to be real you would just simply give thanks that Alex is being raised, trained and coached to grow in the true fear of the Lord by his mother. In addition, this is the first time I have ever heard you call him son. In the context of you calling me mother and yourself Daddy, you are maintaining confusion in his understanding and not acknowledging the fact that there was no true beginning and the "separation" was final. I know you cannot get involved in all these intricacies of explaining to Alex but I leave it up to you to find a way to express genuine truth to him.

In regards to Naomi's letter. Naomi already sees through your patronizing, can't you find anything in her growth of character to acknowledge and encourage her in? Why do you need to tell the children you are praying for them? Are you trying to convince them of your change when they hear from me the contrary? Your behavior is defiance, not cooperation. Why do you practice sanctimonious religiosity and not genuine faith, despite the monumental efforts toward your salvation. You cannot truthfully say you heard the Lord's final word. If you keep on thinking that you have changed, I can assure *you that as a man thinketh, so is he. All your change is thinking you have changed. The mouth speaks from the abundance of the heart; therefore, if you don't experience a radical change in your words with which you describe any situation, you're still way far away from change. Can the Leopard change his spots? If he can, you really changed. Your spots are all over the place.*

In your letter to Zoe, you are listing all these people to her and poor you are missing. There is not a hint about her, who she is becoming, or what concerns her on a true level of reality. Your letter pulls and tugs at her for a space in her thoughts as if she may forget you if you don't. Who are you really thinking of? Not her.

Let me tell you this, you can never change until you believe that genuine change is not ever going to be a license for you to realize your old dreams, wants, expectations and hopes. Genuine change does not keep anything from the past. Unless you believe that genuine change is a raging fire in your house that would compel you to run for dear life naked, it won't happen.

Paige

There is so much that is wrong and wicked with her comments, but I want to focus on one thing she wrote in her notes about Naomi. She said, *"Your behavior is defiance, not cooperation."* Those are chilling words to read, especially for anyone who has ever been a part of a cult. Paige labeled my attempt to maintain my role as a Christian father who loved his children as defiance of her and Uncle Robert. When it came to the beliefs of Paige and Uncle Robert, there was never room for disagreement; there was only defiance. No matter how wicked or bizarre the thoughts, ideas, words, or actions of Paige and Uncle Robert were, you either agreed with them or you were defying them. This is classic cult-like behavior—you're either completely with us or completely against us. Uncle Robert had convinced his little group of followers that the vast majority of the world was indeed against us. Thus, when people criticized his moronic beliefs, it became a self-fulfilling prophecy and strengthened his mind control even further. And even though I was effectively being kicked out of the little cult by Paige, my mind was still not free from the control of the group. So, when I read that I was in *"defiance"* of Paige, I shuddered. I ask you; if defying Paige and Uncle Robert made me, a man of nearly fifty years, shudder, how do you think my three young children felt living in that atmosphere?

I DIDN'T KNOW it at the time, but I wasn't the only one receiving angry letters from Paige during the summer of 2017. Two of her friends in the Bozeman area did as well, which they shared with me years later. The anger, judgment, and vitriol they contain were astonishing. I include these in this story only to illustrate just how much condemnation and hatred Uncle Robert had poisoned Paige with. I find it truly remarkable to read these letters and realize they were written by the same loving woman I married. But the difference between Paige in 1997 and Paige in 2017 was frightening. The first, to Sandra, dealt with their relationship in the multilevel marketing company, doTERRA. I am including only a portion of the letter. Baked into every sentence were the thoughts and ideas of Uncle Robert; his leaven affected everything she did, said, and wrote. Her letters were blunt, free of nuance, diplomacy, or doubt. And if Sandra or others rejected her because of her words, that was something Paige was glad to accept, for in her mind, suffering rejection due to allegiance to Uncle Robert was the exact same thing as suffering for following Christ.

You are run by a tyrannical mind that never delivers on any of its promises. The Word of our Lord is abundant in speaking about humility and receiving instruction and only a fool rejects instruction. Ask the thousands of girls who enlist in the Army and let them tell you about their training. There is not one word in their training manual or exercise that hints at suggestion, it's all command and they accept it because they committed themselves to being instructed, to being trained and to being changed. The foundation of all civilization is the Ten Commandments, they are not suggestions and one of them says, "Thou Shalt Not Bear False Witness Against Your Neighbor." I will show you in detail that your whole email [this email was in response to one Sandra sent Paige] *falls into the category of a false witness, first against yourself and then against me.*

How audacious of you to say, "careful thoughts, consideration and prayer." If it's careful thoughts consideration and prayer, then to whom are you praying? It must be to yourself because you said later in the email that you must listen to yourself. The lack of confidence that you lavishly describe is all of the sudden summoned richly in your statement, "I am confident you should not be my mentor." How can you "know yourself pretty well"? If you really knew yourself you would reject self for the horror of self and you would have the confidence you say you lack. How can you know yourself without the confidence of knowing? You are contradicting yourself so badly that it doesn't matter to you that your words have a conflicting meaning. You keep saying to yourself and once to me that I ask you the same questions over and over and over and you conveniently forget that you are in the same place, the same state of mind and the same condition. How in the world can you not see that if you are not the lead dog, the scenery remains the same? Because you are not humble but self-centered, and it is clear that you are not a disciplined person, you live in the foggy world of thought. "The Lord resists the proud and gives grace to the humble. Humble yourself under the mighty hand of God and He will lift you in due time." You pretend to be humble and that is the epitome of pride. This is a false witness because you refuse to deal with reality, the reality in the interpersonal relationship for success. Reality is interpersonal relation with freedom and respect and this is success. You despise reality because you despise instruction. You label experiential instruction as a command. Why not take it as a command even if it wasn't meant to be? Try being successful in doTERRA or the Marine Core [sic] or any other credible profession without taking the instructions as a command. ...

You are very confused and yet you think you have the ability to bamboozle others into thinking that you are not confused. All your pretending demonstrates a slick, hypocritical tendency to keep you safe in your false assumptions.

If you didn't know Paige's background with Uncle Robert, it would be hard to read that letter and not think she has a problem. With knowledge of Uncle Robert and his beliefs and influence over her, it's easier, I think, to see how she could write such a bizarre letter.

Because neither Paige nor I told anyone what had happened to our marriage and family, people naturally wondered what was going on. Where was Paige? Where were the younger children? Was everything okay? Of course, the answer was that everything wasn't okay, but Paige didn't want others to know, especially those in the Bozeman area who knew us because they would see through Paige and Uncle Robert's absurd lies immediately. In June, a neighbor, Cari, noticed something amiss with our family and casually asked me if everything were okay. I lied, telling her everything was fine. She then made the mistake a few weeks later by asking Paige the same question. Here's a portion of Paige's response to her.

> *Are we on trial in your mind? You said you do not need to know details but just to know basically. Why? What recourse to* [sic] *we have once we come under your suspicion? That is not a friend. That is someone who is sticking their nose into someone's affairs to satisfy curiosity or validate judgment. We, as believers are to keep away from busybodies. 1 Peter 4:15, 1 Cor 10:29 and Col 2:18.*
>
> *People want to know private things to use them against the person once they suspect that someone is not transparent. They have to poke into private affairs to be able to dismiss the person and distance themselves from the person they suspect. The reason the "old mind" wants a little bit of evidence is to distance themselves and put the other person under condemnation and legitimize un-fellowshipping them and feel self-righteous in doing so. Self-Righteousness is righteousness by reverse osmosis not by faith in our Lord Jesus. When they see the*

"wrong" in others, they feel righteous about the wrong in themselves.

The sad truth about this letter is that Cari truly did care and is someone who would never *"poke into private affairs"* just so she could *"dismiss"* someone. Furthermore, the very thing Paige accused Cari of doing, "un-fellowshipping" someone, was exactly what she was doing to Cari and others. I can't say for certain that Paige felt self-righteous by un-fellowshipping so many people, but I can say that this is exactly the behavior and sentiment I observed in Uncle Robert on several occasions. Unfortunately, the more Paige isolated herself in the company of Uncle Robert and her parents, the more bitter and angry her communication became. Paige continued to send angry emails the rest of the summer. I realize reading these emails can be disturbing, but they are an important part of the story. They help remove the veil of secrecy Uncle Robert sought to maintain, and in reading them, the mind of a narcissistic cult leader is exposed so you, the reader, can be aware and spot potential Uncle Roberts lurking in your life.

IN LATE JULY, Paige informed me she had enrolled the children in a private school in Northern Idaho. I was furious, scared, and probably still in denial; furious she had done it without discussing it with me first and scared they were settling into Northern Idaho for the long haul and not planning to move back to Bozeman any time soon. Both exposed my denial of reality. When Paige asked if I'd like to contribute to the school cost, I said yes, then called the school and set up a payment plan to cover the whole cost of the tuition. This was perhaps poor communication on my part, but when she found out she was enraged.

On the 16th of August, Paige dropped the children off to see me for a few hours. In a text before she arrived, she informed me that Thomas, my oldest son, would be in charge of the younger three children and they were to go to him with any questions. Aside from the monumental disrespect that directive showed me, it also pitted me against my son, which was unfair to both of us. Thankfully, nothing happened while she was gone that required adult intervention, and there was no confrontation between Thomas and me.

However, there was an ugly confrontation between Paige and me. Alex wanted to target practice in our backyard with me and I readily agreed. When he retrieved the BB gun, I suggested we use the .22 rifle. He said his mom wouldn't allow him to use the .22, only the BB gun. I rolled my eyes at this comment but went along with her directives and we shot the BB gun. The next day, the 17th, when Paige dropped the children off again, I approached her as she sat in her car, ready to drive off. I asked her why she didn't want Alex to use the .22 rifle with me right there supervising. She sternly told me I had no right to question her choices for the children and she would be the one making all decisions regarding them. For nearly a year, I had completely given up my authority as husband, father, and man. Now I began to realize how wrong that was. When I disagreed and tried to assert my rights as their father, she got out of the car and stormed into the house, refusing to talk with me any longer until she had witnesses. For witnesses she called our teenage sons, Thomas and David, into the office. She then proceeded to call me insane and not a true father but only a "sperm donor." When she started calling me a "sperm donor" in front of the boys, I got angry and cut her off and said that wasn't true. That was the second time I ever raised my voice at her in anger. I held the door open, hinting that she should leave, which she did.

About a week later, another email showed up, addressing the

recent confrontation, as well as the private school tuition.

Peter,

You had absolutely no right to make the decision to set up an account with NICS [North Idaho Christian School] *for the tuition. You never consulted me about this point and I never asked you to be responsible for their tuition. I simply inquired how much you would be capable of contributing. Any decision for the children's education does not require your consent or consult. The decisions I make for them are precisely to do exactly what is best for them with the desired result of helping them overcome all the influence you have exerted in their lives which has created problems for them on every level of character, intellect and will.*

You say you want my courtesy, how have you extended courtesy to me by going behind my back and interfering in a responsibility that is mine? Your brazen lack of respect and consideration for my decisions for the children, which are under my care, demonstrates your inability to interact on a level of courtesy. You cannot say you love the children when you repeatedly bully and disregard their mother. You are a tyrant and I do not want your financial assistance when it is linked to such an attitude of control and manipulation. I included you in knowing my choices for the children's education on the basis of giving you the opportunity to be a positive part of their progress and freedom from tyranny. You have rendered yourself unworthy of even this basic consideration. You're the last creature on the face of the earth to speak about courtesy. I extended courtesy to you by inviting you to contribute what you can and that courtesy should have shown you your limited involvement and that your chosen financial contribution was the only decision for you to be involved in. In other words, you can decide whether to contribute or not, this is the nature of your decision and not one inch beyond that. ...

You cannot operate under any pretext of being a father when all you have is total disregard for me. It must be absolutely clear to you that you are in one world and I am in another. You must succeed in erasing this fiction from your mind that allowed you to consider tyranny and abuse, marriage and start at least pretending to be civil - rehearsed civility. Your unstable conduct when I brought the children for a visit August 16 and 17, not only was belligerent, bullying and badgering, but you showed utter disrespect for me and the children. You lied and you denied you lied ...

Paige

I had discovered that reading emails like this from Paige sent me into a tailspin. Every time I received an email from her, my anxiety level would skyrocket, adrenaline and cortisol pumping furiously through my body, and I had a hard time concentrating on anything. I simply wasn't strong enough yet to read her words objectively. So when I saw an email from her show up on my laptop or smart phone, I would immediately forward it to a few people—my brother, a friend in Idaho, my lawyers, and my counselor. I would usually call one or more of them, ask them if they read it, and did they think it was safe for me to read. This ritual sounds funny to me now, but at the time I really needed that level of support.

SOME OF THAT support came from the law firm I had hired earlier in the summer. I never wanted to file for divorce, but because of Paige's behavior, I was strongly encouraged by my family and friends to seek legal counsel. Thankfully, I listened to them. However, I was so concerned with people in the local community finding out about my current situation that I refused to look for lawyers in Bozeman; with the help of my oldest brother, we located an excellent firm in Missoula. My first visit to their downtown offices was very cloak and dagger: I didn't tell anyone in the entire state of Montana (other than the lawyers) where I was going or what I was doing. I assumed hiring lawyers would be translated as an unpardonable sin by Paige and Uncle Robert. What would they do if they found out? Would they cut me out of their lives forever? What would I say if they asked me why I was hiring a lawyer?

Prior to this, Missoula held a special place in my heart. It had been romanticized by one of my favorite movies, *A River Runs Through It*, and during my first adventure to the northern Rockies, a post college graduation trip in the spring of 1990, I was charmed by Missoula's historic downtown that is bisected by rivers and flanked by mountains. Now, as I snuck into town, I wondered if this association with attorneys would forever stain Missoula for me. We met in their small downtown office, and I was a nervous wreck the entire visit. I didn't want to be there. I wasn't supposed to be there. I wasn't supposed to be secretly meeting with lawyers to discuss my failed marriage. I still held out hope for my marriage, for Paige and me. So, when one of the lawyers asked what I wanted to do, "divorce or separate?," I was tempted to jump out the window.

The most serious concern was protecting my right to be a parent to our youngest three children, and with that in mind I was strongly encouraged to file what is called a parenting plan. A parenting plan is an agreement, filed in a local court, between two disagreeing parents that spells out exactly how they are going to raise the children. My family and lawyers all wanted me to file in July, but I wasn't ready. I still held out hope that Paige and Uncle Robert knew what they were doing and things would get better. But things didn't get better that summer, and with Paige's "sperm donor" tirade in front of the boys and her nasty emails in August, I was finally convinced I needed to take action. Before I did anything legally, I gave her one more chance and emailed her asking to discuss coparenting arrangements. Below is what she sent back in reply.

> *Peter,*
>
> *I disagree with your disagreement,*
> *I reject your rejection*
> *And I deny you your denial.*
>
> *If you cannot accept my assessment of you and the awful way you treated me and the children recently, you are a non-parent. You are devoid of any parenting abilities or qualities. Since you are void of any parental quality, you only have love for and affection for yourself and you will employ anybody, including the children to claim the dispensing of that love and affection. I am not denying you the instinctive attachment to the children which is found on all levels of life including the animals. With no merit whatsoever to the instinct of any individual parent. I am talking about the predatory, serpentine and chameleon attributes of character that mainly worked out the revelation and the awful discovery of who you really are. Only by stealth and deception was there a relationship which was totally non existent [sic] in reality. I have struggled to insulate and protect*

the children all these years from your manipulative destruction and I am vehemently, adamantly and insistently determined to continue to protect them from your parasitical influence.

You are not responding to my statement because you cannot adequately respond. You had to have some help to derail the situation and not respond to my multiple indictments of you. The time you took to reflect was the time you sought help and if you really wanted to respond, you would respond to the substance regardless of the tone. When you begin to speak the truth to me and to the children, that is the first sign you are on the way to qualify for being a good friend to the children to help them discover the father that is more than a biological factor. But you show you don't want them to discover you because you keep hiding, and you want to impose on them the biological determinism that you are a father. The father is far above the dad and the children and I know it very well. What about you? Don't you know it by now? It is a blasphemy to claim "I am the father" when you know you are far from it. As long as you don't see and accept that I am trying to help you be what you have never been so that you can do what you have never done, you will remain lost in the foggy and tormenting hell of your Satan self.

Paige

I was still terrified of how Paige would respond, but after that email, I felt I had no other choice. I needed to file the parenting plan. As for Uncle Robert, I was sure he'd be livid too, but over the summer, I spent less and less time talking with him on the phone. I knew he was behind most, if not all, of Paige's self-righteous anger and I could no longer ignore his incredibly negative, condemning attitude toward me. Calls with him started to feel like muggings. Similar to being triggered emotionally by Paige's emails, I found the same thing happening whenever I called him. It seemed no matter what Paige did or said, she was always right in Uncle Robert's eyes and I was always wrong. I started to dread calling him, so I stopped.

CHAPTER 26
INVOLVING THE COURTS

———◈◉◈———

LATE IN THE afternoon on September 18th of 2017, I found myself pacing up and down the halls of the Gallatin County Courthouse with the signed and notarized parenting plan in my hands. I was there to file the plan with the court, but even at this eleventh hour, I was still nervous. Was this the right thing to do? Had I given Paige and Uncle Robert enough time to show a change in direction? How mad would they get? And what would this do to my relationship with my children? Would they be angry with me? I called several people to discuss the wisdom of filing the plan, practically begging them to talk me out of it and opt for more patience. None did. I had waited long enough, far too long most thought. So, I filed the plan and started bracing for Paige's reaction.

The next day, during our weekly staff meeting, I finally told everyone at my real estate office what was going on with Paige and me. I thought for sure they knew already, but the only ones who did were the owner of the company and his family. The only reason they did was because I had privately told them two months earlier, and per my wishes, they kept it secret. As for everyone else in the office, I was astonished that my puffy red eyes from crying all the time, dramatic weight loss from lack of appetite, and interminable walks around town to knock the edge off my anxiety weren't dead giveaways. But

I was wrong, they were all surprised. And it taught me a valuable lesson: very seldom are we aware of the troubles people are going through. The rude clerk at the grocery store, the guy that cut you off on the highway, or the distant coworker might all be suffering silently through a traumatic life event. So instead of reacting in-kind, be kind. And be compassionate.

ON THE 28TH of September, Paige was finally served with the parenting plan at her parents' home in Idaho. I expected the earth to shake with her anger, but I didn't hear from her right away. Then a few days later she emailed. She wanted to come to a resolution on a parenting plan without the courts or lawyers involved. She proposed we use a mediator. You'll never guess who she suggested.

> *A mediator who knows both of us and all the facts would best serve our situation and I am willing to have a meeting with such a mediator. Who do you know under all of Heaven who knows us, the children and all the facts other than the one who had been your counselor for the last twenty years, Uncle Robert? All of the sudden, you are now seeking someone else? Also, Uncle assured me that you have prepaid for these consultations. If a face to face meeting is not possible with your current schedule, we can have a three way call.*

I briefly discussed this with my attorneys and they strongly advised not to meet with Paige and Uncle Robert. A possible meeting with the two of them reminded me of the funny but true definition of a democracy: it is nothing more than two wolves and a sheep voting on what to eat for dinner. I had no interest in being dinner, so I let Paige know I wouldn't be showing up to a mediation session with them. In the same email where Paige suggested we use Uncle

Robert as our mediator, she also included a thinly veiled threat to put me in jail: *"Please note that your "Petition for Parenting" contains multiple points where you have purgered* [sic] *yourself under oath and you signed your name to it, a course that would inevitably lead you to where you NEVER wanted to be."*

For years, I had been mildly claustrophobic, but in my twenties, I used to go into jails and prisons with Prison Fellowship or other local ministries to share the Gospel with inmates. I stopped going, however, when it became too uncomfortable being locked up. As the years progressed, my claustrophobia became more pronounced, possibly a byproduct of Uncle Robert's intense mental manipulation. Paige knew the last place I ever wanted to be was in prison and was clearly trying to scare me into submission. She didn't tell me what these multiple points were that caused me to commit perjury, but my older boys assured me that all it would take was one word from Uncle Robert and I'd be in jail. In fact, their response had the biggest impact on me.

Not long after telling them about the parenting plan, I had two extremely difficult conversations with Thomas and David. The things they said and their choice of words made it clear they were being heavily influenced by Uncle Robert, either directly or through Paige and her parents. It was hard to be angry with them because it was so obvious they were being poisoned by Uncle Robert's unique brand of hatred and condemnation. They said, among other things, that by taking their mother to court, I proved I wasn't a Christian and I was just a "bloodline" rather than a true father. In the last few months, I had been accused of being a "sperm donor" and a "bloodline" and imprisoning the children through "biological determinism with all its miserable attachments." The sick irony is that just a few years earlier Paige was determined to protect the bloodline of Uncle Robert by bearing him a grandson. The sperm, bloodline, and biology of Uncle Robert were considered nearly sacred, but now these inescapable features of fatherhood were being used to insult and attack me. Sadly, the adults who Thomas and David looked up to couldn't hide their hatred of me, and thus, understandably, the boys soaked it in. So, in my second meeting with the boys after telling them about the parenting plan, they brazenly threatened to move away, have nothing to do with me, and change their last name, unless I removed the parenting plan from the courts.

Once again, terrified, I took the boys' threat seriously and huddled with my lawyers and advisors on what to do. I wasn't about to mediate with Uncle Robert, but shortly before the boys delivered their threat, Paige delivered, via email, a proposed parenting plan that she wanted to agree to outside of the courts. Under her plan, the younger children would continue to live with her in Idaho but it allowed me to see the children every other weekend and split up the summers and holidays. We went back and forth on it and, in a matter of days, had negotiated a workable agreement. I then removed the official parenting plan petition from the courts and hoped we were done with the courts, at least, for the time being. I was wrong.

Two weeks later Paige asked for a divorce. I was devastated. For some reason I still thought we might be able to work it out, that the parenting plan would buy us some time, and once we started coparenting again she'd soften toward me. She didn't file for the divorce right away but told me this is what she wanted and then asked for my thoughts. I immediately set about writing her a letter stating very clearly why I was opposed to our divorce. The next day, she sent me an email, of which a portion is below.

The divorce is already in place since we were never truly married, and Jan 14, 2017 marks the date I formally stated my acknowledgment that we were never joined together in the spirit of truth and commitment, so let's make a clean legal break too. Then, you go on to becoming a true man and I continue to become a true woman and we will see where that places us. If the future provides that we have the choice to choose the other as a partner in life in one mind and accord, then that choice would be made without the presence of guile and self-deception. Primarily, the children will have the fantastic and life-altering example of being obedient to the Lord and the transformative Grace of the Lord Jesus Christ.

How our children were supposed to learn a "life-altering" lesson on obedience to the Lord through watching their mother divorce her faithful husband of twenty years was beyond me. I was desperate to change her mind and help her see the madness of it all. I had so much I wanted to say to Paige, so much that I had kept bottled in and not shared over the past ten months. I had been mute when she left me in January and refused to make that same mistake again. I poured my heart into the letter I sent her, some of which is below.

This point must be crystal clear: I never left you. On January 14th of 2017, you left. You left your husband, you left our marriage, and you left the family. And you are the one who rejected me and our marriage. You are the one who tore our family apart.

You, Paige, decided to leave. I have admitted my mistakes, my faults, my shortcomings and my sinfulness, and I have repented and asked for forgiveness for them all. But I never left. You did.

If you chose to continue anyway and seek a divorce,

then it will be fully transparent to all that you left, you sought the divorce, you sought the dissolution of our marriage, you sought the dissolution of our family.

I offer no justification or credentials or attributes to convince you to love me or to desire me as your life partner. I am relying on faith that the Lord Jesus Christ will work through this situation for the good of those that love Him... and I love Him! I have no conditions attached to my faith, including you coming back. My faith is in the Lord. No matter what happens I will rely on the Lord and trust Him.

If you were to come back, I believe it would truly be a miracle. But the Lord has provided many miracles for us over the years. When David was born 8 weeks premature, his little body struggled to survive. His tiny chest cavity rose and sank with every excruciating attempt to breathe. He had to be kept in the ICU and fed through a feeding tube and on more than one occasion nearly died. Yet our gracious Lord in Heaven saved David and allowed him to thrive. He is truly a miracle.

13 years ago, we had two children and no prospects for any more. You knew the Lord wanted us to have more. In faith you approached me and asked me to reverse our decision. In faith we trusted the Lord to provide even though there was a strong possibility we would still not be able to have more children. But the Lord blessed us threefold. That was a miracle.

Who could imagine giving birth to a daughter one day and handing over the sweet little bundle of life to a doctor so she could have brain surgery on the second day

*of her life. Two years later we were in the same predic-
ament with sweet Naomi when we found out she had
diabetes. But the Lord protected her then and continues
to do so. She too is a miracle.*

*Perhaps you never imagined a life like this. Perhaps
you never envisioned watching your children suffer and
be so vulnerable. Perhaps you never imagined a divorce
twenty years into a marriage that has disappointed you.
The curves in the road our lives have taken has led us to
some very challenges places. Are we in another curve, a
detour, or the end of the road?*

*What a miraculous journey we've been on, a jour-
ney that does not take place without our union, our
marriage. Without you and I together as husband and
wife there is no Thomas, there is no David, there is no
Naomi, there is no Alex, and there is no Zoe.*

*Look at all we have learned from the trials, tests,
and miracles of parenting. Are you really telling me these
miracles and our five children were never intended to be,
never the will of God? Did the Lord work these amazing
miracles only to see you leave and divorce your husband?*

*I will not just allow you to go down the road of
divorce without pointing out what you're doing: what
you're doing to yourself, what you're doing to me, and
what you're doing to the children. What you're doing is
awful and tragic.*

*I never rejected you. Even now I don't reject you. I
reject the idea that we were never married. I reject the
idea that we are already divorced. I reject the idea that
divorce is the right choice for us.*

283

I can't prevent you from getting a divorce, Paige. I can't prevent you from tearing our family apart. I can't make you love me. I can't make you honor me or respect me or desire to share your life with me. I can't make you honor your marriage vows and honor your word that you gave before the Lord.

You have your wings of freedom and can go wherever you want. The door of your self-imposed cage has swung open. You're free. The question is, what will you choose? Will you choose to give up - to give up on us and give up on our family? Or will you choose commitment? Will you choose family? Will you choose love?

Immediately after receiving this letter, she officially filed for divorce. Reading Paige Young had filed a "Petition for Decree of Dissolution of Marriage" against me was gut-wrenching. I had a few weeks to officially respond to her petition for divorce with the court but didn't want to wait that long.

RIGHT AFTER AGREEING to a parenting plan with Paige in October, I started seeing the three younger children every other weekend. Some weekends I would drive up to Northern Idaho and rent a room at a bed and breakfast where the four of us would hang out; other times I would bring them home with me to Montana. The day before Thanksgiving, I drove to Missoula where Paige met me with the children. Missoula was roughly halfway between Bozeman and Hayden, Idaho, and it was here that we would exchange the children. They would be spending Thanksgiving in Bozeman with me and their older brothers. On the drive up, I listened to the book *The Four Agreements* by Don Miguel Ruiz. While I don't agree with everything the author wrote, I loved the book. The four agreements that he urges readers to make with themselves are:

1. Be impeccable with your word
2. Don't take anything personally
3. Don't make assumptions
4. Always do your best

I especially loved the second agreement, don't take anything personally, because it was so applicable to me at that time in my life. Paige was saying and writing such horrible things about me it was very hard *not* to take it personally, but Ruiz's book helped. Encouraged by the words in the book, I asked Paige if we could speak alone for a moment. While the children waited inside the gas station where we met, the two of us went outside. There in the cold and dark of a long Montana night, I calmly and lovingly asked her to consider withdrawing her petition for divorce. I told her growing up with divorced parents wasn't good for our children and that the Lord could perform a miracle in our lives and bring us back together. She searched my eyes intently, looking for any sign of doubt or fear or weakness like she always did. But there was none. She didn't explode with cruel words or furrow her brow in anger. Rather, she gave me a subtle smile, then left. Her smile stuck with me as I drove off with the children. It was a brief glimpse of the old Paige, the one I married, the one who used to smile at me all the time. My heart was happier than it had been in a very long time.

The children and I drove to a nearby restaurant for dinner before heading home. A few minutes after sitting down Paige called me on my cell phone. She told me my statements at the gas station had caught her off guard, and her answer was not only "no" but "a thousand times no," we will not get back together.

UNTIL THIS TIME I had asked my family to refrain from

contacting Paige. This was partly to avoid upsetting Paige further, and, knowing how she really felt about them, partly to shield my family from one of her angry diatribes. But now that my long letter to Paige had little to no impact, I thought other voices might help. In hindsight, I should have encouraged my family and others to reach out to Paige earlier and provide her with voices of reason, truth, and love to balance the insanity she heard daily from Uncle Robert. So, when my family started to contact Paige, they naturally had lots of questions, most of which boiled down to one: Why are you doing this? On Thanksgiving, Paige wrote her answer to my mother, the bulk of which is copied below.

> I spent 20 years of my life working to make something false into something real. In the last 3 years and after about 300 hours of biblical counseling, Peter has revealed that he does not love me, he does not keep my word with the children, and he left me long ago.

The "300 hours of biblical counseling" is a reference to all the time Uncle Robert spent with me on the phone and at our Conferences. I have no idea how they came up with that exact figure.

> When I met Peter in October 1996, I believed I was a Christian, I believed he was too and I liked him very much because I thought he was kind and fun and I could see his potential to be a solid man. The Lord revealed to me, about 3 years ago, that I was not seeing Peter through the eyes of a woman in the Lord but a female who was subject to the collective social mind which dictates and desires all attention for selfish end.

The notion that the female and the woman are not only different, but at odds with each other, is another Uncle Robert teaching, along with the "collective social mind." According to him, being undisciplined in the mind and following what society says is right and wrong was something to be avoided at all costs. Again, there is much truth to that, but the moment you stopped believing just one thing he said, you were in danger of falling prey to the "collective social mind."

My self-deception can be documented beginning with a letter I wrote to my parents January 1997, telling them about Peter. In this letter I even said "am I a fool in love? and "if I am, I will accept the consequences for my actions" then I never sent it (I was in the habit of setting aside important letters to add or change something before sending. I found it by accident January 2017. I had not remembered writing it but the Lord had me find it on the 20 year anniversary of the day I wrote it!) Later in January 1997, the Lord revealed to me in no uncertain terms that I was false and living a lie. I was humbled and crushed and so grateful to be shown the truth and I surrendered my self-life to the Lord Jesus Christ February 12, 1997. I wish I had remembered the letter and gone back to the beginning in my assessment of Peter before I agreed to marry him. I know if I would have reevaluated, I would have found the early stages of what I saw develop over the 20 years and stayed as far away from him as possible. I certainly would NEVER have married him! If I knew then 10% of what I have come to see in him these past 20 years (more intensely the last 6 years), I would have refused to marry him. Yet, as a new believer, still functioning in my old habits and perceptions of the female self, I deceived myself into believing that Peter really did love me for who I was and that he was a believer because he said he was and he said all the right things (even though he declined to share his testimony of belief at a family gathering the previous November 1996.) I wanted to believe Peter, my still fresh female pride did not want to admit I could have been so wrong and I must find someone else to share my life with. ...

Several times over the years, I reached out in desperation to my parents and Uncle Robert and Aunt Staci and they guided me to "become Peter's maturity and persevere" in all things honorable as a wife and mother.

I never gave up, he gave up. He gave up on me the moment he asked me to marry him because he was not truthful. So, you can look at it like there never was a marriage, or that he divorced me from the beginning, but you cannot say that I gave up or left, because he left from the beginning.

These last few sentences were hard for me to read because I had been so used to holding Paige in high esteem and revering her word as the gospel truth. But there was no getting around the fact that what she wrote was pure gibberish. Remember that analogy I gave about Uncle Robert's communication style being akin to giving you the recipe for the chocolate chip cookie versus actually giving you the cookie? It seemed by late 2017 his recipes were going haywire because this nonsense clearly came from him.

According to the Word of God, Peter must accept me and my sole authority as the believer in the lives of the children, but he did not ever accept my way of life or will for the children. Sanctification is based on one mind and one accord, it is not automatic. He verbally said he wanted to stay with me but in reality he had left me a long time ago, before the first day of marriage. Because he is dishonest, he is a male, not a man, and there is no manhood or ability to love in him whatsoever. His hating me and divorcing me from the beginning shows his violence toward me, Malachi 2:16, and willingness to stay only if he could manipulate me and make my life miserable, to the point of putting the children against me.

There's a verse in the Bible that says, "*When words are many, sin is unavoidable, but he who restrains his lips is wise.*" Proverbs 10:19. As her letter went on and on, consistently revealing the hidden hand of Uncle Robert, I couldn't help but think of that verse. And sinful is but one word to describe using Malachi 2:16 to accuse the spouse who doesn't want a divorce of being violent and hateful toward the spouse who has actually filed for divorce. Malachi 2:16 says in part, "'*The man who hates and divorces his wife,' says the Lord, the God of Israel, 'does violence to the one he should protect.*'" Using that verse to prove that I hated Paige from the beginning was instead doing violence to the English language and rational thought.

From the beginning, Peter consistently became upset over my statements of discernment regarding other people and evidence of whether or not they were walking the walk as believers, as if he was working on preventing me from discerning him. … His greatest fear was that I would leave him. Why? I never even considered the thought of leaving him and believed that I had to make it work no matter what. I never saw divorce as an option for a believing relationship and I was right; "What God hath joined together, let no man separate"

289

is true. Yet, when he became revealed as an unbeliever, it was clear that God had NEVER joined us together as God would NEVER join a believer and an unbeliever, since to be married requires the two to be of one mind and one accord. This was the root of his fear, that I would leave him when I discovered that he was not a believer and not willing to stay with me. In the Spring of 2015, when Uncle Robert told me, in front of Peter, that even if he is an unbeliever I should stay, Peter said he was no longer afraid I would leave him. His most recent display of utter disregard for the safety and wellbeing and total lack of love for the children and myself was in September 2017 when he endangered my life and the children's lives by going to the courts for co-parenting instead of presenting a plan to me on his own.

The accusation that I endangered Paige and the lives of our children by filing the parenting plan was repeatedly leveled at me by Paige and later our children. It turns out Paige not only told the children I had endangered their lives by filing the parenting plan, she actually read them portions of the filing. How I endangered their lives was never fully explained to me by Paige.

In this court action, Peter purgered [sic] himself by signing his name to several lies about my choices and the overall situation we had previously agreed upon together. His last 8 page declaration of how I need to honor him does not have one word about him honoring me, and is a classic piece of blasphemy. He will say anything he wants to say to in order to get what he wants, but I said all the things I ever said to him in the effort to build him up as a wife who loves her husband. This declaration of his negates all his attempts to come to the reality of the truth. He was ever learning and never coming to the knowledge of the truth. You described Peter as being brainwashed for your own reason, and it is true he is brainwashed but it is even worse than that, he is unpredictable, untrustworthy and he is never the same from one interaction to the next except in his habits. He is a master in the art of presenting himself like a con artist.

If it were not for strength in the Lord Jesus and the encouragement of my mom and dad and Uncle Robert and Aunt Staci to stick with it and persevere, I don't know how the children and I could have remained sane in that environment for so long. As a wife true to her commitment, I truly loved with all my heart all that I believed Peter was and could be, but as the Lord hates a liar, so do I hate the liar that Peter is. He deceived the female in me and the woman in me, in Christ, woke me up. In January 2017, I gave him my final word that it is over. I would not accept one more minute with him if he would not accept my way of life and uphold my word with the children. I am grateful that the children are given the chance to have answers to all their questions that nagged them and created double mindedness in them. The dichotomy was strong and I was stricken to my heart with the knowledge that all five of them were lost in the same abyss with Peter, the abyss of self that has no heart, no conscience, and can only exist as a parasite, taking and taking from those around it. Praise God for His Truth that set us Free!!

That Paige would use that last line about truth in a letter justifying her desire for a divorce seemed rather ironic to me. As I read this letter, combined with the other emails from Paige over the past year, I knew there was something seriously wrong with what Uncle Robert was telling her. It was becoming clear to me that Uncle Robert was twisting the Bible to give Paige theological cover for wanting to divorce her husband. But I was still on the fence. On the one hand, I saw Uncle Robert orchestrating this divorce and the nasty things Paige and the boys were saying to me; on the other hand, I still admired him for his strength of will and intellect.

I was, however, not on the fence when it came to divorce. Just the sound of the word repulsed me. I hated the idea of divorcing Paige with every fiber of my being. I still loved Paige and would have taken her back in a heartbeat. Divorce represented the worst failure in life. It meant you had failed at the most important thing in life. And after so many failures in other areas of my life, I didn't want to fail at this. Staring divorce in the face revealed an ugly truth about me. Whenever I heard someone say they were divorced I instantly judged them. I thought to myself that I was better than that person. I didn't care if you were a successful businessman or athlete or coach or whatever, if you had been divorced, then I had something to hold over you. I had a happy, healthy, wonderful marriage with a beautiful wife. My marriage was strong. I would never get a divorce. I was better. And my great marriage made up for all the other shortcomings I experienced in life.

That was no longer the case. My marriage had fallen apart. I had failed. Whenever I heard someone else talk about going through a brutal divorce, I cringed inside and made sure not to even whisper a word about my situation. Now that Paige had filed for divorce, I hated the word even more and was determined to fight it. I would fight to save my marriage. I also started to realize I had more to fight for. While everyone else who was aware of my situation had come to this conclusion months prior, it took me longer to realize there was a real problem with the way Paige was parenting our children. I could see a bit of it in the way the two older boys were treating me, but during my time with the three younger children at Thanksgiving it became alarmingly clear. (In an effort to protect their privacy as much as possible, yet still expose the magnitude of emotional abuse the children suffered, I will credit words spoken by one child to all three of the younger kids).

The day after Thanksgiving, the children told me I was a liar, a thief, a robber, and had endangered their lives. They said I endangered their lives by filing the parenting plan, and when I objected, they said my objection meant I was calling their mother a liar. They also claimed I never loved them or their mother because I refused to uphold the word of their mother. There was a familiar anger and defiance in their words and voices. They carried the same self-righteousness that I'd been hearing from Paige and Uncle Robert. It was scary to see their mood swings. One minute we'd be playing and having fun, then if I said something as benign as, "I'm your father and I love you," they would become angry, almost enraged, and claim that was a lie because I never loved them.

When I took the children back to Idaho a few days later I was reminded where they were being taught to be so angry and judgmental. As soon as I pulled into the parking lot where we were to meet, Paige walked up to the car and opened my door. Before any of us could even get out of the car, Paige began her lecture. With her father standing behind her, silently approving of all she had to say, Paige objected to me taking her aside the other day at the gas station in Missoula and asking me to drop the divorce petition. She said she would not. She said it was a miracle the Lord rescued her and the children from the prison I had put them in. She objected to my mother emailing her asking her to stop poisoning the minds of the children and said the poison came from me. She said I indeed had endangered their lives by filing the parenting plan. On one point she actually agreed with me, sort of, that the children would be better off with a mother and father ... but only if the father was a *true* father. The children sat quietly, absorbing all the words of their mother, soaking in all the anger and hatred. Whereas moments before, the car had been filled with the sounds of laughter and love, now the children were stone-faced and cold, barely acknowledging me as I said goodbye.

The children got into Paige's car and I drove off. Shaken by what just happened, I tried to process it and remember what was said. I had a long, dark drive ahead of me, so I decided to call my brother, Brad, to talk about the event. He too had news. He and his wife, Janet, had just met with Paige's sister, Rebecca, for the first time in nearly twenty years. If anyone knew the depths of hatred and condemnation that Paige and Uncle Robert were capable of, it was her. And if anyone could anticipate the savage hatred that was shortly to come my way, it was Rebecca.

CHAPTER 27

HATRED

———◦●◦———

WHEN PAIGE AND I were married in 1997, Rebecca was Paige's maid of honor and my brother, Kevin, was my best man. Prior to our marriage, Paige and Rebecca were roommates in Pocatello, Idaho, and, by my estimation, best friends. That's how my family remembered Rebecca, the fun-loving, energetic friend and younger sister of Paige.

Years later, when Rebecca was shunned, very little was shared with my extended family. My parents or brothers would ask questions, and both Paige and I were evasive with our answers. The message was clear: it's none of your business. As the years passed, they stopped asking questions and Rebecca simply disappeared from our lives. But after informing my family about Paige leaving me and taking the children, I leaned on them heavily for love and support. As I shared more about what had been said and done by Paige and Uncle Robert, naturally the old questions came up again. What *did* happen with Paige's family all those years ago? Why was Rebecca shunned? During the summer of 2017, I still wasn't ready to talk about Rebecca, nor did I see the need to contact her. She had been so thoroughly vilified by Paige and her parents, I was happy to maintain the distance. And I figured if I were to contact Rebecca and Paige found out, Paige's rage would reach new and terrifying heights.

It was also true that in the summer of 2017, I had yet to completely break ties with Uncle Robert. Despite all the difficult things he was saying to me, I still considered him a wise leader and the ultimate authority on Christianity, and I refused to talk negatively about him. Witnessing firsthand what I was going through and having read many of the recent emails from Paige and Uncle Robert, Kevin knew there was a lot of backstory that hadn't been shared and wanted to uncover it. And he knew where to find it. That summer he searched for Rebecca online and found her. They first spoke in September. When Kevin told her Paige had left me and taken the children to Idaho, Rebecca burst into tears. She recovered and they had a good talk. She shared with Kevin things about Uncle Robert and the Klassens that he had never heard before.

When Kevin told me he had spoken with Rebecca, I was furious with him. I asked him why he did that. Didn't he know that if Paige found out she'd be furious too? He said he didn't care what Paige thought, and he didn't need Paige's approval or mine to call Rebecca.

He was absolutely right, but at that moment, I was taken aback. He didn't care what Paige thought? Those words were hard for me to digest. I had been conditioned to view everything I said or did based on how Paige would respond to it. That Kevin would make decisions in his life and not care what Paige thought about it (or what Uncle Robert thought either) seemed as dangerous as juggling chainsaws. But as time passed, I eventually rediscovered a world where I didn't need to gauge my every decision based on the responses of Paige and Uncle Robert.

Rebecca had discovered that world seventeen years prior. At first, she was devastated over being shunned by Paige and her parents. Then, with help, she moved on with her life. She grew close to her two brothers, Lance and Phil, who had also been shunned, as well as her Canadian relatives. She even went so far as to ask her Uncle Tim Klassen, Jack's older brother, and his wife, Peg, to adopt her, which they informally did. She married, had three children and settled in Las Vegas, NV. After talking with Kevin a few times, Rebecca reached out to my brother Brad's wife, Janet, and started communicating with her. At my wedding, Janet and Rebecca hit it off. Like many others in our family, Janet was sad and confused when Rebecca was shunned. But Paige was now her sister-in-law, so Janet didn't push or pry. Since they all lived near the West Coast, it didn't take Janet and Brad long to set up a face-to-face meeting with Rebecca and her family. That first meeting was very emotional for Rebecca. It was the first time she had seen anyone from my family since she said goodbye to me, Paige, and two-year-old Thomas back in 2000.

On the phone that night, as I drove home after dropping off the children in Idaho, Brad made it clear that after talking with Rebecca, he and Janet were convinced all the blame for the disintegration of my marriage and family lay with Uncle Robert. Had he said that a few months earlier, I would have been angry and argued with him. But not now. I may not have agreed with him wholeheartedly, but it was becoming easier for me to see Uncle Robert's role in my situation. It would be a few more weeks before I spoke with Rebecca, but by then, I was more than ready to hear her side of the story.

IN NOVEMBER, IT had been months since I talked with Uncle Robert on the phone and I had only emailed him during that period two or three times at most. In late November, after my lawyers and I filed my official response to Paige's divorce petition saying I didn't think our marriage was "irretrievably" broken and I wanted to share parenting time and custody of the children, Uncle Robert wrote me a testy email.

> *I am asking you with every iota of my being to <u>Stop</u> <u>the</u>* **theatrics** *especially your reinstating what you had withdrawn from the court and the coming* **mediation**. *You say you are for the best interest of the children. I commend you for that. That is the real you. But when you adopt a hellish methodology to prove to no one except the wrong you that you are for their best interest you become a liar and a deceiver and the children will not forget the dishonor and humiliation and that is hardly ever consistent with their best interest.* [Emphasis his]

Turns out that email was just the appetizer for what was to come. A few days later, on December 8th, Paige came by the house to drop off the three younger children so they could spend the weekend with me. As soon as she walked in the front door and entered the living room, she asked all the children to gather and listen, she had something to say to Peter. In front of all five of our children she launched into a furious tirade, her voice loud and strident, her face contorted in rage. At first she wondered why I had refused to accept her divorce petition, then moved on to a lot of name calling. She said she hated me; I was a devil and she hated the devil in me; I didn't display any fruit of the Spirit; I wasn't a Christian but a fraud and fake; I had no right to quote the Bible; I was a horrible person and she felt bad having to bring the children here to spend time with me since she would never want to spend another minute in my presence. I said little in return, and when I did, she mockingly laughed at my words. In the presence of such blinding rage there wasn't much to say.

When she finished her lecture, Paige glared at me, her face red, features hard, eyes taunting, daring me to say something so she could throw it back in my face. I didn't say anything so she turned and stormed out of the house. What I saw that night was a completely different person than the one I married. The once kind and loving Paige was now consumed with hatred. It was an astonishing and scary sight. The children silently listened but also laughed when she did. After she left, I told them, "I'm sorry you had to hear that." All five said, "I'm not." One even said, "I'm glad she told you that."

Amazingly, the children were able to recover from that awful experience and have a fun weekend. There were, however, a few comments that broke my heart. One of the younger three out of the blue said, "Dad, just so you know, when I come here, it's not to see you but to see Thomas and David." It was said with so little emotion and certainly no hatred, that it had the sound of something rehearsed. Also rehearsed or coached was the response I had now received more than once by several of the children: "How can you say you love me when you endangered my life?" This was clearly a phrase given to the children by either Paige or Uncle Robert, and they delivered it as if reciting a memory verse. Arguing with my children about this wasn't something I wanted to do, nor did I think it was going to accomplish much, so I simply told each child I loved them and didn't endanger their life and left it at that. I didn't say anything to the children that was in any way negative toward their mother. But I did read them Proverbs 10:12: "*Hatred stirs up strife, but love covers all sin.*" Two days later Paige came to pick up the children to bring them back to Idaho. She didn't even come in the house.

Later that same night, I could tell Thomas and David were up to something. By this time, we hardly talked at all. Most weekdays, I would make them breakfast, then they would go to school and I to my work. At night, I would cook dinner, they would do homework, and then they would go to bed. It was abundantly clear they sided completely with their mother and probably viewed me the same way she did. But this Sunday night, they were whispering to each other and acting nervous. Finally, they asked to speak with me. In calm, clear voices they reiterated the demands they had made back in October when I had filed the parenting plan, only now I must agree to everything Paige asked for in the divorce decree. If by the coming Friday they didn't have written proof I had agreed to the divorce and reinstated all of Paige's demands, they would move out of the house, disown me, change their last name, and have nothing to do with me. I was far more emotional than they were and had a hard time containing my frustration and anger. I told them they were blackmailing me. They disagreed. I told them they were dishonoring me, a direct violation of the fifth commandment for children to honor their parents. They disagreed, instead responding that they were honoring me by doing this. As the conversation became heated, my voice elevated, and one of them called me a devil with no soul. After that, it was my turn to storm out of the house. It was cold and dark out as I stumbled across the street to my neighbors' farmhouse and collapsed in their entryway in tears.

PAIGE'S ANGRY ERUPTION on December 8th kicked off a week of absolute chaos and gut-wrenching pain for me. It also demonstrated the power of prayer and Christian fellowship. Without the aid and assistance of so many believers, I would have been in far worse trouble that week. After leaving the house that Sunday night, I was comforted by my salt of the earth Christian neighbors. After filling them in, I called several people. The unanimous consensus from all I talked with said I should not cave into the boys' demand and thus teach them this kind of behavior was acceptable. My brother Kevin said if this wasn't a family emergency, he didn't know what was. His opinion was shared by the rest of my family, so my father and brother, Steve, immediately made plans to come out to Montana. After four hours, I kindly thanked my neighbors for their incredible love and support and walked home. Nearly midnight, the cold air bit at my face, stars filled the sky and the distant horizon shimmered with the lights of Bozeman. The house was dark and quiet, the boys were asleep, and I went to my bedroom exhausted. Dealing with emotional pain this severe is challenging enough, but without sleep, it becomes almost unbearable. Thankfully, I was able to get some sleep that night.

The next morning, Monday morning, I went to Manhattan Christian School where David still attended and met with the administration. With his threat to move out, I felt I could no longer hide from the school what was happening in our family. They were incredibly understanding and offered to support me and David however they could. I met with several other people in town, updating them on my situation. They too offered unconditional love and support. I was also on the phone and emailing frequently with friends, family, counselors, and attorneys, each one fulfilling a vital role as I navigated this challenging time. I also received another email from Uncle Robert, most of which is below:

Dear Peter,

1. Paige is not coming back ever.

2. You are not capable of loving her the way she wants and deserves to be loved because as a result of refusing to know yourself as God knows you, you refuse to honor her. You are taking your stalking of Paige to a lower level by insisting on the retrievability of a marriage in total disregard of her being.

3. You are not capable of wanting true change. That is why you keep promising and going back on your word.

4. Tithes are and should be evidence of victory on your part--not the double mindedness that you demonstrate, the narcissistic evidence of your self-absorption and failure to achieve your fantasies and unrealistic purpose in playing your court theatrics to defame Paige in rummaging through her notes and cards she wrote when she still had some hope in your recovery even when you had the audacity to say I still love her you are defaming her by milking your narcissistic fantasies in public. [Emphasis his]

I didn't read Uncle Robert's email right away, but when I did Tuesday morning, I went into a tailspin. Thankfully, I had people there to help. I was confused and scared. It felt like my world was not only crumbling around me but also seeking to crush me in the process. First Paige left, then she poisoned the children against me, now Uncle Robert was attacking me.

The boys' Friday deadline weighed heavy on my heart and mind. What should I do? If I didn't cave in to their demands, would I guarantee their departure from my life for the slim chance I could spend more time with their three younger siblings? I spoke with my attorney, who told me a fight to get the three younger children in my care could be long and ugly. She also said in her thirty-two years as an attorney, mine was the worst case of parental alienation (where one parent damages the relationship between the children and the other parent) she had ever seen. Did I have the strength for a long and ugly court battle? Or should I cave, hoping the damage to my relationship with the two older boys wasn't beyond repair, but, in so doing, consign the three younger children to a life without their father? On Friday, the two older boys were flying to California to spend a week with Uncle Robert at his home. The trip was arranged and paid for by Paige and her parents. I had only recently been told. I knew that no matter what I did, my choice would be the topic of much discussion and criticism while the boys were there.

Tuesday afternoon, my father flew into Bozeman. Wednesday, the four of us—my father and I and my two boys—planned on having pizza for dinner. When I left to get the pizza, my father stayed behind to talk with the boys. When I got home the tension in the room was palpable. My father sat by himself at the kitchen table and the boys were standing in the kitchen, texting furiously on their phones, no doubt to either Paige or Uncle Robert. I heard one of the boys mention Luke 14:26 and knew exactly what was being inferred. The verse says, *"If anyone comes to me and does not hate father and mother, wife and children, brothers and sisters—yea, even their own life—such a person cannot be my disciple."* Such a grotesque misuse of this verse to justify what Paige was doing to me could only originate in the twisted mind of Uncle Robert.

After my father prayed for the meal the boys walked up to the table, got their food and declared that eating together has long been a sign of fellowship. With straight faces, void of any doubt, care, thankfulness or love, they further asserted that they had no fellowship with either me or their grandfather and said they would eat elsewhere. Apparently, their twisted use of Luke 14:26 now applied to my father as well, for the fellowship the boys sought (on the advice of Paige) wasn't with other Christians but believers in Uncle Robert. They took their food and went downstairs. Flabbergasted and upset, my father and I took the rest of the pizza and went to eat at his hotel room.

On Thursday, my father flew back home and my brother Steve arrived. I also started receiving text messages from Paige that Naomi was sick and she was taking her to the doctor in Coeur d'Alene. A little while later, she texted Naomi was worse than initially thought and she was taking her to the hospital in Spokane, Washington. I didn't know exactly what was wrong, but Naomi's diabetes was clearly a contributor. Not sure how serious things were, I packed a bag just in case I needed to drive to Spokane. I told the boys I may be driving up there and left to go meet with my brother. Minutes later one of the boys texted, imploring me not to go to Spokane as he was sure I was the reason Naomi was in the hospital, and, if I went, I would only make her more ill.

While I leaned toward not acquiescing to the boys demands, I made it official by not saying anything to them on their Friday deadline. A lady I'd never seen (probably an Uber driver) pulled into our driveway and picked up the boys to take them to the airport. My brother was at the house with me, but both boys barely acknowledged him or me as they walked right past us and left without anything in writing from me regarding the divorce. Thankfully, Naomi's situation stabilized and she headed home a day later.

NOW THAT YOU'VE made it through that crazy week, take a deep breath, because the next week contained some fairly breathtaking hatred as well. While Paige and her father always seemed the most devoted to (and controlled by) Uncle Robert, his ability to influence and control other people's minds was incredibly strong. And just as Paige used to come back home angry and judgmental toward me after being with Uncle Robert, so too did the boys soak in his hatred. A few of my family members were hoping I could intervene legally and prevent the boys from visiting Uncle Robert. I assured them I could not, nor at the time did I see the need to. However, at the end of their weeklong stay with him, the danger that I had earlier missed was too obvious not to see. Both boys sent me two emails. The words they used, the writing style, sentence structure, and remarkable focus on hatred and condemnation made it clear the emails were heavily influenced by Uncle Robert, if not in part written by him. I only share a few sentences from these emails to demonstrate that the same hatred, condemnation, and judgment that Uncle Robert had poisoned Jack, Cathy, and Paige with was now being fully absorbed by a third generation. They wrote:

> ... *know that I will not be pushed aside, and will not stand idly by to watch my sibling be used as pawns for your demonic self-fulfillment.*

And:

> ... *we will not carry your last name and through our actions lend any sort of honor or respect to that name by which you or the Young "family" might benefit. The natural conclusion of this affair lies in the complete extinction of any chance for you to have a legacy, as Naomi, Alex, and Zoe have incredible potential now to overcome you and become some of the strongest people of this generation.*

On January 4th, 2018, not long after sending those emails to me, the boys, now back in Montana, followed through on their promise and moved out. When I drove home that evening, I saw Jack Klassen's truck in the driveway and knew it was there to help move the boys' belongings. Rather than force a showdown, I backed my car out of the driveway and waited at the neighbor's house. Now I was all alone in my house and I hated it. Every room, picture on the wall, or piece of furniture was a ghost of Paige or the children, ready to bait me into painful and tearful reflection. I spent as little time at home as possible. I had no idea where the boys had gone and was concerned for them. A few days later, I emailed them asking where they moved to. Addressing me as "Mr. Young," here is the reply I got.

> *We cannot divulge our new address to you for our safety, as you have proven yourself to be a bully who does not honor his word and whose unpredictability puts the safety of all around in question. We wish for you that through these difficult times you finally hit rock bottom with enough life left in your mortal body to experience a subsequent ascension. Until you have come to the end of yourself and there is nothing of you left, we must be disconnected from your criminal actions lest our honor go down with you.*

As I read these emails from the boys, I wondered if Rebecca had received similar letters and emails when she was first kicked to the curb by her sister and parents. Was this how it went? Was this the beginning of me not seeing my two oldest boys for years, if not decades, to come? Desperate for answers, I knew the only people who would have the insight I craved were those who had been under the spell of Uncle Robert and managed to escape. I knew of only two people who met those criteria. Would they be willing to talk to me? Was I ready to talk to them?

CHAPTER 28
SEEKING CLARITY

———◦◉◦———

I HAVE BEEN asked repeatedly if there were other people or other families besides mine and the Klassens who followed Uncle Robert. As far as I knew there wasn't anybody else other than Michael Erving and George Bookman. Michael was Uncle Robert's quirky sidekick who, when he wasn't bowing down to Uncle Robert or getting chewed out by him, often fell asleep while trying to listen to him. I actually liked Michael and, under different circumstances I could see being his friend. I don't recall Michael being around much during the first few years of my marriage to Paige, but George was.

George had a checkered past that included drugs, booze, and a few wives. When he met Jack Klassen in the early 90s, he was on the road to recovery and starting to straighten his life out. When I traveled to meet Paige's parents during Thanksgiving of 1996, George was there. George seemed like a part of the family, and every time Paige and I traveled to see her parents, we saw George as well. George attended our conferences with Uncle Robert and talked about him in the same glowing terms Jack did. It seemed the three of them, Jack, George, and Uncle Robert, were the best of friends. Recall that the infamous showdown where Rebecca confronted her family about Uncle Robert happened at George's house.

When George married Patty, his darling wife, in 2003, he grew less and less attached to our little group. He and Patty stopped coming to the conferences. We didn't see them as much. I heard some nasty comments directed toward Patty, and it seemed she was being blamed for George's absence. I wondered if they had been shunned like Rebecca and the other Klassens. If they had, it was with much less vitriol because, over the years, when Paige and I would travel to Northern Idaho, we would occasionally meet George for lunch or stop by his office to say hi.

Come January of 2018, several years had passed since I had last spoken with George. I needed to talk to him because I wanted answers, I wanted clarity. Did he still follow Uncle Robert? Did he still regard him as the biblical expert in his life, a man from whom he would seek advice on any and all topics? And, more importantly, was I justified in entertaining doubts about Uncle Robert? On January 4th, the same day the boys moved out, I called George out of the blue, having no idea if he knew what had happened with Paige and me. Would he be willing to talk, or would he speed-dial Uncle Robert to tattle on me?

When he answered his phone, he was the same George I remembered, friendly and upbeat. When I asked him what he knew about Paige and me, it was clear he didn't know much. Paige had stopped by his office in the summer of 2017 and told him our marriage wasn't doing well, but that's all he knew. He said he hadn't spoken with Jack Klassen and Robert Booty in years. He also revealed he and Patty had recently moved away from Northern Idaho and would rather I not share that information with Robert Booty or the Klassens. He had happily moved on with his life and didn't want them back in it. But, as for me, he was happy to talk and invited me to come visit. I jumped at the chance and, less than two days later, drove to George's home.

I had a wonderful stay at George and Patty's home. Similar to his personality, George has a warm and inviting face, completely bald on top with white hair, white beard, small nose and rosy cheeks. He would make the perfect Santa Claus. He and Patty were clearly happy together and enjoying life. After I updated them on what happened between Paige and me, we spent the weekend comparing notes of our experiences with Uncle Robert and the Klassens. Confirming all my suspicions, he was convinced the Klassens, Michael, and Uncle Robert were a small cult. Like me, he had some bizarre stories involving Uncle Robert, some of which I knew, some I didn't. And some were scary. When he asked about my personal safety and urged me to be cautious, he wasn't the first to do so, but coming from him, with his knowledge of Uncle Robert, it sunk in.

Before I left, George gave me a book to read, one he had recently finished and enjoyed. *Joy for Today,* written by Daryl Kraft, is a daily devotional based on the book of James in the Bible. This book was incredibly impactful for me. They say time heals all wounds, and there's no question 2018 was a much better year for me than 2017. But it wasn't just time that healed my wounds. Reading this book helped me grow in my faith and move beyond the pain and suffering of 2017 and replace it with the joy that only comes from closely following the Lord. I could still hear the dismissive, self-righteous voice of Uncle Robert in my head, but it was no longer the dominant voice whenever I read the Word of God.

A FEW DAYS after returning from my trip to see George, I had my first long phone call with Rebecca. It was surreal, at first. I hadn't heard her voice in nearly eighteen years, and it instantly brought me back to the days of Inkom. I thoroughly enjoyed the talk, even though I experienced a few brief moments of apprehension; I was, after all, speaking to the forbidden redhead. Like George, she shared some stories that I'd heard before and others I had not. Quickly all traces of unease over speaking with the redhead disappeared and we started talking often. She proved to be very helpful as I processed all that had been said and done by Paige and Uncle Robert. Even after all they had done to her, she held no animosity toward Paige. It was a different story with Robert Booty.

"Why do you call him Uncle Robert?" she asked in one of our early conversations. I was taken aback by the question. I was so used to calling him Uncle Robert, it was as if his first name was Uncle and his last name Robert. It just rolled off my tongue. But it bothered her and she encouraged me to stop. Calling him *Uncle* Robert gave him legitimacy and authority in my life, positions he didn't deserve. She simply called him Booty. She was right; so, I too dropped the Uncle.

Speaking with me, which resurrected old wounds and memories of Paige, Booty, and her parents, was hard for Rebecca—but, she assured me, it was something she knew would be helpful for her. She shared some stories from her childhood interactions with Booty that made my skin crawl. With nearly everyone else I talked to at length about my situation, I shared some or most of the email correspondence I was receiving from Paige and Booty. I did this for a number of reasons. First, so they would know I wasn't making all this up, and, secondly, so they could help me craft an appropriate response if needed. But Rebecca wouldn't look at any of the emails from Paige or Booty. To do so would trigger her PTSD. Just me telling her some of the things they had recently said or written brought her right to the edge of mental and emotional trauma. The words and writing of Booty were so unique, so easily recognizable, that, I'm sure, George, Rebecca, and I could easily pick out the one sentence from Booty hidden in a hundred pages of writing.

THERE WAS ONE other man who, while never under the spell of Booty, could provide valuable insight and help me fit all the puzzle pieces together. That was Tim Klassen, Jack's older brother. Tim was retired and living just outside his beloved hometown of Vancouver, British Columbia. I hadn't seen or spoken to Tim since I saw him at Phil's wedding in 2000. When I called, Tim took me back to the days when Jack first met Booty and the changes it brought to Jack's family and the rest of the Klassens. Things had never been the same since. Like the rest of us, he too felt Booty's influence over his brother's family was cultish and considered Booty a false teacher. He astutely observed that Booty used guilt to control Jack and Cathy (recall Jack's reaction to the cockroach comment). He and his wife had been praying for Paige and me for years and had hoped, back in 1997, that, by marrying me, Paige would be able to finally escape the control and manipulation of Booty.

AFTER SPEAKING WITH George, Rebecca, and Tim, it became clear to me that Booty was indeed a bad influence on Paige, her parents, my children, and me. You, my dear reader, may be scratching your head wondering what in the world took me so long to come to this conclusion. I've heard it said that you don't recognize you're in a cult until you've left, or, in my case, are kicked out. Whether or not Booty and the Klassens were a cult was still open for debate in my mind, but the adage held true for me—I wasn't able to accurately discern Booty's wicked influence until I was no longer under his mental control. Even though I was *never* completely comfortable around Booty, I did spend the better part of a decade learning to appreciate and rely on his wisdom and roughly two years in the tight grip of his undue mind control. And now, thanks to the help of friends, family, diligent prayer, and the Holy Spirit, I finally had my eyes and ears opened to the truth. Likewise, now that I fully recognized Booty's negative influence on me, I also had a better appreciation for the warnings signs so many people had been sharing with me regarding my children. Booty's influence was just as dangerous and damaging to my children as it had been to me. And I needed to do something about it.

Enlisting a Guardian ad Litem to protect my three youngest children was first suggested back in the summer of 2017 by my lawyers and a counselor I had been seeing at the time. I had no idea what a Guardian ad Litem (GAL) was. What was it—a French bank, a foot ailment, some obscure legal term? A GAL is actually someone appointed by the court to look after the "best interests of a child" and is usually involved in high-conflict divorces. As I shared the emails from Paige and Booty, the team supporting me were becoming alarmed. Their alarm increased in December thanks to Paige's outburst in front of the children on the 8th and the chilling emails from my older boys while they were visiting Booty. When the idea of bringing in a GAL was brought up with Paige, she was staunchly against it. She didn't want any outside professionals involved with our case and still wanted Booty to either be the mediator in our case or, at the least, be at her side during mediation. As my lawyers and I continued to push for a GAL, Paige continued to add fuel to the fire.

On the first anniversary of her leaving me, Paige gave me a letter. It was a Sunday and I was dropping the children off with her in Hayden after spending another weekend with them. I found the handoffs with the children during this time to be tense and awkward. She was standoffish and cool. The letter she gave me was so outlandish that I've included it in its entirety.

Peter,

It has been one year since I announced to you the divorce and left the false union with you, who cannot and did not love me. In fact, you despised me and led me to believe a lie that I was loved for who I am including all my visions, dreams, hopes and desires. I have told you in so many ways throughout the year in communication by phone and email that it is over but you do not listen to what I am saying, you never listened for the last 20 years, because you are only able to hear your **false assumptions** which are detailed depictions of your own desires and hopes. Without holding any grudge or resentment against you because you are not **real,** I cannot love you, I do not love the "you" that you actually are, and I cannot imagine spending one minute in your presence. I will never be able to think about you without remembering the hellish venture into my self-deception and your chameleon pretending that made me **think** that I fell in love with you. I did not fall in love with you, I fell in love with my imagined potentials in you. Despite the encouragement and support I received from my family to stay with what I **thought** was you, I lived 20 years trying to realize the potential into credentials but never found them. On the contrary, I found the exact opposite. All you care about is repeating your pleasure experience and lighting the candles in the bedroom to entice me to join your idea of intimacy, but from the beginning, you never looked at the candles of my heart or valued the substance of me, and deliberately put them out in rejecting who and what I am.

*You with outrageous audacity, claim "you never left me" yet I am the one who knows that you never earned the place in my being from which you could leave. Now, you so **willfully** prefer to stay in the business of **nurturing** and **nursing your illusions** and existing in the swamp of your lie which amounted to the children and I being indentured slaves. You are trying so hard to prove to society that you are somebody when in **reality** you are a social conglomerate.*

*In all your efforts to keep what you never had and to be what you never were, you will continue to be wrong, live wrong, and die wrong. Give it all up and experience true surrender. Up to this very minute you have never given it up in true surrender. You already lost the older two boys and you will lose the younger three children too if you do not let the children be free to choose you instead of forcing yourself on them as you did on me for 20 years. Only a free person would acknowledge the free choice of his children. If you truly acknowledge who you really are, as you outline in your list of confessions, you would, as you were wisely advised, stay away as far as possible from being all that you listed so you would not influence the children with those horrible traits you describe as you. Just as Jesus says in Luke 19, to him who has much, much will be given, but to him who has little, even what he **thinks** he has will be taken from him.*

Paige [Emphasis hers]

The influence of Booty can be seen in nearly every sentence, especially in phrases like "social conglomerate." But most importantly, the letter also contains the obvious threat that I will lose the three younger children just like I lost the two older boys. Threats like this forced us to act quickly. Paige didn't even try and hide the fact that she was attempting to alienate me from the children. I would imagine she didn't feel the need to hide it because she was supremely confident she was in the right. Shunning and alienating relatives who didn't follow Booty was what Paige had been doing for years. Why would she stop now? Why would she think there was something wrong with it now just because it affected me?

BY FEBRUARY OF 2018, we had a court order appointing a GAL. I would imagine Paige's lawyer convinced her the judge would eventually appoint a GAL with or without her approval, so it would be better if she agreed to it ahead of time, which she did. There was already an abundance of evidence that demonstrated both extreme parental alienation by Paige and cult-like behavior from Booty, Paige, and her parents. Both are considered a form of emotional abuse. Sadly, the evidence continued to mount. To restate, my goal is to keep the children out of this narrative as much as possible. However, they are an integral part of the story, and during the three months the GAL investigated our case, there were several examples of Paige and Booty's negative influence on the children. I will only briefly share three of them here.

The first example took place in February on one of my weekend visits to Idaho to see the younger children. While eating Sunday breakfast at a local restaurant, I decided to read to them from the Bible. For some reason, this triggered an angry, emotional response from them. They told me I never loved them and that the fifth commandment of the Bible, the one that says children should obey their parents, didn't apply to me because it only applied to fathers who loved their children. Obviously, they said that because that's what they were told. There were more angry words from them, words and phrases that clearly came from Paige and Booty, but you get the gist.

The second event took place in March when the younger children came to stay with me for spring break. The day after they arrived, Thomas and David showed up unannounced to check on their siblings under the guise they needed checking up on. I hadn't seen either of them since they moved out in early January, nor had I spoken with them on the phone, so their appearance on my front stoop nearly three months later was clearly coordinated with Paige. I met them outside the door of our house and told them due to the things they had said and written to me, they weren't welcome until they apologized. After a brief and tense showdown they reluctantly left and promptly called the sheriff. Thankfully, the younger children and I had already planned to go visit friends and left shortly after the boys left, so we were not at home when the deputies arrived at my house. Not satisfied with the boys' efforts, Paige also called the sheriff. Still at our friends' home and oblivious to the sheriff's involvement, I finally checked my cell phone around 9pm. Seeing a message from the sheriff, I returned his call, found out Paige and the boys had called him, and did my best to fill him in. He quickly realized there wasn't a problem and said he'd call Paige back and put this to rest, which he did.

During that week of spring break, other painful instances revealed the stress and pressure applied to the children so they would conform to the paranoia and secrecy demanded by Paige and Booty. When friends of mine, who knew the children well but hadn't seen them in over a year, asked innocuous questions like where were they going to school, the children's faces turned to stone, their eyes fixed straight ahead, and they replied, "Ask my mother." There were several more incidents of inappropriate and outrageous behavior from Paige during the week of spring break, but again, you get the gist.

The third, and perhaps most heartbreaking incident happened in late May. Nearing the end of her investigation, the GAL traveled to Idaho to meet with Paige and her parents as well as see where the children were living. At Paige's request, Booty traveled from California to Idaho so he could share with the GAL his pearls of wisdom regarding me, Paige, and the children. When I found out Booty would be in Idaho for the GAL's interview with Paige and her parents, I was instantly worried. I had broken off all contact with Booty in December, and, although I realized he was the root of the problem, I was still somewhat in awe of his speaking skills and powers of persuasion. Would he be able to use these skills to fool the GAL and hide the true nature of his relationship with Paige? Would the GAL be disarmed and fall for his charisma, something Booty oozed during first impressions? I brought my concerns up with one of my attorneys and he assured me that having Booty there at the interview was the best thing that could happen. Based on what he knew, there was no way Booty would be able to hide his true identity and come across as a normal, rational family friend. He was confident all the anger, judgment, and condemnation Booty was spewing toward me and filling Paige and the children with, would come out in the interview. He couldn't have been more correct.

Two days after the GAL's meeting in Idaho, I met Paige at a coffee shop in Butte to pick up the children for a weekend with me in Montana. Paige seemed especially angry and surly and didn't say a word to me. The children also hardly acknowledged me when I showed up. On the drive from Butte to Bozeman, we passed through Whitehall. You'll recall that the entire Whitehall church congregation had been vilified by Paige, her parents, and Booty. As we drove through Whitehall on the interstate the children literally held their breaths. I knew what they were doing and why, but when I asked them why they were holding their breaths they exploded. During a tirade that lasted roughly fifteen minutes I was called a snake, devil, bully, tyrant, and more. They said they didn't want to see me or spend time with me and when they grew up, they wanted to be nothing like me. At one point a little voice said, "Dad, if I were a devil, I'd want someone to tell me." There was, as you probably know by now, much, much more, but you get the gist. After they had temporarily purged the poison inside them, we drove the rest of the way in silence. When we got home, I fed them a snack, played a few games with them, and, once they got in bed, I laid down with them and told them a bedtime story, just like I'd done for years.

Just as Booty constantly poisoned Paige with anger, hatred, and judgment, so too he poisoned the innocent and impressionable minds of my three youngest children. They had just been around Booty, quietly listening and absorbing all his venom. Once they got in the car with me, they couldn't hold it in any longer. It was so clear to me that night that there existed a direct line of hatred and condemnation that originated in Booty and passed through Paige right into the kids. I was so disturbed by what I had just heard that, as soon as the children were asleep, I emailed the GAL. She needed to know how bad it was, and needed to see what my children had to be protected from. I had failed to protect them from Booty while Paige and I were still together, and now that I realized the magnitude of the threat, I knew I needed help. The idea of involving the courts in my family repulsed me, but a friend wisely told me that the courts existed for situations just like mine. He was right.

THE ONE AREA of my marriage to Paige that, in my mind, caused the most tension (other than Booty) had been the disciplining of the children. I tended to be a bit laissez faire, and, at times perhaps too much so, while Paige was far more strident and overbearing. However, over our nearly twenty years together, when it came to discipline, we consistently drifted (or I was pushed) in her direction. It is easy to see the influence of Booty in Paige's desire for swift and firm disciplinary punishment. Booty would often use the word "crush" when describing the process we must go through to be saved and sanctified as Christians. Our sin must crush us, the law must crush us, Christ's perfection must crush us so that we realize there is nothing good in us except God. While that is true, Booty and Paige sought to apply the same crushing when it came to discipling the children. We were to crush our child's will, crush their ego in order for them to submit to their parents' will, for a child not submitted to their parents couldn't submit to God.

True, children are called to honor their parents, but parents are to discipline and nurture their children with love and patience. It seemed to me the desire to crush the will of the child and administer stern discipline in order to produce immediate results was akin to trying to push the river. One can't push the river in order to make the water flow faster, nor can the farmer speed up the harvest by pulling on the shoots. The farmer who is so eager to help his crops grow that he walks into his fields to tug on the shoots will, in the end, go hungry. Put another way, if the apple tree isn't growing straight and its branches are a tangled mess, the farmer who crushes his trees will end up with dead trees and no apples. But the farmer who wisely prunes his trees will enjoy the apple harvest. Patience is needed. And in Paige's zeal and devotion to follow Booty, she pushed and tugged far too much. The same crushing attitude and approach to whatever Paige saw as wicked was evident in the way she lashed out at me in anger and condemnation. It could also be seen in the children, as their smiles and laughter evaporated whenever I drove into the parking lot to drop them off with Paige.

THE GAL REPORT came out in mid-May. It was a stunning rebuke of Paige, her parents, and, mostly, Robert Booty. The GAL detailed the abusive cult influence of "Uncle Robert" as well as the most egregious case of parental alienation she'd ever seen. In addition to all my friends and family who had already seen the red flags, we now had a neutral, third-party observer who saw it. Throughout the investigation, Paige and Booty were confident, almost arrogant, in their feelings of superiority. Paige emailed the GAL shortly before her trip to Northern Idaho that, *"Uncle Robert will make a special trip up to Idaho to meet with you,"* oblivious to the fact the GAL was also making a *special* trip to Idaho. But everything Uncle Robert did was special in the eyes of Paige. Likewise, Booty described Paige to the GAL as a "perfect" mother, which stood in such stark contrast to what Paige's real uncle, Tim Klassen, shared at our wedding saying neither of us were perfect, but we were perfect for each other.

Now twenty-one years after Uncle Tim uttered those words at our wedding, with a fifty-page GAL report chronicling not only the mental and emotional abuse of our children, but also the breakup of our marriage, the implosion of our family, and the destructive cult of Booty, the question of whether or not Paige and I really were perfect for each other stared me in the face.

CHAPTER 29

KICKING THE OGRE OFF THE MOUNTAIN

ON SEVERAL OCCASIONS, Paige claimed the Lord never intended for us to be married because He would never marry a believer with an unbeliever, me, of course, being the unbeliever. She was certain the Lord didn't bring us together and that our marriage was a mistake. In fact, she didn't even think our marriage was seen as a marriage in the sight of the Lord. She considered our wedding day the worst day of her life and agreeing to marry me the worst decision she ever made. Having shared these opinions about me and our marriage, it was clear she didn't think we were perfect for each other. But did I? The answer was still yes, unequivocally yes. The more distance I put between myself and Booty's influence, the clearer things became for me. The more the Lord opened my eyes and ears to the truth, the more it became clear Paige was a victim just like I was, just like our children were. With a simple search on the internet, I found all kinds of results for indicators or signs of a cult. Reading these articles about cults made my jaw drop. Almost every indicator mentioned was clearly present in the small cult of Booty: Charismatic leader who is above criticism, control through paranoia and shame, dishonoring of the family unit, separation and isolation, etc.

321

In 2018, I read a book on Rasputin, the controversial spiritual leader and advisor to the last Tsar and Tsarina of Russia. The parallels between Robert Booty and Rasputin were fascinating; fringe religious figure with an obscure background, poor, prone to wandering, totally devoted to his beliefs, able to cultivate a small but fanatical following, and, some would say, a preoccupation with sex. I discovered that Rasputin had been preceded by a lesser-known guru by the name of Monsieur Philippe, who was said to be possessed with the ability to determine the sex of a child just by looking at the face of the pregnant mother. Of course, everyone has a fifty-fifty chance at being right in this endeavor, but the Tsarina was convinced Monsieur Philippe could do it flawlessly. Obviously, he could not. Similarly, Paige believed Booty possessed this extraordinary ability. That is but one small example of many that continued to pile up and provide me with irrefutable evidence that Booty had brainwashed Paige. At what point he did this, I still didn't know, but it didn't matter. Just like my children needed rescuing from this destructive cult, so too did Paige. So, I started praying every day that Paige would have a Road to Damascus type moment, just like Saul did when he turned from persecuting the Church and became Paul, writer of nearly half the New Testament. After living her entire life under the control and manipulation of Booty, it would truly be a miracle if Paige recognized the truth about him.

The first order of business, however, was protecting the children. A few weeks after the Guardian ad Litem report came out, the judge in our case adopted it as the interim parenting plan and ordered the children to be returned to my care. The order also prevented Booty from having any contact with the three younger children. I, along with everyone on my team, was ecstatic. In early June 2018, I met Paige in Missoula and picked up the children to bring them home. It was a rocky first few weeks as the children got used to being around me and began to understand that I wasn't all the horrible things Booty and Paige accused me of being. As the summer went on, the children and I made incredible progress. Progress was also made with the older two boys when they called me to apologize for their recent actions and seek reconciliation. It was slow going with them as well, but it was a start, and I was so happy. When I got off the phone with each of them, I cried tears of joy.

In early July 2018, Paige and I were scheduled to have our first mediation session. Since we hadn't agreed on a parenting plan—I supported the findings in the GAL report, Paige refused to give it any credence at all—we needed to go to mediation and, after that, a possible date with the court. Having been knocked back on her heels by the GAL report, Paige needed to change her plan of attack. I imagine she assumed I would simply roll over and give in to her demands when she filed for divorce back in 2017, as that is what I had done for so many years in our marriage. But I didn't. I fought back, I fought for the children, and I fought for our marriage. I suspect that when I first stood up to her and Booty, she was enraged by my refusal to cave. Her explosion of vitriol in front of the children in December was testament to that fact. While the rage may still have been simmering under the surface, a new and conciliatory Paige and Booty emerged. While I had been reading books on cults and marriage, she had read the book, *How To Make Any Divorce Better*. Through phone calls and text messages to me, she made it clear she wanted us to ditch the attorneys, bypass the courts, and hash out our divorce between the two of us. It was also clear she wanted to ditch the GAL report too. However, disregarding the GAL report meant disregarding the parental alienation and abusive cult influence of Booty, which wasn't acceptable to me.

The day before we were to have our first mediation session, I was at my real estate office waiting for my attorney to arrive so we could discuss our strategy. Suddenly, Paige walked in unannounced. Wearing a colorful summer skirt and blouse she confidently strode right up to me and, smiling, asked for a few minutes of my time. Reluctantly, I agreed and we went into our conference room and sat down. I listened as she started reading from a proposed parenting plan that she had written. It was very controlling and demanding—down to the type of water I had to provide the children to drink when they stayed with me—and made no mention of Robert Booty or acknowledged any of the issues raised by the GAL report. Sadly, she was in denial, but I detected a hint of softness and humility in her that I hadn't seen in years. After reading just a portion of the plan she handed it to me, then made an attempt at apologizing, saying she was sorry for not acknowledging my role as father in the lives of the children. Then, on the verge of tears, her lip quivering, she said she never meant for things to get this far. It was a surprising admission on her part. I hardly uttered a word the entire time we were sitting together, but when she said that, my mind screamed, *Then who did?* I wanted to say it, but I'm not sure it would have done any good, so I didn't. Everyone knew who did. Everyone except Paige.

A moment later, my attorney walked into the room. Yeah, it was a bit awkward. She had no idea Paige was there. I introduced the two of them. Then my attorney, who had been momentarily flustered, recovered and asked if we needed more time together. I said no. Paige smiled, reached out, shook my hand, and left. I don't know why, but it immediately brought me back to the fall of 1996 when Paige boldly reached out and shook my hand at the singles Bible study in Pocatello, Idaho. When she walked out of the room in 1996, I was lovestruck, but when she walked out of the conference room in

2018, I didn't know what to think.

OUR MEDIATION THE next day was postponed at the last minute because Paige came down with a migraine and couldn't attend. A few days after that I received letters of apology from Paige's parents and Booty. The Klassen's email was brief and seemed sincere. Booty's is below.

> *Dear Peter,*
>
> *This is a letter to express my sincere apology to you.*
>
> *Over the years, you and I have communicated often either by phone, email, or occasionally in person. The communication between us the last year was intense in its personal and family focus. The nature of my relationship with you has been mainly that of pastor, counselor, "best advocate" and friend. In all these years, I never hesitated to share with you privately the whole counsel of God in love, trust, and liberty. In the course of our conversations, I was adamant and confrontational because this is the way I communicate how important your best interest is and my deepest commitment to it.*
>
> *I apologize for the pain and the disappointment I caused you. And I am sorry for my failure to meet your noble expectations.*
>
> *Most sincerely,*
>
> *Robert A. Booty*

This "best advocate" and "friend" called me, among other things, a snake, liar, chameleon, sorcerer, devil, and narcissistic. This man's "deepest commitment" to my best interests prompted him to accuse me of stealing Paige when I married her and stalking her when I objected to a divorce. The whole counsel of God from this so-called "pastor" and "counselor" included binding me in my sin and claiming I was incapable of receiving Christ's forgiveness.

Do you remember the book Booty had us read prior to our 2016 Conference, *A God Who Hates*? At the beginning of the book, author Wafa Sultan tells a fascinating story. It isn't clear to me whether or not the story is hers, but I want to retell it here. It goes like this … There once was a young man who loved to travel and pick up wisdom and knowledge from the places he visited. When he came to a beautiful village set at the foot of the mountain, he wondered why all the inhabitants looked sad and sluggish. He sought out the local wise man who told him the people in the village were terrified of the enormous ogre who lived on top of the mountain. The wise man said the villager's *"fear of the ogre has sapped their intellect and depleted their physical powers, reducing them to despair and hopelessness."* Despite warnings from the wise man not to risk his life, the young man set out for the top of the mountain to confront the ogre and ask him why he was frightening the villagers and not letting them live in peace. Then,

> *when the young man reached the peak, the ogre did, indeed, seem large at first; however, what he found as he walked astonished him. The closer he got, the smaller the ogre became. By the time he arrived he found that this great ogre who terrorized many was smaller than his littlest finger. The young man flattened his hand, held out his palm, and the tiny ogre jumped onto it.*
>
> *"Who are you?" the young man asked.*
>
> *"I am Fear," the ogre replied*
>
> *"Fear of what?" the young man asked.*
>
> *"That depends on who you are. How each person sees me depends on how he imagines me. Some people*

fear illness, and they see me as a disease. Others fear poverty, so they see me as poverty. Others fear authority, so they see authority in me. Some fear injustice, others fear wild beasts or storms, so that's how I appear to them. He who fears water sees me as a torrent, he who fears war perceives in me an army, ammunition, and suchlike."

"But why do they see you as bigger than you really are?"

"To each person I appear as big as his fear. And as long as they refuse to approach and confront me they will never know my true size."'

I wouldn't be surprised if, in the deep recesses of Jack Klassen's mind, Booty stands on top of a mountain terrorizing him with tales of cockroaches performing their fatherly duties better than him. To Cathy, Booty might be strutting around as a giant stallion ready to leap off the mountain and occupy her body once again. To Paige, Booty is so many things that she doesn't recognize—a wicked overlord who demands perfection, a menacing tiger ready to take her life, a conniving mentor willing to sacrifice the lives of her children if he doesn't receive proper respect. To me, Booty was a mysterious guru who held the keys to the Kingdom of Heaven and my wife's affections. Displease this angry ogre, and I risked losing both. But I had long since gone past the point of no return. I had greatly displeased the ogre and lost my wife. With eyes to see and ears to hear, the Lord led me to the top of the mountain, and I finally saw my fear was just a little fat man who loved to hear himself talk. He shrieked at me with his judgmental voice, but it had no effect on me anymore. I walked right up to him and kicked him off the mountain.

Robert Booty,

The Montana district court where Paige filed for divorce has issued a binding order that provides that you are not

to have any contact with David, Naomi, Alex or Zoe.
Any contact by you with any of them will be a violation
of a legal court order. I am committed to protecting my
family from your destructive, parasitic influence. I will
do everything in my power to make sure that the court
order is followed.

I do not want you to have anything to do with my
family. Please do not contact us.

Peter Young

In earlier versions of this email, ones I didn't send, I kicked the little ogre much, much harder.

FOLLOWING THE EMAILS to me from Booty and Paige's parents, Paige sent emails of apology to my parents and brothers. It was a kind gesture, but the apologies strained credibility and hinted at a disconnect with reality. After the surprise meeting at my office, I saw Paige a few more times that month of July. We would meet at a nearby cafe where she would give me some of the children's clothing and other personal items. The meetings were brief and she usually had a friend there as a witness, but her demeanor was far less confrontational than it had been. She also called me on the phone a few times. In one call, she asked me to write my outcome goals for the divorce, and, in another, she asked if I thought we should remain married, to which I said yes. She then asked if I would be willing to see a marriage counselor. Again, I said yes. Sadly, that conversation went no further and she never brought up reconciliation again.

She did bring up my outcome goals, repeatedly. I would imagine it was one of many tasks suggested in the book *How To Make Any Divorce Better*. Rather than email them to her, I asked to meet, and we did on July 19th, 2018. It was our twenty-first wedding anniversary.

Just like twenty-one years earlier, it was a beautiful warm day, the sun high in the sky, not a cloud in sight, but neither of us mentioned our anniversary. We met at the same cafe just down the road from where I lived and sat at an outside table. This time, her friend didn't come; it was just the two of us. I told Paige I didn't have any outcome goals for a divorce and I never would. The only outcome goals I had was for her to experience a Road to Damascus moment where the Lord would open her eyes and ears to the incredible pain and heartbreak her decisions had caused, and also recognize the wicked and destructive presence Robert Booty had been in her life. I told her the best outcome for our children would be for her to completely break free from all of Booty's oppressive mind control and manipulation so he could no longer harm them or her. I finished by saying I wished that our children would know their mom and dad loves them, the Lord loves them, and that they would have the chance to live with a mom and dad who love each other. That is the biblical blueprint for a family and that was what I desired.

She listened politely but was dismissive of my assessment of Booty and asked, somewhat rhetorically, if I really thought him capable of such mind control. I said yes. We talked a bit more about lawyers and the kids, but that was it. She thanked me for sharing, shook my hand, and left.

A few days later, we spoke on the phone again, and this time she was more defiant. She claimed that the GAL report as well as the opinions of me and others regarding her and Booty could be chalked up to a simple "misconception." Further, she boasted she could prove it was a "misconception" in a court of law. But when it came to matters of the law and our divorce, Paige was clear; she didn't want anything to do with the GAL report or lawyers. She continued to push for a facilitated mediation without lawyers and without the GAL report. My lawyers had given me great advice and support, and the children were living under my protection thanks to the GAL report, so I wasn't about to change course now. I took her calls, was polite on the phone, responded to her emails, but I held firm—I wasn't going to move forward without legal representation, and until she acknowledged the issues in the GAL report, there was little to discuss. With that, the encouraging signs of humility and civility she showed me in July soon evaporated.

EARLIER IN THE year, someone asked me if Paige had accused me of abuse. When I said no, they said, "Get ready because it's coming." Sure enough, months later, in the fall of 2018, Paige fired off a notice to the court accusing me of emotionally and psychologically abusing her for nearly twenty years while simultaneously bullying our children "into submission all their lives." The accusations of emotional and psychological abuse became a reoccurring theme. Our first mediation session, held in Missoula in October 2018, lasted nearly all day but didn't accomplish much. A month after that, we had a hearing in front of the judge in Bozeman. It was an emotional and draining afternoon. Paige's attorney was blundering but unrelenting in his cross examination of me and the GAL as he tried to discredit both of us in an effort to get the GAL report overturned. In the end, it was a brutal day for Paige as the judge upheld every aspect of the report.

To me, the most interesting piece of testimony from the hearing came from Jack. He and Cathy drove down to attend the hearing and both were called as witnesses by Paige and her attorney. Well aware that Booty was a central figure in the GAL report, they tried to normalize their ties with him. When asked about his relationship with Booty, Jack called him his friend. And when asked about his relationship with his children, Jack said he was mostly their friend and denied ostracizing or shunning any of his five children. I was stunned he had the audacity to say such obvious lies under oath and hoped my lawyer would pounce, but, in the end, it wasn't necessary.

As I thought about his comments, I started to piece together the puzzle. When Jack said he was going to leave Cathy, back when Paige and I were living in Inkom, he told Paige her real father was Booty. For years Jack had been calling Booty "Dad." When it came to any and all important decisions in his life, Jack always consulted Booty. So, when Jack said on the witness stand that he was mostly a friend to his children, it was because he had abdicated his role as father and given it over to Booty. Then, as I took a closer look at the emails from Paige and Booty in the spring of 2017, the ones that bemoaned biological determinism and encouraged me to just be a friend, it became clear that the plan was to strip me of my role as father to my five children and let Booty take over. This makes perfect sense when you consider one of the most prevalent indicators of a cult is the assault on the family. Traditional roles within the family are erased and everyone—father and son, mother and daughter—are all on the same level and compete for attention and praise from the cult leader. That is exactly what happened with the Klassens and Booty.

While the court hearing was another victory for me and my team, and I was happy the children would remain safe with me and sheltered from any of Booty's influence, I felt sorry for Paige. She was stern and defiant during the entire hearing, but at the end, as the judge came down on her hard, she finally broke down in tears. It pained me to see her like that. Between Booty, her parents, and her lawyers (she was on her third at that point), she was getting such horrible advice. I kept hoping and praying that with each successive defeat she would finally see the awful consequences of following

Booty and be ready for her Road to Damascus moment. I prayed for it every day, but also knew it was in the hands of the Lord. And He knows what He's doing. If the Lord intended for Paige to have her eyes opened to the truth of Booty or have an epiphany—call it what you will—then it would happen. Patience was required, and I prayed for that every day as well.

IN ADDITION TO praying for patience, I also asked for wisdom, and the Lord gave it to me. Of this I am absolutely certain.

"If any of you lacks wisdom, you should ask God,
who gives generously to all without finding fault, and
it will be given to you. But when you ask, you must
believe and not doubt, because the one who doubts is
like a wave of the sea, blown and tossed by the wind."
James 1: 5-6

My days of listening to Booty were dominated by waves of doubt. But the Lord rescued me from that awful situation. Slowly, over several months, He helped me see the truth. In 2018, I turned the corner mentally, emotionally, and spiritually. But questions still remained, such as when did things start to go wrong in my marriage? And, if I could go back and fix things, how far back would I have to go? Then I made several unexpected discoveries that started providing answers.

---◉◉◉---

CHAPTER 30

FINDING BURIED TREASURE

THE DISCOVERY OF hidden treasures has always captivated me. As a child, I collected baseball cards and dreamt of stumbling across some garage sale where a shoebox full of old baseball cards bought for a few dollars, were later found to be of inestimable value. I once took a metal detector around our backyard in Inkom hoping to find a farmers long forgotten coffee can of silver coins. Instead, I found a bunch of metal junk. But the search thrilled me. I'm not alone in my fascination with old things. Exclusive auction houses like Christie's and Sotheby's routinely sell historical artifacts for vast sums of money. For instance, in 2010, the original typewritten draft of the rules of basketball by James Naismith sold for $4.34 million. And in 2012, George Washington's personal copy of the U.S. Constitution, with his handwritten notes inside, sold for $9.83 million. I too have a long-forgotten treasure in my possession. My grandmother and her brother, Joe, grew up in Springfield, Illinois, in the early part of the 20th century. When Joe was just a boy, an old house in town was torn down. Rummaging through the rubble, Joe found an ancient looking diary, which he kept. Somebody (whether it was little Joe or someone else, I'm not sure) discovered a fascinating entry on one of the pages. On September 5th, 1854, it said, *"Let A. Lincoln have $50 on Co. claim."* The diary was later framed, opened to that page with the reference to our sixteenth President, Abraham Lincoln. I inherited it many years ago, and it still hangs on the wall in my office.

There are plenty of reasons for our fascination with old documents: they can be a tangible link to the past, a remembrance of a departed loved one, or provide clues to solve a long-lost mystery.

AFTER PAIGE LEFT me in January 2017, she returned to our home on several occasions, each time picking up personal items for herself and the children and taking them with her back to Idaho. She returned one final time in June 2017 while I was away and picked up most of her remaining personal effects from our home. However, she left behind several of her books and old papers. In the fall of 2018, I was going through a small metal filing cabinet in my office and came across a letter Paige had written to Booty. It was written in late November 2016, during our so-called reconciliation period. I'm not sure if she never sent it to Booty or scanned and emailed the letter to him. Regardless, it reads like a love note. She started out by saying *"I am missing you..."* and *"You and Aunt Staci are so precious to me..."* then transitioned to her upcoming trip to see him in California. *"My days are filled with the tasks here while I look excitedly at the calendar that says California soon. I am glad that Jeff gets to come and Zoe but I will miss being so spoiled when I am the only one."* Apparently, the tasks at our home in Montana made her weary because she went on to say, *"I am remembering that I am not to grow weary in doing good. I would love it if all the good I had to do could be by your side helping you.*" It was fascinating to read that second sentence because for a brief time, I too, was caught up in the importance of Booty's work. Everything he did seemed significant with world-changing consequences. He spoke with heads of state and was on a first name basis with Congressmen. Of course, I never saw him speak with a congressman or head of state, rather I faithfully believed all the stories about him rubbing elbows with the powerful were true. These stories, true or not, were successfully tailored by him to firmly place himself on a pedestal above us. This made the work we did in our ordinary lives feel meaningless and wearisome.

Near the end of her letter was the most surprising statement. "*I know the expectation will be for me to stay and 'work on my project of Peter' but I am not seeing that as the needed use of my efforts and focus. I need to be with you and Aunt Staci and my parents too. We need more of you and I am willing and ready to realize the Lord's plan as it unfolds.*" I had never before heard of the expression "my project of Peter" but it sounded straight from the mouth of Booty. I suspected the goal of the project was to help me become a Christian. But this no longer interested Paige. She wanted to leave her husband and be by Booty's side. And in regard to her last sentence, it is shocking for a married Christian woman to say she needed more of another man, and further, that the Lord's plan for her would be to divorce her husband so she could be closer to this other man. However, if you see yourself as Abigail, your husband as Nabal, and the other man as King David, then it makes sense. Finding this love letter helped drive home the point that Paige left me so she could draw even closer to Booty, her cult leader.

THE NEXT PIECE of buried treasure I found was hidden in plain sight on my laptop computer. For a while, the only good computer we had in our family was the laptop I used for work, so Paige would borrow it occasionally. In looking through saved files I discovered her written testimony from our 2015 conference in Hayden. Recall that at that conference Booty asked everyone to share their testimony. She wrote the letter about a month after the conference, but I read it for the first time when I found it in 2018.

> *The Lord revealed himself to me through the witness of Uncle Robert and Aunt Staci as a young girl. I knew I was loved through them and I found the example of what love is through them. ... It was at this time I remember asking the Lord to change me and make me a good person. I did not understand the full gospel message or what it meant to be saved, I just knew I did not like who I was. I decided to be a better person.*
>
> *... Then, in Jan. 1997 the Lord gave me a dream about a Tiger in our house that threatened to jump out when we least expected it to and kill us. In the dream I did not want to kill the "beautiful" tiger, I just wanted to know where it was so we (my mother and a college friend) could be aware and protect ourselves. Also in the dream, I came to the decision that it had to die or we would never be safe. Just then, the front door opened and a tall man in black entered with his rifle and asked where it was. I told him the closet in an upstairs room. He went upstairs and killed it. I was grateful and relieved. He was my knight in shining armor and sent from God for my protection. This dream spoke to me of the hidden tiger of my ego I had harbored and protected all those years. The Lord got me on the hook when I was 10 but I was not on the boat yet. I wrote a letter to*

Uncle Robert telling him of the dream and asking him how one knows they are a Christian. He sent me a 13 page letter with many biblical references and directions to read them completely. ... I was disturbed. ...

The dream about the tiger was a pivotal moment in her life, so important that she mentioned it in her testimony nearly eighteen years later. The funny thing about memories is that they can fade over time. Names and dates and other details can get confused. That's why the historian is always searching for the written word. The ink may fade, but the words don't change. And while Paige was able to accurately recall the importance of her tiger dream, she forgot some of the details. More on that to follow. But first, the rest of the testimony.

On Feb. 10, 1997, I flew to North Idaho for work and stayed with my parents. I was overjoyed to find that my dear Uncle Robert was there visiting my parents. On Feb. 12, Uncle Robert drove me to the airport in Spokane, WA. As we were driving there, I told him that I had read and reread his letter and the verses and I did not believe I could be a Christian. ... He asked me a few questions and asked me what I wanted. I told him that I wanted to be a Christian and no longer live as I was. He asked me "Why not make today the day?" He prayed with me as I surrendered all that I was into the hands of the Lord Jesus Christ for him to do as he wished with me and save me from myself. That was the best day of my life! ...

That was the beginning, and since then I have had to face my old self and tendencies time and again. In July 2000, I was chastened by the Lord when I failed to stand up for the truth when the one who led me to

Christ was being attacked. I am ashamed to say that I stood by and waited, therefore, condoning the words and actions of the one viciously attacking him. The Lord allowed me a chance, however, by letting my pregnancy of the time become endangered through an amniotic fluid leak. I knew at once why I was there in the hospital with my unborn baby's life in danger. I called Uncle Robert the next morning and confessed and apologized through tears of anguish at what my lack of action had caused. ...

Even since then, I have faced numerous challenges and temptations to waiver and stay in the small lifeboat instead of getting on the big ship which does not feel the swells of the waves of life. Uncle Robert and Aunt Staci have been my anchors when I have been drifting off into despair, self-pity or listening to my old thoughts.

Paige's testimony focused so much on Booty, it is at times hard to discern who saved her, Booty or Jesus Christ. Booty was Paige's anchor, but was he also the "big ship" she sought refuge on? All the important moments in her testimony center around Booty: the tiger dream and his letter, the meeting with Booty at the Spokane airport, and failing to stand up for Booty when he was being attacked by Rebecca. Booty may not have been her savior, but he was clearly something close.

WHILE I ALREADY discussed the extraordinary difficulties surrounding David's birth in Chapter 6, the third document I found revealed Paige's bizarre understanding of those events. One day in 2019, I was looking for old photos and found a forgotten CD in a box in our basement. Curious, I popped it into our computer and stumbled across this remarkable document Paige wrote in late 2000.

> *In early Fall of 1999, it began as a very small seed planted by my earthly sister, Rebecca. I took her word at face value and I accepted the seed of slander and hate she offered against Robert Booty, my brother in Christ. This seed took root in my life, and in effect, I rejected my life in Christ. If not for the mercy of God on my soul, I would be lost forever. … Uncle Robert has been an advocate and a brother in Christ. He has also been like an uncle to me, and the best friend I had through my youth. He has been an intercessor for me in Christ since I was very young. I have learned much and been truly loved through him and his wife, Staci. I am sorry for the hurt I caused them and I am sorry for rejecting Christ. In a blinded effort to do what I thought was best, I essentially rebelled against God through my disobedience.*

These first two paragraphs are quite remarkable, for Paige claims to have rejected Christ, rejected her life in Christ, and rebelled against God, all because she accepted the seed of slander against Booty. How could believing in something your sister said about another man mean you rejected Christ? Rebecca wasn't slandering Christ; she was sharing what she had observed in Booty. In 2018, Rebecca reached out to Paige and sent her a long, heartfelt letter, reaffirming this fact (Paige never responded).

Paige's confession letter from 2000 continues.

> *Rebecca came to me like a wolf in sheep's clothing pleading her case against Uncle Robert and seeking my support. (I can see now how she had prepped and*

readied me ahead of time with subtle things she said and alluded to.) I should have obeyed the voice of the Lord and rebuked her at that very moment... but I did not. I knew something was not right about everything she said and I should have asked Uncle Robert about her accusations against him, but I did not. This began my slide off the mountain of life that I had been given in Christ, and I was nearing the cliff which gives way into the abyss of darkness.

Because she failed to rebuke Rebecca, Paige was now losing her life in Christ and about to fall into an "abyss of darkness"? Would Christ take away Paige's "mountain of life" because she didn't take a stand for Booty? Acts 4:12 says "*Salvation is found in no one else* [Jesus Christ], *for there is no other name under heaven given to mankind by which we must be saved.*" What would supposed slander against Booty have to do with Paige's salvation? The third commandment says not to take the Lord's name in vain; it doesn't say anything about Robert Booty or his name.

I continued to listen to individuals in my earthly family who were building their case against Uncle Robert. ... I began to believe the lies and came to the point where I was willing to rebuke Uncle Robert if he ever tried to interfere with my family and me! I had come to view the messenger of God as an angel of death!

...

Then came a change in the whole scheme of things, my dad, Jack Klassen, 'succumbed' to Robert's way of life. All involved in the slander of Robert were saying, "this must really be a cult he is leading, to have so much power over Jack and convince him he needed to 'join'!" I went along with it, blind and dying.

I remember around this time one of Paige's relatives saying Booty was a cult leader. I was happy when I heard it but didn't dare say anything to Paige. I hoped more of Paige's Klassen relatives would speak up and help her see the problems with Booty. I'm sure they all saw the problem, but other than Rebecca, I don't recall any other relative directly confronting Booty. As for me, I don't think I saw him as a cult leader back then, but I would have been more than happy to see him leave us alone.

After all the trust I had in Uncle Robert and the value I had placed on his friendship, why did I buy into the possibility that the lies about him were true? ...Also, while growing up I had always had a little uncomfortable feeling about the relationship between Uncle Robert and my dad, so perhaps I thought I was seeing the roots of those feelings. Little did I realize, however, that the problem was with my dad who had been acting the wolf in sheep's clothing for many years, and not with Uncle Robert. I had disobeyed God and readily taken sides with my earthly family over my family in Christ, and with great consequence.

Using Paige's own words, I started to piece together a sad story of a girl pressured to idolize and honor a man who, deep down, she didn't want to. Paige said she always had an "uncomfortable feeling" about the relationship between Booty and her dad. In her testimony, she said Booty's letter about the tiger dream "disturbed" her. In the end, whom did she blame for these unsettling feelings? Did she listen to her sister, her relatives, her intuition, her husband? No, in the end, she blamed everyone else and Booty remained blameless and pure. I think back to the card at her fortieth birthday party and can't help but feel sadness for that beautiful young princess who was dominated by the wicked overlord. As Paige wrote this letter of confession in 2000, she was not only completely unaware of how dominated she was by Booty but also how uncomfortable and disturbing her relationship with Booty seemed to me and many others.

> *I had accepted a position on the wrong side of the battle: The dark side. I kept telling Peter that something was not quite right about the things said about Robert. Yet, I still tried to ascertain what it was on my own; I intellectualized it. I somehow felt that I must be able to understand it all and see the truth since I had been reborn in Christ a few years past. But I did not recognize my vulnerability in my infancy in Christ, and that I must always rely on Him for 'everything.'*

I've never heard another Christian mention being vulnerable as an infant in Christ. Christians shouldn't feel vulnerable; we were vulnerable *before* we were saved, but now that we're saved and have victory in Christ, we are *invincible*. The only reason Paige would feel vulnerable as an infant in Christ, three years after supposedly being saved by Booty, was due to the teaching and manipulation of Booty. Paige's words plus Jack's tears of anguish that were always close to the surface are testament to the fact that everyone who followed Booty would always remain vulnerable.

> *At first, our Father in Heaven had mercy on me and allowed me to suffer mental anguish which I could not explain or understand. A veil had been brought over my eyes and I could no longer see the Way. .... I saw myself becoming more and more wretched and dark inside. I kept asking, what is it, Lord? What am I missing, please show me and convict me. Finally, I was saying, I will*

pay any price to be free of this wretchedness!!

I had allowed myself to be manipulated by the adversary and had become like them. Void of life, destructive, and without discipline, the Lord began to work on me. The starkest realization the Lord allowed me was that I had once called Robert uncle, friend, brother, and now I was spitting on him. I never even went to him and spoke with him like a brother or friend. Instead I convinced myself that things would work themselves out and I was not going to involve myself. But I was involved the moment I became his friend and sister in Christ, and now I was ever more involved through my choice to disobey God and turn against Robert. Something was very wrong, and my father was going to have mercy on me and show me the truth, but it would be a soul wrenching process I shall never forget.

There is no question Paige's pain and suffering were real, but to think she became "void of life" for not defending Booty is preposterous. When we believe in Jesus Christ the Holy Spirit resides in us. Would God remove the Holy Spirit from Paige, in essence make her void of life because she didn't take a strong enough stand in defending Booty? Do you think God is more concerned about the reputation of Robert Booty than He is about His own good name? And the fact that Paige was praying to the Lord for answers proves she didn't doubt the Lord and wasn't "void of life." Rather, she was indeed going through a "soul wrenching process" but sadly missed the whole point of it.

He placed me in the hospital to sit in bed with my unborn child and be confronted with my sin and rejection of the Kingdom. Now it was not only my life at stake, but also the life of my child.

How could Paige possibly think the Lord would endanger the life of our unborn child simply because she agreed with someone who had the audacity to confront and criticize Robert Booty? In Psalms 139:13, it says the Lord *"Created my inmost being; you knit me together in my mother's womb."* Was the Lord going to start knitting David in Paige's womb and then purposely kill him because someone offended Robert Booty?

> *On the second day of my hospital stay I was in emo-*
> *tional and mental anguish. My anguish was more about*
> *the rift that was between God and I than the future of*
> *my unborn child, but I knew they were related. I prayed,*
> *I cried, I pleaded with the Lord to have mercy on me*
> *and open my eyes to the sin I could not see but knew*
> *was there. On Friday, July 28, He removed the veil and*
> *opened my eyes. I wept with repentance and asked for-*
> *giveness for disobeying Him, accepting what He rejected,*
> *and rejecting Him as far as to spit on one of his servants.*
> *I asked Uncle Robert's forgiveness. I asked for my dad's*
> *forgiveness, and the forgiveness of my brother Jeff, both*
> *of whom stood firm in the truth during the slander. I*
> *also asked Peter to forgive me for accepting darkness into*
> *my life, and consequently into his life.*

Booty excels at convincing those he manipulates that there is a "rift" between them and God. He did it to me, Rebecca, Paige's parents, Paige, and who knows who else. And when Paige claimed that she accepted what the Lord rejected, what exactly did she mean? She accepted the words of Rebecca that were critical of Booty. Did the Lord reject Rebecca? Did the Lord reject any and all criticism of Robert Booty? As for Paige asking for my forgiveness for "accepting darkness" into her life and mine, I don't recall that conversation. With the benefit of hindsight, I now know that a form of darkness did enter my life, but it was well before 2000, and it didn't have anything to do with Rebecca.

> *I had hated my brother, I had joined forces with those of the darkness, and I essentially was throwing away my salvation and life in Him. I say throwing because by the grace of God I had not yet stepped off the cliff into the abyss. However, the moment he opened my eyes I could see that I was at the edge and with my next step I would be falling.*

She was throwing away her salvation and life in Christ because she didn't stand up for Booty? Really? It seemed Paige found salvation by believing in Christ but could easily lose it by not believing in Booty.

> *The Lord also had mercy on our unborn child, David. He is alive and healthy today, a true testament of the Lord's grace and mercy.*

Indeed, David did survive and grew into a strong, athletic, mature young man. Unfortunately, Paige drew even closer to Booty after this incident, and every voice that had been critical of Booty was now gone. Other than my brief alarm at Booty's bizarre statements related to the events of September 11, 2001, even my critical voice was largely silent.

THE THREE DOCUMENTS, all written by Paige, paint a sad and remarkable picture of undue mind control. What is also remarkable is so much of the history of Paige and Booty's relationship, Paige's parental alienation, and the cult influence of Booty on Paige, is in writing. Between the GAL report, Paige's emails and letters, and all of Booty's correspondence, there is a voluminous amount of written documentation. Instead of a he-said-she said argument over what happened, I have all the evidence I need to support the claim that Robert Booty successfully exerted cultish undue mind control over Paige, her parents, and my family. This small cult of Uncle Robert that ensnared us was a spider web of secrecy, paranoia, exclusivity, shame, guilt, and a twisted interpretation of the Word of God. But when you're under the sway of someone else's mind control, it's very difficult to see the truth and recognize the danger. You don't know you *are* in a cult, you only know you *were* in a cult. And the most obvious example of Booty's undue mind control and manipulation, that is also in writing, is the story of the tiger dream Paige had in 1996.

BY FAR THE most important and fascinating discovery I made was when in the fall of 2018 I found the original letter Booty sent to Paige regarding her dream about the tiger. Like the other documents I found, I was rummaging through a file cabinet in my office when I stumbled upon it. At first, I didn't know what it was, but when I realized what I was holding, I was stunned. I hadn't seen it since Paige showed it to me in 1996, soon after we started dating. I had no idea she'd kept the letter, and finding it was similar to discovering one of the long-lost documents that people buy at auctions. Better yet, it was like starting a home remodel project and pulling up old carpet or tearing off ancient wainscoting and discovering an old photograph or letter that had been accidentally hidden, some vestige from your youth that instantly brings you back to a bygone era.

When Paige first showed me the letter, we had only known each other about a month. I remembered the letter being long and written by Booty in many different colors of ink; it discussed at length Paige's dream about the tiger and mentioned a tall man coming to get rid of the tiger. I recalled a few more details, but not much more than that. At the time I had no idea how important this letter and dream were to Paige. I had yet to meet Booty and see firsthand how devoted Paige was to him. I'm fairly certain I only read the letter once, by the dim overhead light in a car no less.

Paige thought the letter was thirteen pages long when she recounted it in her 2015 written testimony. But that was inaccurate; the letter was actually twenty-four pages long; the many different colors of ink the result of several pens running dry on Booty. What was completely accurate was Paige's 2015 recollection that the letter "disturbed" her. It is a disturbing letter.

It's also a typical Booty letter in that it rambled on and on. And in that rambling were several details that I had forgotten. The most important was that in 1996, Paige had been baptized by the same pastor who, later in the year started the singles Bible study where Paige and I met. I wasn't there at Paige's baptism because we hadn't met yet, but, surprisingly, Booty wasn't there either. And that drove Booty nuts. So much so that he filled several pages of the letter berating Paige for being baptized without him there, or without him doing the baptizing. He went to great lengths to proclaim that his feelings weren't hurt, but then detailed how hurt his feelings really were by what Paige did: *"It is that 'callused' attitude with which you went about it with very little regard to the real people, who labored in your life, that is my concern!"*

Clearly Booty saw himself as the only "real" person who labored in Paige's life, everyone else was … well, you'll see shortly. *"It never hurt my feelings one way or the other if it was just baptism! It was your way of identifying with these people, for whatever reason you may have had!"*

Booty loved to pretend being superior to everyone else in that he was far too emotionally, mentally, and spiritually mature to have his feelings hurt. But it was clear that Paige's baptism amongst "*these people*" hurt him. The world according to Booty was filled with "*these people*," and over the years, he convinced Paige and her parents that everyone not in their tight-knit circle might as well be "*these people*." He continued:

> *You 'acted so independently,' and that is the concern.*
> *Not so much the independence, that is great to be inde-*
> *pendent! But in this respect what you call independence*
> *is really 'defiance', and for what? Just to identify with*
> *these people with this kind of price?"*

Booty also loved to tell us the reasons and motivations behind what we did because he claimed to know us better than we knew ourselves. So, in this case he stomped on Paige's act of independence and called it defiance, specifically, defiance of him. And that was simply not something he was going to allow. For Paige to act independently of Booty and "*identify*" with other Christians presented a grave threat to him. There was no "*price*" Paige needed to pay for being baptized by someone other than Booty, nor did she need to be baptized by him. But Booty was determined to make Paige pay a price, for if she didn't, then *he* would be the one paying the price. Why? Because Paige provided him legitimacy. She was tall, beautiful, well spoken, confident, and well-educated with two master's degrees. Booty's homely physical appearance, odd manner of speech, bizarre beliefs, lack of career success or achievement, and tiny following made it difficult for him to appear legitimate. Spend twenty minutes with him over a cup of coffee and you too would come to the conclusion he was a crackpot, perhaps a funny and engaging crackpot, but a crackpot nonetheless. However, with Paige by his side, doting on his every word, Booty had instant cachet. Paige was, by far, Booty's most important convert, and when she got baptized without him and didn't even tell him about it right away, it represented a clear and present danger to his little cult following. Booty needed to swiftly intervene and suffocate Paige's new independence while it was still in the cradle. And that he did with the tiger dream letter.

After he had sufficiently dismantled Paige's motivation for being baptized by someone other than himself, Booty went on to disparage her testimony at her baptism as a mere *"story."* He bluntly told her she was wrong and, just for good measure, called the pastor who baptized her and all the friends she had made at that church in Pocatello, *"Pharisees."*

I've never seen a baptism where the person being baptized wasn't asked to publicly declare their faith in Jesus Christ. But, just to be sure, in February of 2020 I called the pastor who baptized Paige and asked him if he always had the person he baptized declare their faith in Jesus? Absolutely, he replied. So, it's safe to say that when Paige was baptized, she too professed faith in Jesus Christ, which would lead me to believe she was a Christian. *"If you declare with your mouth, 'Jesus is Lord,' and believe in your heart that God raised him from the dead, you will be saved." Romans 10:9*

You may have heard the philosophical question, "If a tree falls in the forest and no one is there to hear it, does it make a sound?" Perhaps the question in the Booty cult is, "If someone confesses their faith in Jesus Christ, but Booty isn't there to hear it, does it count?" The question is relevant because Paige, her parents, and I all professed faith in Christ without Booty present, only to have that faith later questioned by Booty. Even though Booty was livid that Paige had been stupid enough to be baptized by a bunch of Pharisees, it was going to take more evidence to convince Paige that she wasn't a

Christian in the first place and thus not ready to be baptized. And that evidence was manufactured in the actual tiger dream.

BOOTY'S LONG LETTER to Paige was in response to a letter she wrote him (which I've never seen), probably sometime in late September or early October of 1996. In his letter, Booty regularly quotes Paige from her letter, especially when it comes to describing the dream. There are not a lot of details and only a few characters involved: Paige, her mother, the tiger, the tall man, and her boy-friend, Chad.

Paige had dated Chad just prior to meeting me. I forget where Paige met him, where he lived, or what he did, but I do remember Paige showing up to the singles' Bible study in Pocatello with Chad in tow. I had just met Paige the week prior at the Bible study, and when she walked in that next Sunday with Chad, my heart sank. He seemed like a nice enough guy, although he was a few inches shorter than Paige, and probably a few pounds lighter too as Paige spent a lot of time lifting weights back then. So, they seemed to me like an odd couple. And they didn't act like a couple either.

Booty talked a lot about Chad in his letter. Apparently Chad loved Paige and wanted to marry her. Paige didn't really know what to do about Chad but made it clear to Booty that she wanted to follow the Lord's plan for her life. Booty's response? *"How would you know 'His Plan'? You would not be able to know, because, to know is to obey from the heart in Love, not in fear!"* Reading Booty's letter in 2018, I found comments like these infuriating. Who was he to tell Paige she wasn't capable of knowing the Lord's will for her life? Unfortunately, the letter is full of similarly insulting remarks, some aimed at Chad, the majority directed toward Paige. If for any reason Booty focused on you, waves of condemnation and condescension were sure to follow.

In the dream, Chad and Paige (and Paige's mother) were in a house trying to find where the tiger was hiding. Once found, Paige wanted to "*isolate it*" so she could "*avoid it.*" She didn't want to kill the tiger. Then the dream took a dramatic turn as the tall man walked in the front door. When that happened, Paige hid and couldn't find Chad. Chad simply disappeared.

When I first read Booty's letter in late 1996, it had only been a few weeks since I'd met both Paige and Chad, and I had no idea at that moment that I would never see him again. But reading the letter again in 2018, I became fascinated by the incredible parallel between the dream and reality. The "*tall man*" walked into the dream and Chad disappeared; I walked into Paige's life in October of 1996 and a week or so later, Chad disappeared. Whether he moved away, Paige told him to take a hike, or he saw the writing on the wall with me around and simply left, I don't know. But when he and Paige left the Bible study together that Sunday, that was the last time I ever saw Chad.

BY FAR, THE most richly described character in Paige's dream was the tiger. Paige wrote that the tiger was "*an independent part of me*" and something "*that has gotten me in trouble many times.*" She also said, "*the tiger represents independence, strength, courage, power, beauty, respect, and many of the other things I value very highly in life.*"

As I discovered through my years living with Paige, these attributes of the tiger were precisely the attributes Paige admired in Booty. Not surprisingly, Booty took great pleasure in psychoanalyzing the tiger in the dream, writing in elaborate circles, quoting dozens of Bible verses, and screeching at Paige like the nasty ogre. He wrote that with her dream and interpretation of it, "*You describe a conspiracy of the mind!*" Booty loved conspiracies, taking nothing at face value, instead seeing conspiracies everywhere he looked. He went on:

And this 'whole' is vividly illustrated in your state-
ment above, both in enslaving you and in 'things you
value very highly in life' - a truly vicious dichotomy and
double mindedness to reject and, then accept what you
rejected. If all these attributes (bottom of page 15) [page
15 of his letter listed the attributes of the tiger] *are the*
Flesh the fallen nature—the World, as it is evidenced by
God's Word, then you are in the Flesh and no amount
of 'avoiding' is going to make you any safer from your
favorite 'Pet'!"

This is simply more classic Booty psychobabble. What he was
saying was the tiger represented Paige's ego, her fallen and sinful
nature; in essence, Paige *was* the tiger. I can only imagine the torment Paige must have felt when Booty wrote, "*The tiger is me* [Paige].
*Because I do not want to kill me. I only want to kill what I deem to
be a little 'independent Part of me.'*" Booty was saying, as only he
could, that Paige wasn't saved. And if Booty told Paige she wasn't
saved, it didn't matter what I thought or her parents thought or any
other pastor or relative or friend thought. Most importantly, it didn't
matter what *she* thought. Only Booty's opinion mattered.

So, was the tiger really Paige, her ego, her old self before becoming
a Christian? Or was the tiger meant to represent Booty? Remember,
Paige had already publicly professed her faith in Christ and acted in
obedience to the Word of God by being baptized, reading the Bible,
and fellowshipping with other believers. Would the Lord give her
this dream to tell her He rejected her baptism, rejected her profession of faith, and that she was only pretending to be saved and thus
was still not saved? It seems clear to me that the Lord gave Paige the
dream to warn her that a man in her life, whom she blindly trusted,

was trying to convince her to reject her true faith in Christ for a counterfeit faith in him.

IN PAIGE'S WRITTEN testimony of 2015, she recalled having the dream and getting the letter from Booty in January of 1997, but this too was a lapse in memory. One of the first things I noticed when I read the letter again in the fall of 2018 was the date on it. Booty wrote his letter to Paige on Wednesday, October 23rd, 1996. The large, dog-eared envelope it was sent in also remained and had been postmarked two days later on October 25th. Paige met me for the first time on Sunday, October 27th, 1996. Thus, I had conclusive proof that Paige had the dream prior to meeting me. And the significance to this? In the dream, Paige doesn't know who the "*tall man*" is because she can't see his face. Below is the most fascinating piece of the entire letter.

> *Thank God 'the front door opened.' Who is that 'tall man'? Who is he in your life? The fact you 'could not see his face', and that you hid near the stairs, and that you did not know where Chad was, and that you were afraid for the tiger, and that you wanted to stop the man, all signify the tremendous energy spent in stopping the Witness of the truth personified for your life.*

Please don't go on until you read that quote again. Seriously, read it again. Neither Booty nor Paige knew who the "*tall man*" was in her dream. I stand 6'5", which, obviously, makes me tall. So, the mysterious "*tall man*" enters the dream, Chad disappears, and Paige wants to protect the tiger from the "*tall man*." It would be genuinely funny in different circumstances to realize that Booty, who stood about 5'6" and had a face Paige knew well, tried to pawn himself off as the "*tall man*" in her dream. But that is exactly what he did. In his letter he had the audacity to write this: *"The tall man=Short man. Tall in reality but short in the illusory body."*

If there is one thing Booty does get right in his analysis of Paige's dream it is recognizing the *"tremendous energy"* Paige spent in trying to stop the *"tall man"* or *"the Witness of the truth"* from exposing the tiger. There is no way I could have known in the fall of 1996, that Paige would resist my efforts to rid ourselves of Booty. As weak and sporadic as those efforts were, I can look back now and see she protected Booty at all times and never once allowed my doubts about him to change the way she perceived him.

When I first read the letter from Booty in 1996, I had a hard time seeing myself as the *"tall man"* but it did cross my mind. Even though Booty tried to take the credit for being the *"tall man"* Paige came to see the *"tall man"* as representative of Jesus Christ. So, I too figured this was the correct interpretation of the dream, at least when it came to the *"tall man."* Sure, I was tall and had just come into her life, but I wasn't about to save anybody. That can only happen when Jesus calls you and you accept Him and His death on the Cross. Paige had already done this, regardless of how much she understood intellectually. She had faith, she believed, she repented, she was saved. Period. Amen. Then, once we are saved, we are sanctified, we mature and grow in our faith and in our understanding. *It doesn't happen in the opposite order.* Without first believing in Christ, we wouldn't understand *any* of the Gospel. Without first believing in Christ, Paige wouldn't and couldn't publicly profess her faith in Christ and have the desire to be baptized. Thus, knowing Paige had already been saved, she didn't need the Lord to come into her life and kill the tiger, *if* the tiger represented her ego or her sinful nature. The Lord already had.

Other than the few times Paige referenced her tiger dream, like in her 2015 testimony, I rarely thought about it. But as my road to recovery continued in 2018, finding the original letter was close to an epiphany. Provided with the hindsight that wasn't available when I first read the letter in 1996, it became obvious to me what the dream was about and its true purpose. It wasn't merely a coincidence that Chad disappeared from Paige's life in both the dream and real life after I, a tall man, showed up; it's not a coincidence that Paige couldn't see the tall man's face in the dream at a time when she hadn't met me. Nor is it a coincidence that after receiving Booty's disturbing letter, Paige listened to the tiger, the entity that had *"gotten me* [her] *in trouble many times"* in the past, and rejected her baptism and rejected her public profession of faith in Christ.

I AM CONVINCED the Lord gave Paige her tiger dream as a warning and a way out. He was giving her a chance to see the truth, warning her that Booty wasn't saving her, but rather destroying her. And the way out was a tall man who truly loved her. I wasn't perfect and didn't look much like a knight in shining armor, but married to me, Paige could experience a life without Booty. She could finally escape the confusing and suffocating world of Booty whose words and ideas distorted her reality like a dense fog rolling in off the ocean. But then Booty turned the dream on its head and made Paige the tiger and himself the tall man. Instead of heeding the Lord's warning, Paige fell prey to the tiger, elevated him to near godlike status, and cut me down as a nonbeliever and, thus, incapable of being the tall man.

Booty's manipulation of Paige and her dream had incredibly far-reaching and destructive ramifications. For as long as he maintained his position of authority and control over her, his true identity was hidden, and our marriage was doomed to failure. And since the tiger dream convinced Paige she needed Booty to be saved, she became convinced I couldn't be saved without the direct intervention of Booty. Unfortunately, this same recipe for salvation also applied to our children, for nearly all had their faith doubted by Booty and Paige.

CHAPTER 31
MIRACLES

AT SOME POINT prior to October 1996, Paige was baptized. She had recently graduated with two master's degrees, had begun to go on dates, and was making a life for herself in Southeast Idaho, far away from Booty. Around this time, she had the fascinating and mysterious tiger dream. She wrote Booty about it, and he sent back a long, scathing diatribe that was insulting, judgmental, arrogant, and disturbing. Then she met me and fell in love. A whole new world opened up before her eyes. She had met someone she wanted to spend the rest of her life with, someone who shared the same goals and dreams she did. But the tiger dream and Booty's letter weighed heavily on her mind. She doubted her faith and she doubted me. Paige finally gave in to the doubts and relied on Booty to save her in February 1997. In July 1997, Paige and I were married. We loved and laughed and lived life together. Over the years, we raised five wonderful children. But like a tiger in the jungle, stalking his prey, Booty was always lurking in Paige's life. And the important people in Paige's life—her father, mother, older brother, and Booty's wife—fully supported everything Booty said and did.

But I didn't. And when the cognitive dissonance of living in both Booty's world and mine became too difficult, Paige chose Booty and left me.

Less than a month after leaving me in January 2017, Paige had a fascinating discovery of her own. Buried in a box of her personal affects, stuffed away in a closet in her parents' basement, was a letter she wrote in January 1997. It was a letter to Booty that she never sent. To Paige, finding this letter nearly twenty years to the day of writing it was a sign from the Lord that she should have never married me. In that letter from 1997 (which I gained access to when Paige submitted it, along with other documents, to the court in early 2019), she wrote, *"Peter claims to have new life in Christ, and from what I know of him and have observed, he does. I really like him. I am 'in love' with him, his heart, with the man the Lord is guiding him to be."*

So far so good. But she wrote this letter just a few weeks before she was supposedly saved by Booty, after which she came back to Pocatello and told me she didn't think I was saved.

> *Uncle, I must apologize for my 1st response to your wonderful letter.* [the tiger dream letter] *I was doubting myself and my salvation and read your letter in defense. As I have reread it several times and given my dad a copy (at his request) I believe I am understanding your words better. Thanks for taking the time to write and for your love.*

I cringed when I read this. Clearly Booty, a cunning narcissist with a strong knowledge of psychology, set out to plant doubt in Paige's mind. His goal was to torment her with doubt so she would eventually find herself needing him to rescue her. He created the gate and conveniently set himself up as the gatekeeper. Yet, she apologized and referred to Booty's letter as *"wonderful."* Paige continued a bit further in the letter:

> *If I do marry Peter, I wish to be a blessing to my husband's life, and to appreciate him, (aware that he*

will not be perfect, as I am not). My heart went out to Peter very early, as we are very compatible in communication, interests, preferences, thinking, feeling, Spirit, and are very attracted to each other's person. I have seen 'physically' better looking men but Peter is beautiful to me, right down to his cute ways and quick smile. Am I a fool in love? Well, if I am, I pray the Lord sustain me for whatever I may suffer because of it. Uncle it has been very important to me from the beginning to be honest and 'real' with Peter as well as myself and everyone in our lives. I am amazed at what a freeing blessing knowing Peter and loving Peter has been in my life!

My heart aches for that impressionable, trusting, twenty-four-year-old Paige when I ponder her words. We weren't fools in love. We were simply in love. And in the midst of the oppressive, controlling, and judgmental environment of Booty, Paige discovered freedom when she started to love someone else. Tragically, the "*freeing blessing*" she discovered was crushed by Booty. And for whatever reason—I wasn't smart enough or strong enough or brave enough—I failed to protect Paige and that vulnerable sense of freedom she was enjoying.

Disregarding all the wonderful things she said in her letter about me and our relationship, Paige focused on this: "*Am I a fool in love? Well, if I am, I pray the Lord sustain me for whatever I may suffer because of it.*" Those two sentences were all the proof she needed to convince herself the Lord never intended us to marry. It was all the proof Booty needed too. He pompously told me that had Paige sent him that letter back in 1997, he would have intervened and prevented Paige from marrying me.

Do you really think the Lord never intended Paige and me to marry, even though we did and stayed together nearly twenty years?

And do you really think it was just an accident that Paige didn't send her letter to Booty in January 1997? I don't think so. I am convinced the Lord intended Paige and me to marry and have five children together. And it wasn't simply an accident that Paige never sent Booty her letter doubting me. Paige didn't send that letter because the Lord was protecting our five unborn children from the tiger.

STARTING IN LATE 2019, Paige and I began attending counseling sessions together. It wasn't pretty and we didn't accomplish much. She continued to deny everything written in the GAL report, all the subsequent GAL updates, and the opinions of the counselors working with our children. She remained adamant that Robert Booty didn't exert undue mind control over anybody and there was no cult. In an effort to make their relationship sound more normal she started referring to Robert and Staci Booty as her godparents, a term I never once heard her apply to them during our marriage. Instead of seeing the truth, she continued to accuse me of emotional and psychological abuse and angrily lashed out at me, calling me a bully, narcissist, unfit parent, and incapable of change. She also accused me of stalking her at her job, hacking her cell phone, putting a GPS tracker on her car, and hiring private investigators to follow her—all of which is utter nonsense and never happened.

Despite her vitriol, I still held out hope. The meetings were incredibly tense with just me, Paige, and a young counselor in a room that felt not much bigger than a phone booth. But I was confident I could, at least, plant a seed of truth in her mind. I wanted to help her see what the Lord had allowed me to see. Finally, one day, the counselor gave me enough time to share with her and Paige many of the things you've read in this book. I brought up her testimony that praised Booty, her desire to extend Booty's bloodline, her belief that

David nearly died because she didn't properly defend Booty from her sister, and I brought up the tiger dream and its obvious meaning.

She listened politely, even took notes, but, in the end, she shrugged it off as a fascinating and outlandish story sprinkled with a few facts. It was so sad.

I FINISHED THE first draft of this book in the spring of 2020, during the strange interruption of our lives instigated by the Covid-19 pandemic. While Montana was, for the most part, spared the death and chaos that engulfed other areas, life here, in the shadow of the Bridger mountains, was derailed too. I can see those Bridger mountains when I sit at my desk. They are what I rest my eyes on when I look up from my computer, my eyes fatigued, my heart as well. During the surprising shutdown, when normally courageous and freedom loving Americans cowered in fear at both their government and a virus, I spent several hours every day writing this book. Sitting at my desk, with the faithful Bridgers posing silently in the distance, I unleashed a torrent of words. It was cathartic, satisfying, and therapeutic.

After a visit to the Montana of his youth and the northern shelf of the Bridgers where his mother died, the great writer, Ivan Doig, wrote his stirring memoir *This House of Sky*. In just over three months, more than one hundred thousand of his words crossed the threshold between memory and paper, and his editor asked for changes on only three pages. While not in the same league as Doig, I too felt the magnificent energy and joy of not being able to move my fingers fast enough to record what was spilling out of me. I spent over two decades toiling off and on before I was finally able to give birth to my first book, *The Blue Team*. But this was different. The emotion, the pain, the discoveries were all balanced on the rim of a cup ready to pour out. And they did.

IN AUGUST OF 2020, I received an email from my attorney's office letting me know the divorce was final. I had prayed daily for years that the Lord would provide a miracle and open Paige's eyes and ears to the truth. I hoped that moment would come before the court dissolved our marriage, but it did not. I still choke on words like divorce, divorced, and ex-wife, but they are now a part of me—ugly, indelible stains on the fabric of my life story.

I can't help but wonder, did Paige ever truly love me? I believe she did, which begs the question when did she stop? Did her love slowly erode over time or was it a quicker transition? Did she spend most of our marriage regretting her decision, hoping for change, hoping I would become someone else, someone more Syrian? I realize I can't go back in time and change the past, but it is hard to keep my mind from playing the "what if" game. What if I had been firm in 2001 and demanded we have nothing to do with Booty? What if I hadn't allowed myself to be brainwashed by Booty and stood up for my faith in 2015? Countless questions like these have crossed my mind, like stars filling up the night sky. Reaching up and touching those stars is impossible, as is trying to find answers to those questions.

While the last few years have been incredibly painful, I know that I am a million times stronger now than I was in the final years together with Paige. I no longer first seek the approval of Paige or Booty or anyone when confronted with life's problems. I seek first the Lord and His wisdom. Like it says in the first chapter of James, we should ask the Lord for wisdom and He will generously give it to us, but we must not doubt. That I have done and the Lord has given me wisdom ... and patience, strength, and deliverance. I have been delivered from a small but dangerous cult, and so have my children.

My marriage to Paige wasn't saved. Booty finally tore us apart just like he tore my family apart, just like he tore the Klassens apart. But I don't give up easily, which makes me either stupid, stubborn, or strong. I keep hearing coach Jim Valvano's voice in my head. As basketball coach at North Carolina State, the charismatic and energetic Valvano won a national championship in 1983. And while cancer took his life before he reached the age of fifty, he fought the disease until the day he died, famously saying "Don't give up; don't ever give up." How do you give up on your marriage? How do you give up on the mother of your children? How do you give up on your dreams?

When I lay my head down at night, I don't dream about moving on, organizing my post-divorce life, or diving into the dating pool. In my dreams, I am a loved father and husband: loved by all my children and by the beautiful and vivacious woman I married so many years ago. My household is a happy and unified place where division, demonization, hatred, factions, paranoia, self-righteousness, and Uncle Robert are distance memories, just like a faded scar. But am I truly dreaming about Paige, or am I dreaming about the myth of Paige, the distant memory of her, the beautiful wife of my youth, the beautiful wife of every man's youth? I don't know. I do know that I envisioned growing old with Paige, sharing many wedding anniversaries as we aged, looking back at the early days with wonder and warmth, telling our story to our children and our grandchildren. But that's not my story anymore.

LIKE A RUBBER ball, my children have bounced back remarkably well from the trauma of living under Booty's oppression. I have apologized for not protecting them from him and have patiently pointed out the destruction he caused. To help them recover, I regularly teach them the message of love and unmerited grace that Jesus

Christ speaks of in the Bible.

If we are looking for them, we will find that teachable moments happen all the time. One such moment happened when I went looking for my old college clock. Accolades and awards were rare during my college basketball career at George Washington University. In fact, I received only two. One was being named tri-captain of the team for my senior year. The other was an award I won at our year end banquet. Every year the team gave out awards, voted on by the season ticket holders and coaching staff. After my senior year, I was given the Desire Award for my outstanding hustle on the court. I received a decorative clock with my name on it, the GW logo, and the words *1991 Desire Award*. That clock sat on my desk for over twenty-five years. I wasn't prone to exaggerate my exploits and wax poetically about the glory days that so many former athletes do, but I did appreciate that clock and what it stood for. I went to GW as a lightly recruited walk-on and, through lots of hard work, managed to carve out a small role on a winning team. I was proud of it.

But at my absolute nadir with Booty, when his sick mind control was working overtime, he asked me if I had ever succeeded at anything. His question dripped with disdain, and it wasn't really a question, but a backhanded slap in the face of a man who could barely lift his chin. I thought about it for a moment and said, "No." It was the closest I came to giving up on life. A short while later, I gave the clock to Alex, who was ten at the time, and living with Paige and her parents in Idaho. I wasn't proud of it anymore and didn't want it, and in giving the clock to Alex, I was pretty sure he would either take it apart for fun, or simply break it. That's what ten-year-old boys do; it's what I would have done when I was ten.

Having bounced back myself, in the summer of 2020 I asked Alex if he still had the clock. He had all but forgotten about it, discarding it in the basement of the Klassen's home in Idaho. As I thought, he'd been rough on it, stripping all the significant markings off of it. When we got it back, I told him I wanted to repair it and put it on my desk again. At first, he protested, wanting to keep it for himself, but then I explained the significance. Robert Booty encouraged me to hate everything about myself; he encouraged me to see myself as a failure, my life a complete and utter waste. For that reason, I gave the clock away, not caring what happened to it because I didn't care about myself. But it was wicked of Booty to do that to me, and no one should ever make another person feel worthless, especially one who claims to care for you. I never became the next Larry Bird like I wanted to, but I played my heart out at the Division I level and people noticed. That clock symbolized not only my success as a basketball player but also my overcoming Booty.

As I held that beat-up clock in my hands, I told Alex that Robert Booty no longer had any control over him or me, and that no matter how much he struggles, no matter how often he fails, I loved him, I believed in him, and he would never be a failure. He smiled and understood. And I bought him a new clock, one that will now have meaning.

MY RELATIONSHIP WITH Paige and Booty gives credence to the phrase "truth is stranger than fiction." It has been a bizarre and odd journey since meeting Paige in 1996. Thankfully, I now have nothing to do with Booty, my last interaction with him coming in 2018 via email when I told him to leave me and my family alone. With Paige, it's only terse messages about the children. As for our children, most are now fully aware of the damage done by Booty. Washed clean of his greasy presence, they too have no interaction with him. I wish I could say the same about Paige for she too deserves to be delivered from the multigenerational curse that has plagued her family for decades. She too deserves to be free from the screeching ogre. As I read all of the letters I had found and thought about Paige and all she's been through, I thought about the story shared at her fortieth birthday party.

> *Once upon a time in a faraway kingdom, lived a beautiful young princess who was held captive by a wicked overlord. Because she had grown up under the overlord's control, she was unaware of how completely she was dominated. As she matured, the princess gradually became aware of how imprisoned she was by the constant pressure to always do things perfectly or else the overlord would be displeased with her. Alas, she was never good enough. The princess tried very hard to escape, but no matter what she did, she was powerless.*

Regardless of all the horrible things Paige has done and said to me, for which she is responsible, it should be abundantly clear by now that she too is a victim. The wicked overlord has been dominating her throughout her entire life. He stole her loving marriage and stole her family. This is why I still pray for her to have a Road to Damascus moment.

DO YOU HAVE an "Uncle Robert" lurking somewhere in your life? In your church? At the office? Tigers conceal themselves when hunting, patiently stalking their prey as they close in for the kill. Don't allow yourself to become isolated. Don't abandon fellowship. I don't care if you have deep doctrinal differences with fellow believers, you and I weren't meant to live in isolation. Lamps are not lit and then hidden under a bowl; rather, they're put on a table to light the whole room. Maintain strong relationships, stay in fellowship, love one another, and don't neglect meeting together as a body of believers.

If you're married, don't let anyone—pastor, priest, parent, child, or cult leader—get in-between you and your spouse. A healthy marriage has Christ in the center and nothing or nobody else. As a couple, pursue mentoring and accountability from those who seek to strengthen the marriage, rather than jealously tear it down.

Miracles happen every day, and the Lord can provide one for Paige. The Lord is the one who will rescue Paige, not me. I know that, but, at times I feel like I let her down, that I didn't do enough to protect her from the tiger. I didn't protect her like a husband should. Then I remember that I'm not perfect, but in need of a perfect Savior.

For Paige and me, this has not been a perfect journey nor was it a perfect marriage. Far from it. It was a life lived by two imperfect people. I truly believe the Lord has a plan for everyone and can take whatever mess we create and use it for His glory. *"And we know that in all things God works for the good of those who love him, who have been called according to his purpose." Romans 8:28*

I don't know what the future holds, but I will continue to pray. And I wonder—if Paige does finally find freedom and the truth, yet we remain divorced, would that still be a miracle? Would it be a miracle for her but not for us, not for me? It's something I've thought about often, and I believe that it would still be a miracle.

I USED TO struggle writing my testimony. I thought it lacked sufficient emotion and drama. For years, I wondered if my wife accepted my testimony as valid. Then, when she openly doubted it, I doubted it. So, it changed, and changed again. I was confused and frustrated and unable to give a simple explanation for my salvation. Sitting over a cup of coffee with a friend during that season of my life, I must have sounded like a colossal idiot as I attempted to convince him that the fifth time I tried to be saved with some guy named Uncle, that's when I was really saved.

He leaned forward on the table, looked me right in the eye, and said, "Peter, you were saved on the Cross two thousand years ago."

He was right, and, sadly, I had lost sight of this. What happened two thousand years ago on the Cross was a miracle, and since we can't save ourselves, *all* testimonies are miracles.

Cult leaders can't perform miracles; only the Lord can. And no one can take away what the Lord has given you.

The best writing advice I ever received was write what you know. This is my story and my testimony. And it's wonderful, messy, bizarre, tragic, and victorious.

It's a miracle.

ACKNOWLEDGMENTS

I am very grateful for the assistance of my wonderful editor, Jamie Downer. She provides skillful guidance, an eye for detail, and a love of language that inspires me to write better. Richard Van Yperen was my high school English teacher back in the 1980s. He teaches still, asking me hard questions and offering helpful analysis of my writing. Thanks also to editor, Wayne Purdin, and the excellent staff at Self Publishing School.

Thank you to the many friends who read early versions of this memoir and provided valuable feedback: Bob Comstock, Steve Bussis, Alan Miller, Randy Pope, Lloyd Mickelson, Nancy Clark, Ray Schaefer, Cristina Giambalvo, Jennifer Smith, Kristi Lahusen, and others.

I am deeply indebted to Rebecca Soto, George Bookman, and Tim & Peg Klassen for their willingness to relive some of the darker moments from their past, which helped fill in the gaps in my memory, and shed light on events I never knew existed. In early 2023, just prior to publication, I learned from George that he was the one who anonymously sent me the book *Combating Cult Mind Control* back in 2018. He knew what I needed. Five year old riddle solved.